Developer Career Ma

Build your path to senior level and beyond with practical
insights from industry experts

Heather VanCura

Bruno Souza

BIRMINGHAM—MUMBAI

Developer Career Masterplan

Group Product Manager: Kunal Sawant
Publishing Product Manager: Akash Sharma
Senior Editor: Kinnari Chohan
Technical Editor: Maran Fernandes
Copy Editor: Safis Editing
Project Coordinator: Deeksha Thakkar
Proofreader: Safis Editing
Indexer: Manju Arasan
Production Designer: Shyam Sundar Korumilli
Marketing Development Relations Executives: Rayyan Khan and Sonia Chauhan
Technical Reviewers: Viktor Grazie and Scott Wierschem

First published: September 2023

Production reference: 1250823

Published by Packt Publishing Ltd.
Grosvenor House
11 St Paul's Square
Birmingham
B3 1RB, UK.

ISBN 978-1-80181-870-4

www.packtpub.com

To my family and friends, for their patience with me as I spent much of my free time working on this book, and specifically for their encouragement, confidence, and support throughout the process.

In loving memory of my grandfather, who inspired me to share my passion, knowledge, and stories with others.

– Heather VanCura

In loving memory of my father, Hamilton. His encouragement early on got me on the path of helping developers in their careers. To my wife, Karina, who supported me during all the craziness of my career. To my friends and mentees, and also my daughters, Juliana and Lara. Everything in this book, I learned with you. To my long-time friend and co-author, Heather, you know this book would not exist without you.

– Bruno Souza

Foreword

An individual person's career is shaped by many turning points. These turning points are often encounters, either with other people, with particular tools or technologies, or even with ideas. More often than not, those moments only become apparent in hindsight. But the ability to recognize those moments when they happen, or shortly afterward, turns out to be an important career skill. One such moment early in my career was when I first met Heather VanCura. It was at an early JavaOne conference. I had just started taking my first steps into the career-broadening world of open standards. Heather was also early in her career but had already started working with the **Java Community Process (JCP)**. This particular event was the first awarding of the JCP Star **Specification (Spec)** Lead program. A "Spec Lead" is a role. It's a person who leads a team that produces a specification for a part of the Java platform. I point to this event as a turning point in my career because it encapsulates all three parts of this important book: first, learn and practice technical skills; second, get involved; and third, create impact. As you'll learn by reading the distilled wisdom from the many colleagues Heather and Bruno have interviewed in this book, the three parts are all a process, not a destination. During your career, you continually learn more technical skills, continually get more involved in existing and new communities, and continually create impact. That first JCP Star Spec Lead event was a turning point for me for the following reasons: I was working on technical skills, then I eventually became a Spec Lead, and then became a Star Spec Lead, and ended up stewarding a community that had a positive impact on our industry. The stories of the individuals profiled in this book follow a similar progression. By reading and applying the learnings in this book, you can too.

This book arrives at a historically important moment for careers in general, and **Information Technology (IT)** careers specifically. Over the over 25 years of my career, I've learned that experienced and expert developers are hard to impress. The more experience you have, the more you can really say, "I've seen it all before." This current **Artificial Intelligence (AI)** moment is different. Not everyone I've talked to is actually "impressed," but they all agree that the current AI moment is different and significant. This speaks well for the first part of the book. You'll learn to push yourself outside of your comfort zone, how to discern which new technologies to absorb, and which to skim, and how to be intentional in assembling your invisible college of fellow developers into a support network. In this hyper-accelerated, AI-charged moment, these meta-skills are more important than ever.

Once you build a process for keeping the skills fresh, the second part will show you how to find an audience for them. Experienced developers know that software development is a cooperative game. You can't do it on your own. You must join your talents to a community. I have personally benefited enormously from applying the lessons in this section. In my case, I applied the lessons before Heather and Bruno collected them in a book, but I can attest they worked for me, and am confident they'll work for you too.

Finally, the last part is where it all comes together. At Microsoft, we have three core leadership principles/bromides: create clarity, generate energy, and deliver success. The third part of the book is all about delivering success, both for your community and for yourself. By the time you get to applying this part in your career, you will understand your own individual actions will have a bigger impact when they are delivered downstream by other actors. You will have learned that your own actions influence others and you are able to benevolently wield that influence to create value.

Heather and Bruno have created an accessible book distilling a career's worth of advice from many individuals, each independently successful. You can think of it like many lifetimes worth of success right in your hand.

Ed Burns

Principal architect for Java, Microsoft

Ed's book *Secrets of the Rock Star Programmers: Riding the IT Crest* (McGraw-Hill 2008) is a good supplement to achieve a broader perspective on the ideas in this book.

Contributors

About the authors

Heather VanCura is a senior director at Oracle, leading the JCP program and MySQL Community Outreach team. With 20+ years of experience at Oracle and Sun Microsystems, she actively engages with the developer community as an international speaker, event organizer, and mentor. She has visited 6 continents and over 50 countries, meeting developers and helping them to engage in standards-related and open source projects. Heather is passionate about promoting diversity in technology and volunteers with organizations such as Women Who Code and IEEE Women in Engineering. Her extensive involvement includes serving on the boards of Dress for Success and FIRST LEGO League NorCal. Heather's dedication to empowering developers and advocating for diversity makes her a respected leader in the industry.

Bruno Souza is a Java Developer and the founder of SouJava (The Brazilian Java Technology Users Society). With extensive experience in large Java projects, he holds the position of Principal Consultant at Summa Technologies. He is also the founder of Code4.Life, an initiative focused on helping developers grow their careers towards a life of freedom and purpose. Developer communities are his personal passion, and Bruno has actively worked to build and nurture several open-source communities.

As the founder and coordinator of SouJava, and the Founder of the Worldwide Java User Groups Community, Bruno has played a pivotal role in strengthening the global Java Community. He is a Founding Member of the Java Champions and has been a Java Developer since its early days. Bruno represents SouJava on the Executive Committee of the Java Community Process (JCP) and holds the position of an emeritus Director of the Open Source Initiative (OSI).

Beyond technology, Bruno enjoys puppeteering and cherishes family time in a country hideout near São Paulo.

We would like to thank all the amazing community members and developers who have been with us along the way in our career journeys. Thank you for sharing your stories with us and trusting us to guide you on your career path.

Interviewees

In this book, we have interviewed the following industry experts. We'd like to wholeheartedly thank them for their contributions:

Chapter 1: Rafael del Nero

Chapter 2: Mala Gupta, Ben Wise, Barry Burd

Chapter 3: Nikita Koselev, Helio Silva, Barry Burd, Scott Wierschem

Chapter 4: Arun Gupta

Chapter 5: Scott Wierschem, Thiago Bomfim, Nikita Koselev

Chapter 6: Edwin Derks

Chapter 7: Elder Moraes

Chapter 8: Rodrigo Graciano

Chapter 9: Mary Grygleski, Trisha Gee

Chapter 10: Ixchel Ruiz

Chapter 11: Josh Juneau

Chapter 12: Jim Weaver, A N M Bazlur Rahman, Mimar Aslan

Chapter 13: Victor Grazi and Wellington Rosa

Chapter 14: Ed Burns

Chapter 15: Yolande Poirier

All the interviewees are personal friends of one or both authors, and they have encountered their own career challenges and triumphs. We have strived to present their experiences in an inspiring manner to encourage and prepare you for your journey ahead. Many others could have shared their stories in this book, but due to time constraints or missed opportunities, we couldn't include them. We extend our gratitude to all who volunteered, engaged in discussions, or contributed in any form to shape this book. Your dedication to your careers is greatly valued and appreciated.

About the reviewer

Douglas Hirsh, a self-taught software developer with 22 years of experience under his belt, is celebrated for his zeal to innovate and unravel complex business and technical challenges. With a commitment to quality and insightful design, Douglas ensures that solutions resonate with both technological and business visions. His adventure began in the early days of .NET, progressing into arenas such as Python, network automation, and AI. From roles ranging from hands-on developer to CTO and piloting his own freelancing venture, Douglas's diverse path has provided a holistic perspective. He's proud of his three-year stint instructing at a coding boot camp, nurturing emerging tech talent.

I'd like to extend my profound gratitude to Bruno for inviting me to be a part of this enriching endeavor. His faith in my expertise has been truly inspiring. A heartfelt thanks to my family for their unwavering support and patience as I dedicated time to this project. Their understanding made this journey smoother and all the more rewarding.

Table of Contents

Preface

There are many books on technical topics and just as many on careers, but there is no guide or roadmap for moving in a technical career from junior developer to senior developer. As experts working in the software development industry, with over 20 years of experience each, this is one of the most common requests that we receive from developers asking for advice and guidance. This book provides that guide, along with examples and stories from our global careers working with developers from all parts of the world.

When we decided in 2021 that we wanted to author a book together, it was a conversation that developed organically, and started with a discussion on how to create a more engaging online social networking event for developers. We had already been working together in the community for over two decades and we shared many experiences both together and separately, many of them in the Java community ecosystem. We both shared during our conversations that we wanted to author a book. Almost immediately our thoughts went to sharing some of the career stories from developers we have worked with over the course of our careers. We worked together at Sun Microsystems for a brief time, and for most of our careers, we have worked in adjacent roles in the **Java User Group** (**JUG**) global communities, in the **Java Community Process** (**JCP**) program, and at various software development conferences all over the world. During these activities, what we see is the influence that participation has on the careers of these developers. During this time, we have both had the opportunity to interact and share our learnings with thousands of developers. We both share a passion for developers, communities, and technology and enjoy seeing and sharing the successes of those three passions coming together for greater impact.

In this book, we will share how you can advance your technical career from a junior or mid-level developer to a senior developer. We will share the steps you will take on this journey, based on our experiences working with developers in over 80 countries as they navigated their careers across the continents of Africa, Asia, Australia, Europe, and South and North America. Along the way, we will share some interesting career stories from developers working in some of the largest employers as examples.

We are excited to have this opportunity to guide you on the way to achieving your career goals and enjoying career success. By the end of this book, you will have gained the knowledge you need to clearly develop a plan for your career progression.

Who this book is for

This book is for anyone who wants to advance in their technical career, no matter their level, but specifically for a junior to mid-level technical professional, engineer, developer, or architect who wants to move from a junior to a more senior level and excel in their professional life.

What this book covers

This book is divided into three main parts, each having a few chapters to help you fulfill the aim of advancing your technical career. Here's a brief overview of what each part covers:

- *Part 1, The Basics: Learn and Practice Technical Skills*: Career growth in the technology world involves being great at a technical level. Although the technical side is not everything, and sometimes not even the thing that will make your career grow, it is needed to be part of the game. *Part 1* will help you go deep into the technical side and get you ready to advance your career faster and farther.

- *Part 2, Get Involved: Participate in the Community*: Although developing your technical skills is a great step, to have an amazing career, you need to go beyond technical skills. Software development is a team effort, and being able to work together with others is a required skill that puts you at the next level. *If you want to go fast, go alone. If you want to go farther, go together* (an African proverb). Building a career is playing the long game. We are not here for the fast, short sprint, but long-term unique results. *Part 2* will prepare you for the long run.

- *Part 3, Create Impact: Share and Lead*: Now that you know how to establish long-term relationships that will drive your career forward, it is time to take the last step: position yourself as a leader, to break all limits in your career growth. *Part 3* will discuss advanced actions you can take that will differentiate you in the market and transform the lives of people around you.

Developer Career Masterplan involves constant growth, a constant feedback loop. You learn and then practice your knowledge. You can network with your peers, and share what you learned. This will open more possibilities for learning, practicing, networking and sharing. This loop will take your career to great projects, and amazing positions. You will grow to senior levels, and beyond.

As you can see in the image below, the three parts of this book have chapters covering each step of the masterplan. You will start with learning and practicing. As you progress, you will do more networking and sharing. This masterplan can be applied over and over, always resulting in career growth. Each step, described in detail in the corresponding chapters, builds on and reinforces the other steps, to help you build your career path, to take you where you want to go.

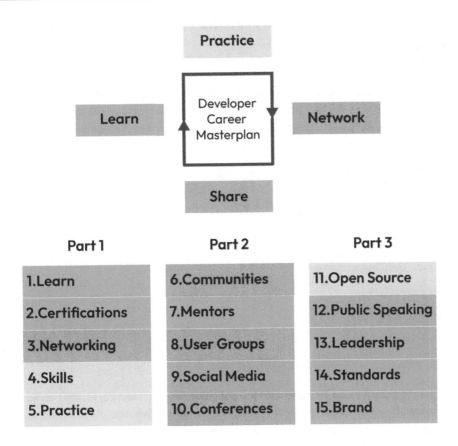

To get the most out of this book

To get started on this journey, you need to understand the importance of emotional intelligence, or EQ, how to grow beyond technical skills, how to strategically build your technical knowledge, and the importance of increasing your visibility.

In a well-known Fortune-500 company, there is an engineering team with a couple of developers who stand out for promotion. There is a developer who has the best technical skills, and a developer who has good technical skills but also is an expert communicator and team player/collaborator. Who do you think will receive a promotion? Based on the tired media trope of a solo programmer working alone in a basement eating pizza, most people would think that the developer with the best technical skills will receive the promotion. However, this is not the case. The developer with communication and collaboration skills alongside the technical skills gets the promotion. These are the skills that make up emotional intelligence.

Many academics have written on this topic with diverse ways of measuring and evaluating emotional intelligence, but to understand the point, it is enough for you to know that most employers today would prefer to hire, retain, and promote a developer who not only has the top technical skills but also a high degree of emotional intelligence. Even if that means sacrificing some level of technical ability, when given the choice, employers will more often choose the individual with better emotional intelligence. The one with the best people skills wins. Emotional intelligence requires skills that you cannot learn from reading a book alone. These are skills that require practice and human interaction. This is true in technical roles as well as non-technical roles.

The World Economic Forum is an international organization that brings together public and private organizations for cooperation purposes. The Forum engages the foremost political, business, cultural, and other leaders of society to shape global, regional, and industry agendas. The World Economic Forum recently issued *The Future of Jobs Report*. The report listed the following skills with growing demand through 2025 and beyond:

- Critical thinking and analysis

- Problem-solving

- Self-management

- Working with people

- Management and communication of activities

Take the time to consider and evaluate your level of emotional intelligence. Identify areas where you need to grow and look for opportunities to practice your skills. While machine learning and artificial intelligence will impact development jobs, and you must learn to work with them, the demand for development jobs will continue to grow and will remain strong even in economically uncertain times.

How do you grow beyond just technical skills to incorporate emotional intelligence? It is easy to think that as a developer, you should only be coding. It may seem to fit into your predisposed view of how you can advance your career to the next level – to focus on the technical skills that you were hired to use in accomplishing your tasks and projects.

Developers cannot expect to write code in isolation and deliver it by *throwing it over the wall* or putting it in a repository and closing the project. Open source and agile methodologies for software development have been just some of the factors that have changed this method of working to deliver software.

The way to grow beyond the technical and develop your emotional intelligence is to practice with others, whether virtually or in person. Look for moments to empathize, communicate, and collaborate with other people. You will see your skills develop through repetition and feedback.

How do you choose the right skills to learn? Many developers tend to want to learn the newest, coolest, or shiniest technology. Often, they will start the process of learning a newer, more innovative technological skill without considering whether it will benefit them in achieving what they really want. Before you start spending time learning a recently released technology, evaluate why you want to learn that technology or skill. Does it align with your goals to advance your career to the next level? Is it worth the time you will lose learning the skill when you could be spending that time in other areas?

It is great to learn new things, but before you add every modern technology that is popular to your list of skills to learn, think about the reason that you want to learn that technology. Is it required for a project you are working on? Or do you think it could be used in such a project? Or do you see the potential for this technology to grow and be useful to you in the future? If yes, then you should invest the time required to learn it.

Employers expect developers to be learning on the job and filling skill gaps in technical areas. The problems arise when we add every recent technology to our list of skills to learn. At that point, it can be overwhelming and can lead to procrastination and stagnation. The sheer volume of new tools, techniques, and technologies can trigger the exact opposite of what you are trying to achieve, resulting in immobility.

Time is finite. It is our most precious and valuable commodity as humans. Take the time to evaluate and consider why you want to learn a new technology before you add it to your career map. You can often gain visibility by getting involved in projects or areas that are valued by senior management. Pay attention to the projects that your line manager prioritizes. Listen to or read reports, listen to podcasts, or read articles where they discuss future directions. Communicate your interest in working in those areas. Learn new skills in those areas. Share knowledge that you have in those areas. Some excellent ways to share include social media, public speaking, user groups, and networking at industry conferences or events.

What we have learned in our own career journeys is that sharing builds communities and trust. The authors of this book share the common desire to help you advance your technical career and build your trust in us to guide you on your way to a senior developer position. Do you have a map ready with some of the areas identified where you need to grow? Take some time to think and get clarity on those items before you move on to *Part 1* of the book.

Conventions used

Tips or important notes
Appear like this

Get in touch

Feedback from our readers is always welcome.

General feedback: If you have questions about any aspect of this book, email us at customercare@ packtpub.com and mention the book title in the subject of your message.

Errata: Although we have taken every care to ensure the accuracy of our content, mistakes do happen. If you have found a mistake in this book, we would be grateful if you would report this to us. Please visit www.packtpub.com/support/errata and fill in the form.

Piracy: If you come across any illegal copies of our works in any form on the internet, we would be grateful if you would provide us with the location address or website name. Please contact us at copyright@packt.com with a link to the material.

If you are interested in becoming an author: If there is a topic that you have expertise in and you are interested in either writing or contributing to a book, please visit authors.packtpub.com.

Share Your Thoughts

Once you've read *Developer Career Masterplan*, we'd love to hear your thoughts! Scan the QR code below to go straight to the Amazon review page for this book and share your feedback.

https://packt.link/r/1801818703

Your review is important to us and the tech community and will help us make sure we're delivering excellent quality content.

Download a free PDF copy of this book

Thanks for purchasing this book!

Do you like to read on the go but are unable to carry your print books everywhere? Is your eBook purchase not compatible with the device of your choice?

Don't worry, now with every Packt book you get a DRM-free PDF version of that book at no cost.

Read anywhere, any place, on any device. Search, copy, and paste code from your favorite technical books directly into your application.

The perks don't stop there, you can get exclusive access to discounts, newsletters, and great free content in your inbox daily

Follow these simple steps to get the benefits:

1. Scan the QR code or visit the link below

https://packt.link/free-ebook/9781801818704

2. Submit your proof of purchase
3. That's it! We'll send your free PDF and other benefits to your email directly

Part 1
The Basics: Learn and Practice the Technical Skills

Career growth in the world of technology involves being great at a technical level. Although the technical side is not everything, and sometimes not even the thing that will get your career growing, it is needed to be part of the game. *Part 1* will help you go deep into the technical side, and get you ready to advance your career faster and farther.

This part has the following chapters:

- *Chapter 1, The Secret to Learning about Technology Fast and Continuously*
- *Chapter 2, Choose Your Best Path for Learning, Training, and Certifications*
- *Chapter 3, Optimize Your Support Network for Growth*
- *Chapter 4, Acquire the Right Skills Deliberately*
- *Chapter 5, Stepping Outside Your Comfort Zone*

1
The Secret to Learning about Technology Quickly and Continuously

Software development is a creative and innovative field. Although the main concepts last for many decades, the applications of those concepts, as well as technologies and tools, come and go in short periods of time. Because of this, software developers need the right skills and habits to continuously learn and adapt.

There is no better way to start a book on technology careers than by going directly into the number one career problem that you may be facing: how to stay up-to-date with the fast pace and changes of the technology world.

In our many talks and presentations around the world, the question of how to learn all the new things is common angst for technology professionals. It is common to find people that reserve several hours each day for learning, and still feel outdated and unable to catch up. To get out of this predicament, the best solution is to stop focusing on knowledge and start focusing on skills.

We, therefore, bring you this chapter, where we'll unravel the secrets to learning about technology constantly and quickly. You'll learn about the following main topics in this chapter:

- Knowledge versus skills
- Finding focus and priorities
- Applying just-in-time learning
- Practicing deliberately to learn a tech
- Implementing important good habits

Let's dive right in!

Knowledge versus skills

Developers around the world ask us a quite common question: How can we keep up with current, ever-changing technology? Developers spend many hours every week trying to do exactly that: learn about technologies, frameworks, APIs, languages, and tools that pop up all the time, hoping that this will amount to keeping up to date with technology.

The problems with this approach are multiple:

- There are too many things happening at the same time, and it is impossible to know which ones are the most important
- Trying to learn many things at once is confusing and you end up feeling tired and overwhelmed by the number of things that need to be done
- Forcing yourself to spend many hours a day doing something that seems never-ending is a recipe for frustration

But there is one thing that gets the crown for being the most frustrating:

- Learning many things that you will not apply right now is not only superficial but the knowledge will neither last nor will it be useful for long

When you learn a new skill, think about how you will apply that skill. Actively search for a way to incorporate your new skill into your day-to-day coding projects. Using the skills you gain right away will help you to build the muscle memory for the new skill and assimilate it into your library of knowledge.

Have you ever spent hours learning something that you are not using in a project right now, and a few months later, when you need it, you remember next to nothing, and have to *refresh* it? And does that *refreshing* feel like almost having to relearn everything? There is a reason for that feeling and it is the difference between knowledge and skills.

An effective way to think about knowledge is that it is a *collection of memories that are disconnected from each other*. Because they are disconnected, it takes some time for you to remember those things when you need them. And once you recover one memory, it does not help you recover other memories. This is like learning about the history of bicycles and how they were invented. Although you may love bikes, it is hard to remember the names and dates and who did what. There is a better way.

Have you ever heard the popular saying that goes like this: *once you learn how to ride a bicycle, you never forget*? This is because riding a bicycle is not knowledge; it's a skill. An effective way to think about skills is that they are collections of memories that are connected to each other. Once you recover one of those memories, they all come *together* and are accessed in a much faster way by your brain.

That is why, once you acquire the skill, you just sit on the bicycle and go. You do not need to remember each fact about riding a bike. It just *comes* to you, without effort. The most important thing about skills for you to keep in mind is that although you can acquire knowledge by reading or listening, you can only develop skills by *doing*. There is no amount of reading, listening, watching videos, or following amazing tutorials that will ever get you to ride a bicycle. The only way is to go down to the park and try, fall, try again, and eventually, do it.

This is the same for every developer skill that you want to master. **To really learn something, you must do things, instead of simply studying to acquire the knowledge**.

When you write your CV or resume or prepare your LinkedIn profile, do you list in it all the books you read and YouTube videos you watched? Do you list all the knowledge you have? Or do you put more focus on the projects you worked on and the experiences you acquired?

Even when just starting, you will clearly be better off including everything you *did*, even if they were just personal and volunteer projects, because, at the end of the day, it is your *experience* and *skills* that really matter.

We started this chapter by talking about how developers spend a lot of time trying to keep up to date, so does the discussion around skills just make it worse? We must spend time keeping up to date, but the outcome we desire is to gain more skills. As we gain skills, we must still do our day-to-day things, so it will take *more* time, not less!

Sometimes, in order to do things, you need to develop a strategy for doing so. This reminds us of a developer we know named Maryna Savchenko. She is a software engineer, based in Germany, and a true believer in software craftsmanship, clean code, and TDD. She finds intellectual fulfillment in accomplishing hard tasks and is passionate about acquiring and improving skills. When we asked her to share a story with us about learning continuously and shaping her career, she shared that what really helped her in her learning journey is a book entitled *A Mind for Numbers*, by Barbara Oakley. By reading this book, she figured out her own "learning framework." Understanding how she learns best helped her to avoid frustration and keep being motivated during learning complex topics. Understanding the best way to learn new skills and gain experience by doing is a crucial step as you continue your path for learning. Let's hear some more from Mayrna.

After leaving Kharkiv National University of Radio Electronics with a bachelor's degree in computer engineering, I did not work as a software engineer. I was told that "I do not have it." And I strongly believed that for some time. When I was offered a job in application support at a software development company, I was glad. I worked hard. I learned accounting by myself (to understand enterprise resource planning systems better) and passed four certifications, only to realize that I was learning the wrong thing. I learned the hard way how focusing on the right thing matters! Why was it wrong? Well, that technology (1C Enterprise) was limited to a number of countries (Ukraine, Russia, Belarus, and Kazakhstan). I could not reuse my knowledge, and working for a company with headquarters in Russia was not right after Russian-Ukrainian War started in 2014. In addition to that, I was making less and less money every day because of inflation. I was paying full price for my wrong decision and for listening too much to other people. At this point in time, I did the first analysis of the Java ecosystem and thought that it may be a good way forward. In the meantime, my husband and I decided to move to Poland from Ukraine. I realized at this time that I needed to think hard about what to do and what to learn next. After one more analysis of the market and technologies, I was sure that Java was a good choice and decided to become a Java programmer. Finding a job abroad without relevant experience is not an easy task. You need to be better than local candidates and prove it. In my case, I needed to prove it to myself also. So, I needed to learn a lot of things, such as the language itself, frameworks, build tools, testing frameworks, databases, design patterns, and so on. In the beginning, I was very slow, ineffective, and overwhelmed. So, I googled how other people learn. Many said they "just learn" and that is it. After some searching, I found Barbara Oakley's book and it was full of the advice I needed. I also discovered a rich and diverse software engineering community (including Java champions, Microsoft MVP people, experienced software engineers, techno bloggers, and tech educators). It gave me an understanding of what I was doing wrong, and I started to believe in my plan. But looking for a software developer job in Poland was not successful for me. I had only one technical interview. When I tried to send my CV to Germany, I realized how geography matters! From sending 13 CVs, I got 6 responses, 2 onsite interviews, and 1 job offer. And we were on our way to a new country. In Germany, I still needed to learn a lot to level up, as well as the German language. Having a learning framework gave me the right tools and confidence to proceed. Last year, I got promoted to mid-level and started blogging (`https://savchenko.tech/`). *Now, I am living in Munich and on my way to improving my career.*

As Mayrna's story illustrates, sometimes you have to find your inspiration and curiosity to continuously learn. Next, we will discuss how to find focus and priorities to help us identify the skills we need to keep up to date.

Finding focus and priorities

Connected to the *how to keep up with current, ever-changing technology* question that we looked at in the previous section, there is a follow-up that we also hear all the time: *Which technologies are important to learn today, and which ones should we prioritize?*

This question is a recognition that there simply is not enough time to acquire every skill, so what do you choose?

There is a simple answer to that: **Choose to learn something that you need to apply right now**.

It may sound simple, but it makes sense. If execution is what develops your skills, then if you prioritize learning about something that you need to use immediately, you will go ahead and use it, which will develop your skill. This is the best way to get yourself to *do* the skill the fastest. This is simple, but it is not very helpful, is it?

Imagine this. You must do something at work, and your boss tells you to learn and apply it. In this case, what we just discussed could be the right answer. However, that leaves you at the mercy of what your company wants you to do, and someone else's ideas of what is important. Not a good strategy for an awesome career, is it?

For you to take control of your career—the theme of this book—you need to proactively go after the things that make a difference to you. For that, you will need to focus and choose what matters to you.

And immediately when you hear that, you may feel a tiny bit of anxiety pop up in your head. There are so many options to choose from:

- What if I choose the wrong thing?
- What if the thing I choose is not the best thing?
- What if I miss the important things?
- What if things change?

If you feel like this, maybe it is because you think that the focus is the technology or the tool that you will spend time mastering and developing the skills for. You may be thinking that the focus is, for example, on Java instead of Go or Ruby.

But that definition of focus is too narrow, and not very useful for your career. Choosing an area of your focus is not about choosing a technology or a tool, much less a framework or an API. Choosing a focus is choosing the problem you want to solve. In a way, choosing a problem is a much more specific and narrow focus.

For example, you can focus on solving the very pressing problem of achieving high performance for large, scalable, Java-based finance applications in the cloud.

This is a very precise problem to solve. It seems much more specific than focusing on Java or the cloud.

However, the tools, knowledge, and skills needed to achieve high performance are actually many and varied. You will need to know about Java tools, cloud tools, performance tools, financial concepts, scalable architectures, and so much more!

Well, this seems too much to learn! Aren't we back to the problem of lack of focus? If you keep the problem in mind, then no. It is the problem that will help you keep your focus.

In our example, you don't need to learn or keep up to date with everything in Java, just the parts that focus on performance. There's no need to follow every single tool that shows up in the cloud. You will focus on the ones that give you an edge on the scalability needed in the financial world.

Finding your focus is finding an interesting problem to solve that you are passionate about. In the next section, we will introduce a concept to help you.

Applying just-in-time learning

Here is where the rubber hits the road. Once you know a problem, even if it is a broad idea of what it is, you have a direction to go, learn, research, and dive deep. How can we mention *broad* and *deep* in the same sentence, and not make that contradictory? This is what we call **just-in-time learning**, which is a two-step process. Let us discuss each step briefly in the following subsections.

Step 1 – Have a broad vision of the market

The first step is to have a broad view of the problem you are going after, the tools, technologies, companies, people, and more.

Once you lean toward a problem or direction, even if it is fuzzy and just defined in general broad terms, surround yourself with related information. Your goal is to go broad, to know what exists.

This will be scary because the more you know it exists, the more you will feel there are too many things you do not know. That is called the **Dunning-Kruger effect**, and it is a cognitive bias that you can learn to control:

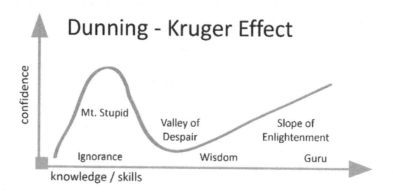

Figure 1.1 – Dunning-Kruger effect

To go broad, use the following techniques:

- Follow people related to your focus on Twitter and LinkedIn
- Search for technologies and projects in that general area
- Talk and connect with people, ask questions, and pay attention
- Attend online and in-person meetups and events
- Subscribe to bloggers in that space

Here, you are looking to have a broad view of the landscape, get a feeling about the terminology, the most mentioned and used tools, the people that are shaping that area, and what they think.

This is a superficial view, but you should also look a little below the surface. When you hear about tools and concepts you do not know, a quick Google search will tell you what they are and what they are useful for.

Keep this in mind: **you need to know that things exist, their general usefulness, what problems they solve, what problems they create, and a sense of their popularity**. You can use your memory, a file on your computer, a notebook, or even tools such as Anki to maintain your general view of your problem space. This is knowledge, and it is particularly important that you are continuously aware of your problem domain.

One crucial point: this seems very time-consuming, right? If you agree, it is because you are thinking about going deep, and spending hours researching every day. But remember, that is not the point but rather a superficial understanding. You should be aware and connected. You should be paying attention to your area. A few minutes a day, or when the opportunity arises, is more than enough for you to build that general idea.

We can almost hear you say, "*This superficial idea will not help me learn things!*" And you are right. The objective of being broad is to know what exists. Then, you apply step 2.

Step 2 – Go deep when you are ready to apply

Now that you know what exists, look for opportunities to apply interesting things in your day-to-day coding and development projects so you can experiment with this approach. This can take many forms.

Look for opportunities to experiment with some of those technologies or ideas in your current project. Even if your project will not use these ideas in production, there are many opportunities to experiment with prototypes and test cases, as tools for you to be more productive, or to build a tool for the team.

Pay attention to what is going on in your company. You may hear of projects or proofs of concept that are being considered, customers that need a new solution, or internal projects that need to be implemented. Volunteering to discuss and participate in some of those may give you a chance to apply the technologies you are interested in.

Find things outside of work that you are interested in. Applying skills at work is your best option, but sometimes the opportunities are harder to come by, and you may need to look elsewhere. Personal projects, volunteer projects for a non-profit, or open source projects are all good options.

In all cases, when you see an opportunity to apply your knowledge, this is the time to go deep with just-in-time learning. Do a deep dive into how to use that particular technology or tool. Spend a few hours during the week creating a small prototype, getting something up and running. Your goal here is to get up to speed with it as fast as possible and go as deep as possible in that time.

The objective is not to become an overnight expert but to be able to apply that new idea to a real project.

What will just-in-time learning do to your skill acquisition process?

First, it will give you a broad vision of what exists and what matters to your focus area. That, in turn, will allow you to identify opportunities to apply that technology.

Second, once you find a real opportunity, you will go deep by learning and applying immediately what you learned, and that will give you the skills you need to advance.

That begs a new question: how do we practice?

Practicing deliberately to learn a technology

If you ask me what the third question that we get all the time is, it is *How can I be a better developer?*

And again, the answer is simple enough: practice.

If what matters are the skills you only acquire by doing, it follows that the more you do (practice) the skill, the better you get at it.

Again, the answer is simple, but not very useful. Because you are probably thinking about your reality, where you barely have time to do your work and what you must do, you can barely keep up with all that goes around you. How can you spend hours and hours practicing something?

This, indeed, is a good point.

First, you do not need to spend hours and hours practicing. Second, as much as possible, you should practice by doing something real, and that, in most cases, means doing your work.

There is a third point too! If this is *your* career, should you strive to be the best you can be?

That is not a rhetorical question. For many people, their job is just a job. And that is totally OK. If this describes you, do not feel bad that you are not interested in putting your best effort into becoming better. All you need is to be good enough to hold a decent job. And at the end of the day, you go home to your family, hobbies, and your life.

There are many developers whose lives and hobbies are more interesting than their jobs. And they are *better* at their hobbies than they are at their jobs. At this moment, Bruno interjects—"*I am one of them.*" I am *better* at speaking, engaging audiences, and building communities than I am at being a software developer. I now spend my time helping developers with their careers.

As a Java developer since the earliest days of the technology, Bruno took part in some of the largest Java projects in Brazil and gained extensive experience in large projects in the government, finance, and service industries. While doing this, his passion was actually communities. Slowly, he combined his developer work with community work and started to participate in Java open source communities and projects, such as the **Java Community Process (JCP)** program, the **Open Source Initiative (OSI)**, the innovation-focused Campus Party Institute, The Developers Conference and much more.

So, although he started as a Java developer, he eventually made his community hobby his main work, and he helped to found **SouJava (Sociedade de Usuários da Tecnologia Java; Java Technology Users Society)**, one of the world's largest **Java User Groups (JUGs)**, and became a leader of the Worldwide JUGs Community, helping the organization of hundreds of JUGs worldwide.

The fact that I was able to turn my hobby into a full-time career is testimony that it can be done.

But if you *do* want to be the best technical person you can be, then you must practice. And for you to not spend all the time you have available practicing, here are a few things you need to know about practicing deliberately:

- **Deliberate practice is practicing with a purpose**: You must practice with a specific purpose in mind. Just sitting down at the computer and hacking away for a few hours is fun, and you should do it because it is fun. But that is not practicing deliberately. Define what you want to improve, by when, and what you are going to do to get there.

- **Deliberate practice is focused**: Choose a specific skill you want to improve and work deeply on it. Focus on the specific thing you need to improve and be better at. Practicing is improving one specific skill at a time.

- **Deliberate practice is intense**: Define some exercises that you can focus on with intensity for 30 minutes to 1 hour. A clever idea is to use the Pomodoro Technique and execute one or two *pomodoros* (25 minutes each). Another technique is to use the rule of three: do three focused bursts with a few minutes or even a couple of hours between them.

- **Deliberate practice is daily practice**: In terms of skills, nothing beats consistency. It is better to practice for 15 minutes every day than to concentrate 4-5 hours at the weekend. Set a daily practice time, use some inactive time during the day to review past practices, and commit yourself to do a small effort (even 5 minutes can make a substantial difference). Anything that helps you practice daily will give you better and more consistent results.

- **Deliberate practice uses proven methods**: As much as possible, follow existing tested practices. Learn how to type on the keyboard using proven methods. Practice code katas that have been created specifically to improve development skills. If you cannot find or do not know a proven method for something, talk with friends or colleagues who are more advanced than you, and see whether you find some common techniques that worked for them.

Practicing proven methods daily, in a focused way, and with intensity, especially when combined with work, can at the same time reduce the number of hours invested and give better results.

You will encounter roadblocks along the way, but you can remind yourself to make learning a part of your career path and journey. To be successful in your technical career, you need to consistently be learning. Consistency with a manageable amount of learning is the key to success in making learning a part of your lifestyle.

But how can you keep the consistency? You keep consistency by making learning a habit. That is why we need to build a few good habits.

Implementing important good habits

Your brain is always trying to optimize the paths and build the neurological structures (the brain equivalent of muscles) to allow you to do what you need to survive. So, it looks for repetitive things that you do, and it tries to codify those repetitive tasks into structures that are easier to access, faster to execute, and require less energy.

That is why we are creatures of habit. Most of what you do every day are habits or routines, codified in our brains, so we can access them easily and quickly.

When those structures help you move forward and achieve your goals, we call them good habits. They are good for you. When they prevent you from advancing, hinder your results, slow you down, or cause you harm, they are vices or bad habits.

Either way, your brain loves to just run with them!

There are a few good habits that can really change your life. We have listed a few steps that we think are particularly important for you to create good habits.

Take action

When there is something that you would like to do, get in the habit of taking small actions. Taking action is the hardest thing for us to do, and not taking action is the basis for terrible vices such as procrastination and perfectionism.

Try to take small actions on things you want to do. Do you want to participate in an open source project? That seems big and fearsome. Take a small action such as accessing the page of the project and looking at it for a few minutes. Overcoming the inertia of things you want to do will help you do things even when you do not feel like it.

Write every day

Our brains can be cluttered with thoughts and ideas. To help you think better, your brain needs to externalize. Speaking with someone or writing about it will help you clarify your thinking.

That is why developers need to write code every day, focusing on solving problems. Take a few minutes every day to write about a problem. It can be writing the text for a blog or article, or it could be more technical and be code and pseudocode to explain or test an idea. It can also be just having a conversation. Doing this daily will help you think better and be more articulate.

Create routines to get yourself started

You know when you start a sports activity, your coach will do some exercises that are always the same? Things like stretching and warming up exercises. This primes your body and gets it ready for the activity ahead. Your brain needs that too.

Create small routines to start working. Start coding. Or any important activity that you need to be very sharp and focused.

A startup routine is a series of small steps, such as saying the following to yourself – before I start coding I will do these things:

- Sit down
- Put away things that are not needed

- Drink a glass of water
- Close the email
- Open the IDE

Try to repeat the same steps, with purpose, every time you start coding. It will prime your brain and get it ready to focus on the task at hand.

Plan your week

We live in a world that is full of distractions and we combat information overload coming from all aspects of our lives. We are busy and it becomes difficult and overwhelming to achieve the things that matter to us. If we focus on the things that are most important to us and that we want to accomplish, we not only gain focus but we also become happier and more productive. This is the idea behind the Three Big Rocks concept. It is a concept that can help us to prioritize our time.

The Three Big Rocks concept is mentioned by Stephen Covey in his book, *The Seven Habits of Highly Productive People*, which can be found on Amazon at `https://www.amazon.com/dp/0743269519/ref=olp-opf-redir?aod=1<`.

In this book, there is a time management expert giving a seminar to a roomful of people. He provides a demonstration of this concept by taking a mason jar and putting large rocks into the jar and asking the audience whether or not the jar is full. The attendees indicate that the jar does appear to be full. The speaker then adds smaller rocks into the jar, fitting them in between the large rocks, and turns again to the audience to ask whether the jar is full. The audience is not sure which way to answer at this point, so he adds some sand to the jar to fill in even more of the space between the large rocks and the pebbles. While pausing and asking the audience again to confirm whether the jar is full, he then pours water into the jar until it is at the point of overflowing. The speaker then asks what the objective of this exercise is. Some people may answer that no matter how busy or full your schedule may be, there is always room to put more things into your schedule; however, the point of the Three Big Rocks example is that if you don't put the big rocks in first, you will never get them in at all.

This is a simplification of the concept and there is much more that you could learn and apply, but this gives you an overview of the main idea behind the term "three big rocks." To implement this concept, at the start of the week, make sure you decide on your three big rocks for the week. They are the three most important tasks you have for the week, the ones where, if you complete them, you will feel that your week was worth it.

Schedule time to do them. To choose the three big rocks, look at your long-term goals, and make sure you choose the things that move you in the right direction.

Deploy habits

Those are just a few examples you can implement. To help you deploy those habits in your life, remember to start small. Your brain will resist any substantial changes.

Habits are implanted faster if you succeed than if you fail. So, it is better to create a writing habit by writing for 5 minutes every day and succeeding every day than trying to start writing for 1 hour a day and failing after a few tries.

Also, daily habits are easier to implement because they become ingrained faster. To implement a habit, experts say you need around 66 repetitions to create new pathways in the brain. That amounts to 3 to 4 weeks if you do 2 or 3 repetitions a day. So, it is better to do something you can repeat every day, multiple times a day, depending on the habit. That is another reason why you should focus on starting small.

Other techniques you can use to help you keep the motivation to implement powerful habits include doing things together with friends in a community (it increases your commitment) and organizing your day or your habit to be easier for you to do than for you not to do (making it easier for you to take action).

Building small habits or routines will help you stay focused and consistent and will lay the groundwork for you to advance fast in your career.

Heather interjects here, as an enthusiastic learner who enjoys having a variety of responsibilities, *"I have found joy in being able to consistently bring new aspects and skills into my life and career by developing habits that set me up to be successful."*

As the senior director and chairperson of the JCP program, in her role, Heather is responsible for the leadership of the community and chairing the JCP Executive Committee. She has led and participated in several initiatives with the community (including JUGs) as part of her role, such as JCP.next, Adopt a JSR, Hack Days, and Java in Education, and is an internationally renowned public speaker at software development events all over the world.

She says, *the work that I do to engage the Java developer community on a global basis is broad and vast – it could become overwhelming to think about all of the areas where I could focus. I have found that by incorporating habits to focus my time, it becomes energizing and exciting to always be evolving and learning. In order to establish consistency and focus to accomplish great things in the community, I have incorporated certain habits that are part of my routine. For example, every Sunday, I review my calendar for the week and block out time for my priorities for the week. I also identify those priorities and set aside time to prepare for the most important meetings of my week. I then identify a list of tasks that should be accomplished during the week. My week also includes time for creation, learning, and networking. I have set habits that allow me to build these activities into my week. For instance, I rise early and take time early in my day to focus on creation or writing, and I plan most of my meetings following that time, in my mid-morning hours. I incorporate some form of exercise in the middle of my day, and my afternoons are for doing tasks on my list. I also try to leave Fridays open for new initiatives or projects that I might be working on, as well as learning and networking. Setting up my habits to include these areas that I have identified as priorities for me has allowed me to grow and expand my career and my areas of influence over time.*

Tips for learning new skills

Assess and focus. You need to identify the skills or knowledge you are missing – be as specific and focused as possible to narrow down the area to learn. Look for skills and knowledge you need to learn right now.

Study and review the skills to build and deploy your habits. Have a plan and stick to it. Look for ways to celebrate and reward your success along the way. Share and communicate those wins to other people.

Get feedback and check your progress. Validate that you are on the identified path. Adjust your learning process and plan as necessary. Ask for feedback from others to check your knowledge and learning progress.

Interview

Rafael del Nero

We would like to share with you the experience of Rafael del Nero, working at Mastercard as an example.

Q: Tell us a little bit about the current role that you have at Mastercard. What do you do? What kind of things do you work with? How interesting are the projects that you work on? Tell us a little bit about that.

A: I'm a senior software engineer at Mastercard, and my work is not exactly related to business requirements implementation. The project we've got is to triple our current cloud project that's deployed only in the US to other continents. We are doing a lot of DevOps work and configuration work for our website, and my day-to-day work is on that.

I'm going to give you some examples of the work I've done. Some of the activities that I've been doing have been migrating Java 8 to Java 11. Another example would be adding partition jobs and out-scaling. I've generally been doing work to enable our services to be deployed in other continents, and we have to make them at least a little bit more reliable by adding out-scaling and basic microservices features.

I'm not doing a lot of coding. But even in my last role in the last company I was working for, I wasn't doing a lot of coding because, as I said, sometimes, for developers, the scenario of software development is changing. You are far more of a software engineer rather than a developer who develops code. I don't see that very much anymore in the market, and that's happening because of the cloud era. Services nowadays are deployed in an isolated way. It's just a natural thing that happens in technology. As technology evolves and gets more mature, the work changes as well. Nowadays, for example, we don't have one big unit. We have microservices, and they communicate with each other using investment brokers, and so on. I've also done a lot of work with message brokers, so it's just software engineering work.

Q: Tell us a little bit about your projects. You have the Java challenges project. Can you tell us a little bit about that, how that got started, and the results you're having with it?

A: Yes. The Java challenges started five years ago.

Basically, they are Java quizzes. They are carefully designed to help Java developers really understand Java features. They resemble the certification questions but are more useful than those questions. I carefully produced them to really push developers to understand the main Java features, such as polymorphism, threads, and inheritance, and new features, such as records, the new switch case, pattern matching, and virtual threads. There are Java challenges for all of those features, and it's fun for developers to understand and master those features.

As for how it started: well, it started with Bruno! If you didn't motivate me to share my knowledge, maybe I would never have done it! When I saw your talk on TDC, you were saying that it was possible. In one talk of yours, someone mentioned mentorship, and I said, "*Man, this guy is crazy. How would Bruno or anyone else need a mentorship?*" Then, you answered, and then I said, "*OK. Maybe that's possible.*"

Then, I started the mentorship program with you, but before starting the mentorship with you, just with that talk I saw on TDC, you had already made me believe that it was possible. By going through your talk, I gave two talks at my job, because I thought, "*OK. I believe Bruno. He said it's possible, so I'm going to do it.*" You were able to empower me to give my first talk, and that was great because after I gave those talks, people were looking differently at me and telling me, "*Rafael, I can really see that you've grown a lot,*" just because I delivered the talks.

When I saw the guy asking that question, I said, "*Oh, this guy's crazy. How can Bruno give mentorship?*" Then, you put up your website, and I said, "*OK. I'm going to write that down and do the mentorship with Bruno.*" At that moment, I decided that I was going to do the mentorship.

Anyway, I learned a lot from you, and then I started sharing knowledge on Twitter more consistently because I wasn't doing that very consistently before. I had maybe five posts on my blog – I didn't have a lot – but then I learned that consistency was so important with you, so I said, "*OK. I'll commit to that. I will start generating content regarding how to have fewer bugs or how to create high-quality code.*" I started creating some blog posts regarding that.

I did a design pattern post on Twitter, and Yolande retweeted this design pattern article and I got lots of views. I wanted to say thanks to her, and then I asked you, Bruno, "*How can I thank Yolande? How can I thank the Java community for that?*" You said, "*Create content for her.*" I thought, "*OK. What can I do?*"

Then, I saw that she was working on a project called *100 Days of Java*. I thought to myself, "*OK. I really like to explore those Java features and I also like games, and I'd like to create some Java code challenges. I will create one daily challenge,*" and that's what I have done. I created one Java challenge every day and I shared them with Yolande and the Java community.

That was an amazing way to help her to share Java knowledge, and it helped me a lot as well because I gained so much visibility. In fact, I had no idea that I was getting so much visibility, but when I had the Java challenge of going to JavaOne in 2017, a lot of people already knew me. A lot of people came to me and said, "*Oh, I know you. I know your job. I know your work.*" I was impressed because a lot of people knew me because of the Java challenges.

The consistency was a game-changer. Sometimes, one simple idea, when combined with a strong will and consistency, can be a game-changer. I was consistent with the Java challenges, and that opened a lot of doors for me. It opened the door to give a talk at JavaOne. That then opened the door to writing a book. That then opened doors to great videos and great articles, and I also wrote a lot of articles for JavaWorld and IDG InfoWorld because of the Java challenges. It's all down to one idea, motivation, and encouragement – you know, there are lots of variables, but at the start was the empowerment of a mentor: that's so important. Bruno was my mentor – he is my mentor. Maybe without that, I wouldn't have been empowered enough. Maybe I wouldn't be doing what I'm doing. I was focusing so much on technical knowledge that I forgot everything else. What happened was that a lot of other people were getting promoted, and I wasn't.

Q: What were the results for you of the consistency, the practice, and the challenges? What happened in your career after that?

A: Well, what happened was that I got visibility, and it was far easier to get interviews, for example. A lot of companies were sending me messages on LinkedIn to do interviews, and when I arrived in Ireland, things were easier. There were doors open already.

For example, through SouJava, I was able to meet the Java group leader when I was touring Sao Paulo. That opened doors for me because I already knew him. In the first week, I remember I went out with the two Barrys, and we had a chat, and it was fun. Then, I could help him build their website, and it was great because I was mentoring a German lady and I was practicing my English. It was good to have these doors open when I came here for the first time.

When I was sharing my knowledge, what happened is that I gained trust. People trusted me, even if they had never talked to me before; I had their trust. Barry Alistair, the JUG leader, told me, "*Hey, Rafael. There is a group of Brazilians there. Go say hi to them.*" I went over to say hi, and one of those Brazilians – Rodrigo Rodriguez – knew me already; he had seen my content. He said, "*Hey. Are you working?*" I said, "*No. I'm looking for a job.*" Then, he said, "*Man, there is a company that's really good to get started with.*" I went to talk to a friend of his, and then I got recommended to this company, and then things worked out.

So, why is sharing so important? You gain trust. Even if people have never talked to you before, people trust you. He only recommended me because he saw the content I was sharing, and I didn't even need to tell him anything. He just said, "*I will recommend you.*" What happened was great because, when you recommend people, in most companies, you get some money. He got some money, I got the job, and so it was a win-win for everyone.

Q: One of the things you mentioned here was practicing and consistency. Can you talk a little bit about how practice was important for you to learn new skills, especially because one of the things that you do is that you help other people practice? How important is practicing to improve and learn things and improve skills?

A: Well, it's highly important. Practice is the key to mastery. You can do only moderate-quality work if you do it once in a while, but you can create a masterpiece if you do deliberate practice. That's why it's so important to build consistency, and it's hard to build consistency because there are days that you don't really want to do whatever you're committed to doing. But on those days, when you push yourself, those are the days that you build up mastery.

It's extremely important to do deliberate practice in whatever skill you want to really build up. In the case of the Java challenges, nowadays, I'm able to create better Java code challenges. It's important to be consistent because that's how you build up your confidence, and when you build up your confidence, you are able to do much more.

And not only that: when you are consistent and do whatever you plan to do for a long period of time, you will excel in that skill. If you do something only once in a while, you'll be only average in that skill. You won't excel. You won't gain mastery of your work. But if you are consistent for a long period of time, and you do what you need to do, even when you don't feel like it, you can build really big things. And that's hard to do because you are fighting against your own mind.

Q. You help people to become better developers. I know you: you help them with the Java challenges project, and you help them to learn new things and be better. What's your biggest suggestion for people to improve their skills?

A: Deliberate practice is the key to the mastery of skills – for example, writing. Writing is a skill that takes time until you get good at it. I started writing articles consistently so that I could get better at my writing skills. Not only that, but I could also improve my writing skills by writing a book.

As a tip for anyone who wants to be consistent, firstly, you have to believe that you can get there. Otherwise, you won't even do any of the work because what's the point of doing such hard work for nothing? The first step for anyone who wants to be consistent is to believe that you can achieve it.

Mentors help so much with that because a mentor is someone who has a much broader view than you, and that gives you the confidence to believe that it's possible. A mentor is a tremendous aid to help you with your confidence.

You'll also have to fight against your own mind because there will be days that you won't be willing to do whatever you're committed to doing. You have to decide, "*OK. I'm going to do that no matter what,*" because you're going to have to do those things on the days that you don't feel like it: that's hard. But when you see the big picture and think, "*OK. If I keep doing that, I know that I will reap good things,*" it gets easier.

It also gets easier when you start seeing results. When you start seeing results, that's a boost for your motivation. But you have to keep in mind that motivation won't get you all the way. Discipline will get you all the way. Motivation is a booster that you have at the beginning, but what makes you continue is not motivation – it's discipline. Of course, you're going to have some motivation boosters – when you see some results, for instance, you're going to have a motivation boost – but for most of the process, you're going to have to be taking action and not getting immediate results. Focus not on the results but on the process, and just keep doing it.

That's the hardest part: to keep doing the thing you decided to do, even when you don't feel like it. It's a war against your own mind. That's the hardest thing about being consistent. Staying consistent on those days that you don't feel like it is the hardest thing.

And of course, do something you enjoy – otherwise, it's much easier to give up. If you do something you like, then you feel more motivated, but keep in mind that sometimes, whatever you choose to do, there will be things to do that will be a little bit boring: that's OK. Sometimes, it won't be so easy – you're going to have to embrace the boredom. I embrace the boredom a lot. You have to keep in mind that it is part of the process: sometimes you're going to do boring tasks. But of course, keep the fun tasks as well – otherwise, if you keep doing only boring tasks, you might give up.

I always innovate. If you are creating content or learning technologies and you end up learning or using the same technology for many years, you're going to get bored. Always find new ways to learn, and that should upgrade your career.

Summary

In this chapter, we have covered how you can always be learning. You now have the tools to identify what you need to learn and what you need to practice. You also have an understanding of how to apply just-in-time learning to accelerate your learning journey. By planning your priorities in advance and identifying what it is that you want to learn, you will be able to keep a focus on the big picture of what it is you want to accomplish on your career path. In order to stay on your path, you know that you must apply deliberate practice methods and focus on implementing important habits to set yourself on a path to be always learning. Now that you have this mindset of always learning, with a dedicated and precise focus, we can move on to discussing some types of learning that you may want to consider as you continue on your technical career journey. As we mentioned earlier, there are both formal and informal learning methods and pathways. Both have a critical role to play in shaping your skillset and career.

In the next chapter, we will cover the essential elements of formal learning and certifications. Formal learning means you are told what you need to learn, and the goals for the learning will be clearly established by an instructor or identified in an online learning course or certification program. Using the tools you have learned about here will help you to select the best formal learning and certifications for your career journey.

2
Choose Your Best Path for Learning, Training, and Certifications

One of the unique advantages of technical careers is the normalization of continuous learning. Learning new skills actually changes and shapes your brain in positive ways. As we mentioned in the *Preface* of this book, employers of this era expect their employees to constantly re-skill themselves. This puts developers at an advantage because ongoing learning, training, and certifications are the hallmarks of developers. While we know this to be true, there is always this tension between formal, informal, and self-taught learning processes. In this context, certifications appear as a crucial way to validate those learnings. This chapter will discuss how to merge and benefit from all the learning possibilities that are available for developers. Therefore, we've included the following main topics in the agenda of this chapter:

- Deriving maximum benefit from formal learning
- Expanding your opportunities through informal learning
- Learning how to learn – self-learning
- Acquiring and benefiting from certifications
- Combining several learning possibilities

So, without waiting any longer, let's dive right into it!

Deriving maximum benefit from formal learning

While formal learning is not the only method to gain technical skills, it can provide a valuable base of knowledge or addition to existing knowledge. In order to derive the maximum benefit from formal learning, you must be conscious and consistent. Sometimes, formal learning is undertaken as a requirement to move on to the next step, whether that be a degree or a position. When you approach learning in this way, it is easy to lose sight of why you are taking the time to learn the topic or skill. This is not what you want to do. Here are a few things we suggest:

- Approach every learning experience by first clarifying and understanding why you are investing your time and money (or someone else's money, if your employer is paying the costs).

- Next, be clear about what you want your learning outcomes to be through this formal learning experience, and keep your mind focused on this outcome throughout the educational experience.

- While it is often not a requirement to have formal computer science learning, it is often an advantage to have formal learning and training, especially for hiring and promotions. You should consider investing the time and financial resources to obtain formal learning experiences.

There are formal learning options offered through traditional university institutions with formal computer science courses and degree programs, corporate training programs, and coding *bootcamps*.

A coding bootcamp is a concentrated course that teaches technical skills and provides real-world training in computer and information technology fields. Coding bootcamps shorten the time and expense that would be involved with a 4-year college degree. They often focus on technical skills that are easy and fast to learn, such as frontend web development. Bootcamps can provide an entry point into a technical career. Through a coding bootcamp, learners can acquire skills that businesses need without spending time and money on a computer science degree. For example, many bootcamps can be completed in 12 weeks. This can also be used as a stepping stone in your career to position you to learn other technologies and languages.

Traditional degree programs provide an extensive foundational base for critical thinking and complex problem-solving. Often, traditional 4-year programs also include instruction on coding in languages such as Java or Python. Arguably, the most critical skill in software development is complex problem-solving. Combined with the essential emotional intelligence skills, this is a powerful combination to propel your career forward. A boot camp-style training program is also a formal learning option. These programs are often structured and short-term, offering an alternative to a degree program, which can be more economical and shorter in duration. They are typically focused on teaching specific skills, such as frontend coding, with the objective of acquiring the skills and assisting in job placement following the completion of the training. These types of programs are often preferred by individuals who are looking to make a career shift or transition into software development technical roles from non-technical roles.

We know developers who pursued a formal 4-year computer science degree at universities who are frustrated when they are not hired for junior or entry-level development jobs. There are other developers who are hired right out of a 4-year university computer science degree program. What works for some developers will not work for others. Do keep in mind that *formal learning is important, but it is not the only type of learning required for a software development career; it is not necessarily always required, either.*

There are also ongoing formal training programs that can be used to supplement any kind of formal university or bootcamp training programs. These can be on specific technical skills, or more theoretical conceptual topics, such as agile methodologies, project management, technical leadership, or similar.

In my experience, there are often employer-provided training budgets and allocations for employees. I am often surprised to find that many developers do not take advantage of and use these employee benefits. When I have asked why people do not utilize their training allocations, it is usually because they are too busy with their day-to-day job or coding project. I urge you to dedicate the time on a regular basis to take the formal training that is budgeted for by your employer, or budget the funds in your own financial planning if you are self-employed or your employer does not provide these benefits. Learning new skills will expand your mind and give you perspective in your day-to-day coding work. Even when it seems you do not need the skills at this time, there is always something new to learn. One of the leadership courses that I took in my earlier career began with understanding the premise: You don't know what you don't know until you know. In other words, until you gain knowledge, you can become complacent in your belief that you know all that you require at that moment. Once you obtain and assimilate new skills, you discover the value of the information that you did not know before.

All of these formal training options have their advantages. Again, keep in mind why you are undertaking the training as you make your decisions on what type of formal training you will acquire.

Expanding your possibilities through informal learning

In Heather's two decades of experience working with some of the top developers around the world, approximately half of the developers I have worked with have been *self-taught*, meaning that they have not completed formal learning to acquire their development skills.

Whether you have acquired your skills through formal learning or not, there is a significant role to play in informal learning. You will expand your career possibilities through informal learning.

There are many forms that informal learning can take. While there are a myriad of online audio and/ or video options available, there are also books (or e-books or audiobooks) and the often-overlooked informal learning option of pair programming. There are also books published by Packt on pair programming. Informal learning has the advantages of being affordable, accessible, and self-paced. You must still keep at the top of your mind the motivation for your learning, being pragmatic in the courses or materials you decide to undertake for your informal learning path. Plan to dedicate an hour or more every day to digesting some of this informal learning. Take breaks as you go, preferably every 20 to 25 minutes, and remember to share and discuss what you are learning with your peers. This can be done electronically or in person, but this important element will cement the learning in your mind and help you to apply your learning in your career.

Another informal learning opportunity is through code reviews. Many developers think of a code review as a negative aspect of software development because it is often difficult to hear feedback on your work, and it is time-consuming to explain and potentially defend the technical decisions that you have made in developing software. However, code reviews are a wonderful opportunity for learning not only technical skills but also critical thinking and communication skills, as you approach and explain how you are solving problems and listen to your peers to learn from them. Listening to learn and understand is vastly different than listening only to have your turn to speak. Listening can become a valuable skill and differentiator for you in your career as you seek to learn and understand.

In selecting topics for your informal learning, look for skill gaps in the projects you are working on, both in your paid development role as well as in any volunteer projects you are working on or following. The number of topics and informal learning options can be overwhelming, so allow yourself to be selective and guided by the need or perceived future need for skills on a particular topic. There is always something new to learn, so make peace with it and accept the reality that you will never know it all. And you don't need to know it all. You don't need to have all of the answers to be successful, or even to be an expert in your field. In *Part 2, Get Involved: Participate in the Community*, of this book, we will share how you can get more engaged in the community to help you to tap into the emerging demands of new technologies.

Select the mode of informal learning most suited to your educational style. Do you retain information better via auditory or written delivery? Often, there are similar materials available in multiple forms – written, audio, and video. Utilize the method that is most effective for you. You may also complement the learning by consuming it in multiple ways to reinforce the materials. I often like to watch a video and then refer to written materials, either a book or online materials, and then find audio recordings that I can listen to after I have absorbed the key concepts. Identify the methods that suit your particular learning style.

Once you find a combination of modes of learning that works for you, you can continue to consume learning materials in that style, whether it is articles, blogs, podcasts, videos, or books. There may be certain times of the day when a mode of learning is more effective for you. For example, I like to listen to podcasts in the morning while I am doing my stretching exercises, and I prefer to read articles or newsletters later in the day. Find experts with opinions that you respect and admire and follow them on social media to be informed when they release new information. Designate times during the day that you can dedicate to learning. There is a limitless amount of knowledge to consume, so be sure to set limits on the time you spend learning versus the time you spend coding and working for your employer or company. Learning is important and should be an integral part of your career map.

One of the best informal learning methods is pair programming. This mode of learning allows you to learn in real time in a hands-on way from one of your peers. You can help each other, learn from each other, and share your learnings. This can happen simultaneously and can also enable you to improve your communication, collaboration, and emotional intelligence skills along the way. If you are not currently engaged in pair programming, look for ways to incorporate this style of learning into your work. You will reap the rewards both individually and collectively. It will also complement your other informal learning methods.

Self-learning – be independent by learning how to learn

While it is important to share your knowledge, it is just as important to be independent in your learning. Part of the excitement in a technical development role is that technologies evolve and change constantly. In order to succeed, then, you must learn how to learn. You need to learn how to adapt to the expectation that you will need to acquire new skills, and those are most often expected to be acquired by employees independently, in their own time.

Once you have identified the way you prefer to learn, self-learning (or learning how to learn) becomes second nature. It is an intrinsic part of the way you perform in your development role. You incorporate learning new skills into your everyday routine and habits. Making learning a habit takes time, practice, and commitment. When you establish the idea that self-learning will be part of your routine, identify the way you learn best, and commit to dedicating time for learning in your daily or weekly schedule, it will become a habit. You will not need to be told what skills you should acquire; you will identify them and seek out ways to learn those new skills and technologies in a way that works best for you. This is an ongoing process. As you learn, remember to share what you are learning with others.

Make self-learning your superpower. Become known for consistently and selectively identifying the skills that are required for your role. This will not only benefit you in growing your skillset but will also set you apart and differentiate you in your organization and career.

I know several developers who are known in the community for evaluating new tools and technologies. They are often sought out for new opportunities either to speak at conferences or to work on new projects. They have built their reputations and careers on learning how to learn.

Tips to build your reputation and career include the following:

- When you decide to learn a new skill, share your experience as you go on social media and with your peers.

- Offer to present on topics alongside speakers, colleagues, or mentors you admire. This is a fantastic opportunity to learn something new from someone with experiences you seek to add to your repertoire. Heather interjects, *"I know of a developer working in Central America who has utilized this method to advance their career."* By selecting a topic you think is advantageous to learn, you can then seek out experts who are familiar with this topic. You can learn from them and discuss their experiences with them. You can also do some independent studying and learning on your own, and then bring your questions and areas of interest back to the expert for further exploration. This will deepen your learning and also strengthen the relationship with the expert in your shared interest. You can look for opportunities to present together on this topic. It is an interesting experience to hear about a topic from the perspective of a long-time expert and pair this with the insights of someone newer to the skill. It is very interesting to hear the viewpoints of a new learner with fresh eyes on the subject. Look to provide your social media followers with a regular cadence of updates to your learning of the skill. Be willing to share when you are making progress, when you are stuck at a certain point, or even when you are lost or falling behind. You will be surprised at the camaraderie that follows when you are willing to be vulnerable to show your successes as well as your struggles.

- Create a presentation on your experience of learning a new skill and share your unique perspectives at conferences, summits, user group meetings, or employer meetings.

- Share the benefits you have realized by learning a new skill on social media and with your peers.

- Offer to be a resource to people who want to learn more about this skill.

Acquiring and benefiting from certifications

Certifications can communicate and verify your expertise with certain technologies. They can differentiate you from others with similar credentials and experience and they can instill confidence in your skills and knowledge. The benefits of certification will vary depending on your role, location, and experience level. There are no disadvantages to certifications, but their value will vary depending on these factors.

For example, if you are an entry-level junior developer, a certification can help to supplement formal and informal learning. You may not yet have work experience to prove your expertise and skills, but certifications can be a way to supplement your education and verify your knowledge.

The value of certifications will also vary depending on the reputation of the certifying institution. The more well-known a certifying institution is and the higher its influence, the more value will be conveyed with the certification. For instance, in the world of Java technology certifications, the Oracle University training and subsequent certification program is well-known and highly regarded, with the expectation being that Java certification comes from Oracle University since Oracle is the steward of Java technology. There are also certifications from other vendors or even some vendor-neutral certifications, but for Java certifications, Oracle University offers the gold standard.

There are some developers in the Java community who are passionate and enthusiastic about certifications and advocate for developers to become certified on the latest versions as soon as the materials are released and available. Indeed, in some areas, this is an essential criterion for some employers looking for Java developer talent. This is also a way for developers to differentiate themselves in the marketplace. I think of certain countries such as India, for example, where this can be particularly important. Employers often seek a developer with a certification when they are hiring, and even once employed, staying current on certifications and providing tips and suggestions to fellow developers can become an area of expertise in your career. There is a developer advocate in India who is known for her advocacy around Java certifications and regularly speaks and writes blogs and articles around Java certifications. In this way, she has made certifications part of her personal brand and area of expertise. Members of the community will look to her as an expert in this field and go to her for advice and questions on this topic.

Some Java certifications from Oracle University include the following:

- Oracle Certified Associate, Java SE 11 Programmer
- Oracle Certified Professional, Java SE 11 Programmer

- Oracle Certified Associate, Java SE 17 Programmer

- Oracle Certified Professional, Java SE 17 Programmer

- Oracle Certified Foundations Associate, Java

- Java EE And Web Services Oracle Certified Professional, Java EE 7 Application Developer

There will most likely be Java SE 21 certifications coming out in 2023. The certification path is typically offered for the Java SE releases that are offered as **Long-Term Support (LTS)** releases. Java SE 11 was the first Java SE LTS release, followed by Java SE 11, and the next Java SE LTS release is planned to be Java SE 21 in September 2023.

There are also certifications available from various cloud vendors and providers (which you can use as a platform to deploy your applications), such as from **Oracle Cloud Infrastructure (OCI)**. In addition, your location will be a factor in the value of certifications. In certain areas of the world or certain types of organizations, there are requirements or expectations of certifications for beginner or junior programmers, as well as more experienced or senior developers. There is also the expectation that certifications remain current and up to date. If you have adopted the ability to learn how to learn, then this will be natural or second nature for you at this point.

Many developers in emerging economies often relay to me that certifications from a reputable source are essential in their communities due to the plethora of different certification options or authorities being offered in the region. Often, in more developed economies, certifications are viewed as optional or nice to have. In these economies, experience is often more valued than certifications. However, certifications are typically seen as either an added bonus or as a requirement, depending on the area.

There are also vendor-neutral certifications available for certain technologies. For example, there are several vendor-neutral and vendor-specific cybersecurity programs. The vendor-specific programs will give you an authority on a specific vendor platform. The vendor-neutral ones will focus on interoperability and how the different offerings work or complement each other.

Once you have obtained your certifications, actively seek ways to apply the knowledge and techniques you have learned in the courses required for your certification. Be confident in asserting your knowledge based on the certifications you have obtained from a source you can trust. Be willing to communicate and share the learnings you have gained and establish yourself as a technical leader in this field. You now have the credentials to back up your experiences and other learnings.

You should also add your certifications to your social media/professional profiles. This will help to promote your skills and drive awareness for you as a proactive learner.

So far, we have reviewed formal and informal learning options, learning how to learn, and obtaining appropriate certifications. In the next section, we will describe how to combine many of your learning opportunities to create a strong foundation for your technical career.

Combining several learning possibilities

As you evolve through your career and learning pathway, you will need to combine all of the methods we have discussed in this chapter to achieve career growth. You will undoubtedly have some formal learning, some informal learning, and certifications, and along the way, you will acquire the ability to learn. Working as a software developer in the industry, you will very quickly learn that the expectations for continuous learning and improvement are real. It can be overwhelming if you have not designed a strategy to approach how you will learn. Remember to evaluate how you learn and why you are learning the skills you have identified. Be purposeful in your approach to your learning. Attempt to combine some elements of all of these methodologies to learn.

Continuous learning and development can also be expensive. Your employer can often be a resource for these expenses as part of your ongoing employee training and development budget. All too often, employees do not utilize these budgets and they are unrealized. Ensure that you are communicating with your management about your ongoing training and development plans. This will not only help with expenses but also will guide your selection of tools and technologies, ensure visibility of your commitment to your development, and ensure awareness of your career development plans and progress. We will talk more about taking responsibility for your career and your relationship with your direct manager in the next chapter.

Ask yourself who you aspire to be. Do you aspire to become a senior developer? If so, commit yourself to an ongoing process of learning and improvement. Enjoy the process of continuous learning as a way to expand your knowledge base and skill set. Many times, developers will ask what type of training they should select to advance their careers. In reality, it is a mix and a balance of activities that must be selected strategically. It is not a case of multiple choices and one answer and one size fits all. You must evaluate the available learning options and let your career map guide you as you make your choices. Always keep the end goal and picture in mind as you decide where to invest not only your money but also your time. Heather interjects here: *One of my favorite and guiding thoughts in my life has to do with time. You could say that I am obsessed with time. Time is a precious resource.* As Steve Jobs has been quoted as saying, the most precious resource we have is time. *"My favorite things in life don't cost any money. It's really clear that the most precious resource we all have is time."* So, when you make decisions on your learning path, bear in mind not only the financial costs involved but also the costs of your time. Economists call this the opportunity cost. Opportunity cost is the value of what you lose when choosing between two or more options. You may lose money or you may lose time, but you make the choice based on whatever you decide will produce more value for you in the end, no matter what you lose, based on making and following through with that choice. Actively seek out ways to learn the skills and technologies you have identified. Look for a base of formal learning, and then supplement it with informal learning and experiences to use those skills. Identify and evaluate whether there are ways to validate those skills through certifications. Think about ways you can share your learning processes to not only help others but also reinforce your own learning and process. Applying your knowledge as you gain it is the best way to ensure that you continue on your path of career growth.

Acquiring knowledge without applying and synthesizing the information provides little value. You must actively find ways to apply your skills. If you have been strategic in selecting what to learn and if you have kept in mind your motivation, or why you are learning, along the way, it will be a natural extension of your learning to apply it in your daily development work and projects.

Interview

Mala Gupta

Q: Can you introduce yourself and tell us a little bit about who you are?

A: I work as a developer advocate with JetBrains. I have written a couple of books on Java, mostly on Java certifications. One was on the new features of Java. I'm a Java Champion, and I also lead two communities: one is the Delhi Java User Group, and the other one is Women Who Code Delhi. Thanks for the opportunity to let me talk about my journey.

Q: Thank you so much. Can you tell us a little bit about how you got started in your career and how you got involved with technology?

A: I did my undergraduate course in computer science. The story of why I am a developer goes way back to when I was in class six. That was when I started learning coding at my school, and I immediately knew that it was the career that I wanted to see myself in, so I pursued it. I did coding at school for a couple of years, and then I did my undergraduate course in computer science. That's why I am a developer.

In the late 1990s, I started my first job. I was working with Visual Basic in the beginning. I liked that, but Java was taking off big time, and I had to make a decision as to whether I wanted to go with Visual Basic or Java. Java had the big promise of "write once, run everywhere." I liked that concept, and so that's how I went toward Java.

For my first job, I was a Swing developer. I made a desktop application in Swing, and that still remains one of the best projects that I think I worked on.

Q: Cool. You said you're a Java Champion and a developer advocate. Can you tell us how you got to your current position and what you do?

A: As I said, I have been working with Java since I started my career. I've been doing development in Java for quite a long time. Around 2010, I started thinking about writing books on Java.

When I graduated from college and started working as a Java developer, I saw that there was a gap between what we were taught at university and what the industry demanded of us. Soon after I joined my second job, I had to complete one of two Java certifications, which was part of the requirements of the job. One certification was Sun-Certified Java Developer, and the other one was Sun-Certified Web Component Developer, which was on server-side Java.

I completed two certifications, and that really helped me learn Java inside out. That was one thing that really stayed with me. I got to know all the basics. I could clear all the interviews after completing those certifications, and it also gave me a lot of insight into how Java works. I was able to write more advanced code.

In 2011/12, I started thinking about writing books so that I could help either new developers or students from college to bridge that gap and gain Java certifications. The certifications involve a lot of exam topics that you need to know about. I used a lot of fun features in my book so that it was easy for readers, and that's how I got into writing.

I wrote a couple of books on Java, and I also started speaking at colleges and conferences. I also started contributing to my community. I became a contributor to the Delhi Java User Group, and then one of the leaders, and then I joined Women Who Code. That's how I progressed.

I met Venkat Subramaniam, who will probably write a book, and he nominated me to be a Java Champion. I was already doing a lot of things that a developer advocate does, and then I noticed a tweet by Trisha, where she mentioned that they were looking for a Java developer advocate to join their team. I reached out to her, and that's how I got into the position that I'm working in now.

Q: That's cool. What is a developer advocate?

A: That's an interesting question. All the developer advocates at JetBrains would give you a different answer, and that would apply to all developer advocates in different organizations.

I work as a Java developer advocate for JetBrains, which essentially means that I help developers know and understand Java better so that they are able to use Java better in their day-to-day jobs. I try to make that simpler for the Java developers because that's where my expertise is. I try to make things simple for them.

I do a lot of things. I write blog posts, create video content, and speak at a lot of conferences and colleges. I have even organized a couple of online conferences with JetBrains, as well as doing a lot of other things.

I work with the Java team at JetBrains. A lot of input goes into figuring out how developers can use the IDE in the best possible manner so that they can get the most from the language by putting in minimal effort. That's another area where I contribute.

Q: Going back to the certifications, has certification had an impact on your career? How does that help you today to help other developers?

A: That's an excellent question.

I'm still reaping the benefits of certification. As I mentioned, a certification has a set of topics that you must know inside out to clear the exam. And so, when I talk about certifications, I'm not talking about the piece of paper that I get at the end of the exam. I'm talking about the process. I'm talking about the journey of people studying for the certification. They have to know the basics, which gives them all the knowledge that they need to get over the baseline and have a very strong foundation. Then, they can talk about going on to advanced concepts such as architecting a solution.

For me, the biggest benefit has been having a very strong foundation. I talk to some developers who have 20 years of experience but they don't know a lot of the basics covered in the certifications. I covered my basics 20 years ago! Every developer should know the basics. What if people don't know the basics and they start working on critical projects? Then, the casualties would be the project itself, their colleagues' time, or the company. The basics learned from certifications still help me a lot, even now, in my day job.

Q: As a developer advocate, you help other developers to grow and to learn Java. Do you recommend any certifications for other people? What should developers do in terms of certifications?

A: Certifications really help young developers when they're starting their careers because, as I mentioned, they can build a very strong foundation if they do a certification. A certification covers all the basics: methods, classes, interfaces, collection classes, arrays, I/O, streams, lambdas, and a lot of other things. It really helps people to know all of that.

Q: Today, do you use certifications to help other developers? Do you recommend that people do certifications?

A: Yes, I do, but not a lot. I am still reaping the benefits of certifications, as I mentioned.

The process that I followed when I was studying for my certification was this: I downloaded the source code of the JDK and I opened the ZIP file. I was using a text editor back then to prepare for the certifications.

The first time I saw the source code of the `String` class, I was blown away: "*Oh my God, this is Java code.*" Still today, I make it a habit to look at the source code of the API that I'm using or any other library that I download. That is just one of the things that helped me as a developer back then, and I'm still using it now.

I give this example to a lot of developers that I talk with. It's about having your foundation. A lot of people ask me, "*Why certification?*" This is what I tell them: if there is another process that sees you cover all these topics, go for it, but if not, then this is something that is established and has been validated by a lot of people. I have benefited from it. I am living proof that, yes, it has benefits, and I'm still reaping them. I definitely recommend it to people who are starting a Java career, and I still use the processes that I learned with it to help the developers I help.

Q: Awesome. People think, "*If I have a certification, I can get better jobs.*" Do you see that? Do you see companies requiring certifications?

A: Absolutely.

What are job seekers looking for? They are looking for good jobs, good projects, or good companies to work with, and they will have some rules or some conditions in place to assess whether they want to work for a company.

The same applies the other way around as well. Companies are looking for talent that has skills that can be validated or certified. If the candidate has a certification, the company doesn't have to reinvent the wheel and ask them all the questions that the certification exam has already asked them. So, it's a win-win for both of them.

Certification is recognized by industry the world over. The exam objectives are updated by Oracle with the latest version. Anyone who's taking the exam will know the version they're working with. A lot of developers are still working on Java 8, so they are not aware of the module system or the new language features that have come in. A Java certification covers all of that. That's good for the projects that these people work on and, of course, for the companies, because they get people with verified and certified skills. In the interview, they can talk about advanced concepts with these people because they know that the basics have been covered.

A good analogy that I always use is this: would you like to go to a doctor who doesn't have a certificate or a degree but they say, "*I don't have a certificate, but I have performed a lot of operations and surgeries?*" Would you like to go there? I would never go to a surgeon or a doctor who doesn't have a degree.

A lot of people say to me that people go to universities to get a degree, so why should they get additional certifications? Well, we need to take a look at the long-term and the short-term goals. A degree at a university is a long-term goal, but when I talk about certification in a technology or a language, I'm looking to certify my skills in that technology. That's a short-term goal.

Ben Wise

As we were writing this chapter, Heather was in Singapore working with the developer community and hosting several events and workshops for students. One of the most common questions from computer science students was how you can prevent yourself from being overwhelmed by all of the technologies, tools, and languages to learn. If you use the techniques we discuss in this book, you can learn the right things at the right time and avoid burnout. However, we know that burnout does happen in all industries, but especially in technology and in times of uncertainty. Around the same time, Heather met Ben Wise, who is the owner and founder of STORYD, story-driven and lead-gen B2B ghostwriting for founders and executives. He shared that he recently saw a therapist because he was struggling with burnout and that burnout was winning:

- I think about work when I don't want to

- I wake up in the night feeling anxious

- I feel sad and stressed

He further shared that it was tough asking his general practitioner for help and telling the therapist his symptoms. He decided to share this information on LinkedIn where his team members, vendors, and clients could also benefit, even though it triggered fears of being judged, perhaps positioning him not as an "authority figure," but as just another vulnerable and fallible human who does not have all the answers.

But, he decided that having worked with founders and executives to develop personal brands that help grow their businesses on LinkedIn, he knows that everyone struggles with this at one point or another, and he wanted to normalize the conversation about mental health. So he agreed to share what the therapist told him and we are sharing it with you here.

She's seen more and more burnout in her patients post-COVID. Working remotely makes it more difficult to get space from work. If that's you, there's nothing wrong with you – have compassion for yourself. Her recommendations were as follows:

- Get dressed for work in the morning and then go for a short walk around the block before sitting down in front of the computer. This "commute" helps differentiate your personal and work life.

- Take another walk after you're done with work. Listen to music, a podcast, or something else that you enjoy. This tells your brain that you're back in your personal life.

- Adhere to strict working hours. If it's 9-5, don't check your email at 8, and don't schedule calls at 6. Protect your personal life because you deserve the well-being that it will lead to.

- Have lunch outside if you can. The change of setting will help take your mind off work. The sun is healing.

- Thinking about work outside of working hours is not helpful. Your brain needs a rest and space from work makes you a better problem-solver. If it's important, write it down in a notebook and leave it for when you're actually working. If it's not, don't engage with the thought.

These are some tips for preventing or overcoming burnout when it does happen to you.

Summary

We have learned that, to advance your technical career, learning is the key to your success. The skills that you have learned in this chapter include how to derive maximum benefit from formal learning, how to grow your options through informal learning, how to be independent by learning how to learn, how to acquire and benefit from certification, and how to apply it all towards career growth.

If you apply these skills to your learning path, you will be one of the employees who are not only skilled and expert in their current role but also ready to take on the next high-profile assignment, promotion, or new role. When these opportunities come along, you do not want to be scrambling to acquire the necessary skills; you want to be the individual who is ready with the skills needed to tackle the next step in your career path and journey.

In the next chapter, now that we have mastered learning, we will show you how to optimize your social network. Your social network can be a valuable asset in helping you to advance your technical career.

3

Optimize Your Support Network for Growth

In *Chapter 2*, we discussed how to choose the best path for learning, training, and certifications. In *Chapter 3*, we will focus on how to optimize your support network for growth. The areas we will cover include taking responsibility for your career, finding support for what you need, holding crucial conversations, developing good negotiation skills, and handling feedback, including criticism and lack of support. There are many people that can help you grow in your career – parents, bosses, leaders, friends, and significant others – but the key word here is "help." They can be awesome assets and supporters, but they can't advance *your* career for you! This chapter will show how you can hold the crucial conversations you need to grow while taking responsibility for your career.

The agenda of this chapter involves the following main topics:

- Taking responsibility for your career
- Finding support for what you need
- Holding crucial conversations
- Developing good negotiation skills
- Feedback – dealing with criticism and lack of support

Taking responsibility for your career

Your career is YOUR career. The only person that is fully responsible for everything that happens for your growth and for your opportunities is you.

That does not mean that you shouldn't request or accept help. It just means that you should see other people that are willing to help as helpers. They can help you advance and they can make your path easier or faster. But the reality is, no matter whether you receive help or not, it's always your responsibility.

What does it mean to take responsibility?

The most basic thing about taking responsibility is to stop blaming others since the most common way to avoid responsibility is to blame others for difficulties or challenges in life.

My company doesn't give me opportunities.

My boss doesn't send me to events.

My colleagues don't help me.

Or even my significant other is not supporting me.

The economy. The inflation. The government.

All of these are ways to avoid responsibility and blame other people for our problems.

That is not to say that there are no difficulties. Of course, our life is full of challenges and difficulties, and often our friends, family, and even company can be a hindrance or an obstacle to our growth. And yes, inflation, the government, and other regulations are out of our control.

But every time we consider that it is their fault and not our responsibility, we end up not being able to do anything. If it is them, there is nothing we can do. We can't change our families. We can't force our boss to do something. We can't single-handedly change our company's policies, or change the government, or the economy for that matter.

There are, of course, some things that are outside of our control. There are problems and issues that we alone cannot solve. If you are facing challenges in your career – and we all do at some point in our career journey – the first thing to do is to identify the problem. Next, you should determine whether it is within your power or control to change or influence the problem. Stop and evaluate your role in this and whether you can solve the problem through your own actions. There will be some problems that we cannot control. In that case, we must decide how we will react and respond, such as in an economic recession. There are other problems that we can directly or indirectly influence or respond to, such as our current job responsibilities.

When we blame others, we are at their mercy.

When we consider that it is their responsibility and for one reason or another, they don't do what we want them to do, we get stuck. There's nothing that we can do. We don't have any action plan going forward. All we can do is stay stuck and sulk.

We stop being protagonists of our life.

That's why it is so important to recognize that the only person able to take action is you.

The only person responsible and to blame for any failures or any problems is also you.

This may sound very despairing; it may sound like a lot of weight to carry on your shoulders. In reality, it's very liberating.

Now that you know that it is your fault and that you are the only one responsible for the direction of your life, then you can take some action and figure out what is missing and why you are not getting results.

That is very liberating indeed. It liberates you to take action, instead of sulking. Believing others are to blame is a limiting belief. It limits what you can do, your actions, and your opportunities. Understanding that we are responsible is a liberating truth. It allows you to search for possibilities, to be creative and imagine alternatives, and to look for and find new paths around the obstacles. Every time you see yourself blaming someone or avoiding responsibility, realize that this is a limiting belief. Every belief, even if it may be true, will only be true if you let it be.

If you're open to giving it another shot and turning that limiting belief into a liberating truth, you have the opportunity to discover something equally valid that can propel you forward.

For example, let's imagine the case where your company does not support your advancement. You could say that it is true that your company does not have a policy that allows you to train or go to events or training. I cannot advance because my company does not support my training. This is true, but it is a limiting belief.

You can turn that into a liberating truth. For example, you could say it is true that you can use the time between meetings to learn something new. I can find 15 minutes a day to experiment with some new technology within my job.

That is now a liberating truth. It is true. And it is something YOU can take action to do.

If you can do that, 15 minutes a day during your work hours, you will start to advance in your job.

You might be thinking that 15 minutes is just too little – I need more time.

That could be true, but the reality is, you're no longer stuck on the previous limiting belief; although, you may need to work to create a liberating truth around the new challenge.

I cannot advance because 15 minutes a day is not enough time.

This is a limiting belief.

I can start with 15 minutes a day, and if I'm consistent, and on some days I have a bit more time, the consistency will make a difference. Consistency is better in the long run.

That's a liberating truth. I can now take action.

That will allow you to continue to take action and to continue to move forward.

You have the responsibility to take these actions. Let's say, as an example, you have a manager that does not seem invested in your career. In this case, remember that you have the responsibility to develop a relationship with your manager and your manager's manager. Take action to meet with them and keep the conversation moving in the direction that you want it to go. Ask the questions to determine what is keeping them up at night. Determine how you can be part of the solution and communicate how you can be part of the solution.

When we talk about taking responsibility for our careers, it's simply taking responsibility for finding the right path and finding something that you can actually do that will move your career forward every day, every week, and every month.

Finding support for what you need

Keeping our responsibility in mind, the reality is that we do not advance alone. Having help and support will allow you to advance faster. That's why it's very important to find the support you need.

Finding support is, in most cases, not finding someone that will do things for you, but the right people that can guide and direct you to the best solution, which you will work on implementing yourself.

There are many ways to look for help. You can reach out to friends and colleagues, ask for help from family, get support from your boss, and even request official support from your company.

Those are the normal ways.

Today, the internet is a great place to find help, even from people you don't know. You can follow experts. You can read books, subscribe to blogs, and watch YouTube videos:

- Read books
- E-learning
- Attend conferences
- Subscribe to blogs
- Watch YouTube videos

When you follow people that you trust and who can help you overcome your issues, even if they don't know you, they can still be very, very helpful.

The one problem you have to look out for when getting help from people that you don't know and that you don't have direct contact with is the lack of accountability. It makes it harder for you to take action.

When you receive help from someone close to you, such as friends and family, colleagues, or your boss, they are able to motivate you, and you have a level of accountability with them. If you don't take action, they will notice, and they will call you out on it. You have a big motivation to take action. You can't ask for help from your boss or your spouse and then not act on their advice for too long!

But that's not going to happen with YouTube videos and blogs! Either YOU take action, or no one knows. People you read or watch can't push you forward without contact with you. The internet has, at the same time, made it easier to get help from people, but also less efficient. Make sure you take this into account when using those means to get support.

Scott Wierschem

Scott Wierschem is a well-known developer. He attributes some of his success to his networking at conferences and his blogs.

Scott is a developer with a passion for legacy code and cleaning up the code in older projects. He found his passion in his day-to-day work, but he did not have many opportunities to expand his network in his role working with long-term clients on their legacy code projects. Once he had the opportunity to expand his network, he applied his skills to create an additional business opportunity for himself. He met Java luminaries in his social network and became an influencer and blogger. His network inspired him to create an impact and share his knowledge beyond what he was able to share in his day-to-day projects. Very early in his career, he chose a poor mentor – but was so naive, he didn't realize it. He shares the following story from that time.

My mentor was very cynical and taught me not to trust anyone, and never stand out. Shortly after we had that conversation, I was laid off, so that seemed to confirm his advice. That crippled my career for decades until I met Bruno Souza. I was miserable and looking for a different career. He encouraged me and helped me to understand that I knew a lot and could help others by standing out and sharing my knowledge. I gave talks at Java User Groups, and at conferences, such as JavaOne. I created a business plan inspired by a talk from Legacy Code Rocks, and it has revolutionized my career – and my life! I now deliver weekly training sessions, write articles and teach lessons. This gave me flexibility and freedom to practice my job, create training lessons, and publish an e-book in my free time. I just wish I had met him decades earlier!

Barry Burd

Barry attributes some of his early career success to his ability to network to form new connections. He is a professor at Drew University, an author, and a trainer/consultant. In the earlier days of his career, he was looking online and found a local user group meeting that interested him. He attended the New York Java SiG and started to grow his social network. Barry found that it can feel lonely to think about networking in a new group, but if you are in the right place, you are growing your network organically. As a professor, talking with developers about their projects and keeping up with technical discussions provides a social network, but also a strong sense of maturity. Conversations can give you an understanding of the context of how technology is used to solve current problems, and an honest view and perspective. Interactions with your social network can provide outcomes you may not expect, but you learn from your connections and enjoy the process and the relationships along the way. As Barry says:

A user group is an excellent place for learning new things, but when I was just starting out, I wanted to find consulting work by joining two user groups. At almost every meeting I attended, no one mentioned the possibility of my working for them. I could have been discouraged. But at two of the sessions (one in each of the two groups), people asked me about conducting training for their companies. Both leads ended up being very profitable for me. I guess the moral of this story is this: when your networking opportunities don't seem to be paying off, don't be discouraged. They're paying off whether you realize it or not.

Asking for help

When you ask for help, you are asking the other person to take time from what they want to do, to help you do what you want to do. It is reasonable that people prefer to do what they want, instead of what you want!

So, when you ask for help, try to help the other person to help you.

That may sound strange because you are the one trying to get help. How can you possibly help the other person?

Make sure that the other person has a number of reasons to help you and the least amount of resistance.

When you ask someone for help, make clear that you just need them for a few minutes. They won't need to spend a long time or make a big effort to help you. Ask for five minutes from them, so they can point the way or help you unblock.

Also, you may want to try a "no" oriented question. People have less resistance to saying "no" than "yes." Experiment with "*Would it be a ridiculous idea if I asked you to help me with this problem for 5 minutes?*".

Another important aspect when you ask for help is to research things yourself first.

There are many places you can go to research. Try looking at some examples on GitHub or in the issue tracker of a related project (JIRA, etc.), or try searching on Stack Overflow, Reddit, or Quora. Artificial Intelligence has recently supercharged your research capabilities, and you should also consider using ChatGPT and other AI tools. If you do your research and take time to educate yourself on the subject, not only will it be easier to ask for help, you will also benefit more from the help you receive.

When you do decide to approach someone about your question and you say, "*I don't know how to do X, can you help me?*", that does not give enough context, even if they want to help you.

When you show the things you did try and how they failed, or where you got stuck, that not only will help set the context of the situation but will also make it more probable that people will help you, and make it easier for them to do so.

When you give the context, people can see where you are, how much effort you have been putting into it, and the challenges you have already overcome. All this context will make it easier to help you move forward in the direction that you want.

One situation that you will commonly need help with is when you need some kind of connection or introduction. Such as when you want to connect with someone that could help you or that you want to invite to an activity. Or, when you want to be recommended for a job position or need to hire someone. Another example could be when you would like help promoting your content, maybe a blog post or your new YouTube video.

All those situations require the person you are asking for help to write a message or a note about you to send to someone else. You can make this a lot easier if you create the note or the email yourself, and offer it as a suggestion. *"If you have a few minutes, could you introduce me to your friend so-and-so? I'd like to invite them to give a talk at my company. If it helps, below you can see a little introduction text I drafted, to help you reach out to them. Feel free to adapt it in any way you want."*

This is not a copy and paste job: make sure the text you draft is written thinking about the person you asked for help, and that they would be comfortable using it.

When you make the effort and make it easy for others to help you, there's a much bigger chance that they will want to help you.

Another way to help people help you is to look for opportunities that turn the fact that they are helping you into something that actually helps them move their careers forward.

For example, imagine you're trying to get help to become an open source developer. A good strategy is getting help from existing open source developers. You may be looking for help in finding a suitable project to join, or you may want help with what you need to do and how to implement the steps.

This is asking for help. You are asking them to take time from what they want to do to help you do what you want to do.

Let's try to turn this around. You do some research and find that the person you want to ask for help is working on her own open source project. Instead of asking her to help you, you could offer to help her with her projects. You could offer help with small things such as promoting the projects, writing a tutorial, or improving the documentation.

With this small but very thoughtful offer, you make yourself helpful first. You are spending YOUR time to help them advance THEIR project. That helps the other person to want to help you because helping you will actually help them advance their own goals.

You help people by thinking of them first. You may think that you are the person that needs help, so you can't help anyone! But no one is so helpless that they cannot help. and at the same time, no one is so self-sufficient that they don't need any help.

Turn things around by thinking about how you can help others. When you start putting them first, you make yourself useful and make yourself (even just a little) important for them, and that's going to bring more help your way.

This mentality of wanting to help will make you a giver, someone that gives more than they receive. Research shows that givers are the people that have more opportunities in companies and the job market. Position yourself as a giver. It will help you achieve all your big goals.

One important comment on asking for help: maybe you try to get help by asking the person to do something for you. Remember that people are usually not interested in doing things for us.

It's your responsibility. If you want anything done, you have to do it!

When looking for help, focus on asking for guidance. Ask for tips to get you unblocked, and for ideas to speed things up. This is a win-win situation. Mindset changes are the most powerful for you and your career because they change the way you do things. At the same time, they take less time from your guide, who will mostly show you the right way of doing things. They may be able to point you to an idea, technique, person, tool, or technology that will help you get unstuck and advance.

With that said, you also have to pay attention and take action! The guidance and suggestions you receive can be extremely valuable and can have a lasting impact on your career, but only if you take action on them. Nothing's going to change your life if all you do is listen and forget about it.

Holding crucial conversations

The best help someone can give you is to have a deep conversation with you, about your current situation and where you want to go. If you have a chance to have a conversation like this, not only should you take it, but make sure you make the best of it.

The more you understand what the person is telling you, what the tip is, or how to apply it, the better results you're going to have. So, when asking for help, make sure that you ask lots of questions.

Many times, I've had people approach me and ask how to do a specific thing and I tell them and can see they understand what I'm saying, but they still don't see how to apply it, or even don't believe it is possible.

Usually, the reason is that they don't see the connection to their current situation.

I may linger for a bit, to see if they will ask follow-up questions, and most times there aren't any. So, I ask questions instead, to try to uncover the context, and get clarity on the real situation. Otherwise, it is hard to connect the dots and help with clear, specific steps.

But most people that are willing to help you will not be that detailed, and they may just answer your questions. To help them help you, make sure to present where you really are. Describe your situation so people can give you help on the right things.

Holding crucial conversations is all about asking questions, from both sides!

Asking questions is sometimes scary. It may feel like it will make us look dumb. Or, it may show that we do not understand. It can leave us vulnerable. We are vulnerable! That's why we're asking for help.

Don't be afraid of asking questions. Make sure you understand how to apply the suggestion to your current situation. If not, ask!

Developing good negotiation skills

For your career growth, negotiation is one of those skills that are fundamental but largely neglected. This is probably because it is a skill not usually associated with technical jobs, and only thought about when we are negotiating salaries.

But negotiation is a skill that we use daily, every time we have priorities and expectations that involve other people.

We negotiate even during our free time – where we will eat on the weekends, where we will spend our vacations, the responsibilities we have at home, how much time we can spend with friends, and what we will do during that time. When we are working, we negotiate what feature needs to be implemented, who will implement it, and how it will be implemented. When we negotiate our career development, we determine which jobs we will take, what salaries we will be paid, which projects we will work on, which responsibilities are ours, which mentors we will have, what bonus we will receive, which stock options we will take, when it is time to move on to another role, when to ask for a promotion, and so much more.

We face many small and large negotiations every day. We can recognize them and be good at that skill, or we may ignore the skill and basically be trumped in most situations in life.

Alexandra Carter is a world-renowned negotiator for the United Nations and wrote the book *Ask For More*. In her book, Alexandra talks about the *10 Questions to Negotiate Anything*. The first five questions are the conversations that you have with yourself. These questions will help you understand what you want, how to ask for it, and help you understand what your approach should be to get what you want.

We have summarized the questions here:

- **Question #1: What's the problem I want to solve?** Sometimes you have to spend time to save time. Think about what it is you really want at the end of the discussion.

- **Question #2: What do I need?** Think clearly about what you need and do not confuse this with your demands. You can visualize what you find intolerable and flip the situation around. Also, be wary of allowing what others think you need to answer this question.

- **Question #3: What do I feel?** Once you determine what you need, you need to face your feelings. Remember never to fear negotiation or to negotiate out of fear.

- **Question #4: How have I handled this successfully In the past?** Your past negotiation successes will often provide clues as to how you can be successful in future negotiations. Think about things that have gone well for you in the past.

- **Question #5: What's the first step?** After you finish asking yourself the questions, you are ready to ask the questions..... *see the information box with five tips for asking questions.

- **Question #6: Tell me….** In this step, you ask the other party to share their perspectives on the problem, scenario, and solution.

- **Question #7: What do you need?** You should never assume you know what the other party needs. Make sure you summarize and repeat back to them what they say and ask follow-up questions.

- **Question #8: What are your concerns?** You want to be able to understand their perspective and what they may be thinking about as they negotiate with you.

- **Question #9: How have you handled this successfully in the past?** Involve the other party in a conversation on how they have handled this situation before to help you work together to come up with a solution.

- **Question #10: What's the first step?** This question helps to establish you as partners and to take action together. Be empathetic to their needs and concerns to establish trust.

Five tips for asking questions of the other party:
- Land the plane – also known as "ask the question"
- Enjoy any silence
- Ask follow-up questions
- Summarize and ask for feedback
- Listen to what has *not* been said

Another useful book on negotiation strategy is by Christopher Voss, a former FBI negotiator. He authored the book *Never Split the Difference*, which lists the tools he uses to improve negotiation. Here are six tips from the book:

- One: **mindset.** To be a good negotiator, you need to have the mindset of a negotiator.

  Negotiation is not a confrontation, but it is a learning opportunity. When you approach a negotiation, you should not be trying to win or to best the other person. Negotiation should be a situation where you try to achieve a result that is beneficial for everyone. That's what we call a win-win-win situation.

  Approach negotiation as a learning opportunity. You are learning what the other person wants, and also what is important for you. You're learning about the challenges in making those things happen, and the consequences of them happening or not happening.

- Two: **listen.** The most important skill of a negotiator is listening. Negotiation is all about listening, understanding the other side. But not just listening – active listening, asking questions

  Most people listen just to be able to answer or just to be able to argue back. This is the wrong way of listening. Listen to understand and clarify what the other side wants, what they think, and what they believe. Once you understand, it's much easier for you to look for a win-win situation.

- Three: **time it right.** Part of negotiation is finding the best time. Try to time your negotiation to happen in the best moment possible

  If you can time your salary negotiation at a moment when your company can see your value and is looking forward to working more with you, you're going to have better success than if you time it for when you are being unproductive or you're not happy with your work

  Of course, if you delay the negotiation and don't plan your timing, other conditions may force you to negotiate at the worst time for you, or at the best time for the other part.

Salary negotiation, for example, is best done as a continuous improvement process for your career at your company. It's not a process where you only engage when you join and you are very happy and when you want to leave because you're unhappy.

- Four: **framing**. The fourth idea around the negotiation is framing or context. When you set the frame and the context, you help other people see what you see

A good way to create a frame is to complete the statements *"Have you ever"* and *"Do you know when."* For example, I could say, *"The best moment to start to negotiate a salary increase is when you just got a salary increase."* This may sound preposterous, unclear, and even untrue! Or, I could say, *"Have you ever noticed that people that have a continuous conversation with their boss about their goals and results are more aligned with their bosses' expectations and can better show their value to the company? That's why the best moment to start negotiating salary increases is when you just got a salary increase, it should be a continuous process.*

Isn't this much more impactful and believable? Can you see that when we add context, you help people see what you see

That's what framing is. Do this for your negotiations, and they will give you much better results.

- Five: **give and get**. Be generous and have gratitude in your negotiations, and you will have much better results

Remember, negotiation can be a win-win discussion. It is not about destroying your opponent and getting all the results you want. That is just tyranny. Negotiation is about finding a place where we all win. You get a better salary. Your family lives better and is more secure. Your boss gets a happy employee that wants the best for the company and is a partner in its success. Win. Win. Win

When you get something in a negotiation, give something. When you are generous while negotiating, you help all parties to be happy with the results

And the same thing is true for the other side. When you give something, expect to get something. You should be generous, not naive

- Six: **walk away**. The sixth and last negotiation principle is about being able (and willing) to walk away. It's important to avoid emotional decisions. Make sure that when you walk into the negotiation, you have the facts, you have the reasoning, and you have clarity about what you want. Make your best effort to understand what others want. Get the facts from their side too. That will help you avoid negotiating only based on your emotions. When you avoid emotional decisions, it's easier to walk away if needed. If you get to a point in the negotiation where things are not converging to a win-win resolution, be ready to just say, *"Thank you, but no, thank you."* Gracefully walk away

That's going to give you the power to really negotiate. If you can't walk away from a negotiation, then you're in no position to negotiate.

For example, if you tell your boss that if they don't increase your salary, you're going to leave, but you don't have another company to move to, or you don't have enough visibility in the market to easily get an offer, you are negotiating from a weak position. Setting aside that putting people against the wall is a terrible way to negotiate (it never yields long-term results), if they don't give you a better salary, you're stuck. Not being able to walk away is going to undermine your position, and even make future negotiations harder.

Negotiation is an important and valuable skill. Don't only think about it when you need it because that is too late. Start now. Practice asking questions. Listen. Negotiate small things in life. Get good at negotiating small things and you will be much better off when big things show up!

The most important things to remember about negotiation are that it does not have to be a conflict or confrontational and that everything is negotiable. Use the techniques we described to partner together to come up with a solution that not only works for you and your career but for the other parties as well, whether in your career or in life.

Feedback – dealing with criticism

When we talk about negotiation, we have to talk about feedback.

Not because feedback is a type of negotiation, but because feedback is an important part of working with other people and trying to achieve results together. To work together, we need to correct each other.

Also, feedback is very important for self-improvement. It's incredibly hard for us to judge ourselves on the things we do since many things we do are not clear and objective. Receiving feedback from other people, such as our peers, and our bosses is extremely important for us to understand whether we're on the right track.

But feedback also hurts. Not positive feedback, of course. That is always fun to receive. Negative feedback shows that we have been wrong or mistaken, and that hurts, but negative feedback is crucial.

If feedback is important, then negative feedback is even more important! It may be nice and fun to know that we are right. But it can be lifesaving to know when we are wrong.

Only when we know we are wrong can we correct it. We can fix it. We can improve.

That's why, for example, in software development, we want a fast feedback loop. When we build and test our code, we want the system to tell us that we are wrong very fast, so that we can correct it before mistakes can spread to the rest of the system.

Can we do the same with our abilities and our daily actions? That's where feedback comes in handy.

So, if we agree that this is important and it will help us improve, why don't we like feedback (negative feedback, of course)? It hurts!

The most likely reason why we don't like feedback is because it shows our ignorance, and it shows where we failed. It also shows our vulnerability. Being vulnerable in your job or in your career is risky.

Maybe you imagine that if your boss sees that you are wrong, you might not get a promotion. If your colleagues see that you failed, you might not get respect.

Feedback also impacts our views of hierarchy. When someone gives us negative feedback, we might feel lower than they are. This is not something conscious, but it is something that impacts our lives.

Yes, negative feedback can really hurt.

However, since feedback is very important, here is a fact-based approach that incorporates some suggestions on how to receive negative feedback in a way that would make it constructive, no matter the intention of the person giving the feedback.

Step 1: Is the feedback a fact?

Not all feedback we receive is fact-based. A lot of it is actually an impression, a feeling, or a person's opinion. There's nothing wrong with someone's opinion, but someone's opinion may be wrong or may be just something that you don't agree with.

So, start by evaluating the feedback and whether it is a fact or not.

If it is an impression or opinion, you can either safely discard it or accept it as feedback to consider later based on the intentions and the source of the feedback. Everyone is entitled to their own opinions. You are entitled to your own opinion too!

For example, if someone says, "*I don't like this book, I think it is badly written*", that's an opinion.

You may agree or disagree with it, but it is just an opinion.

Now imagine someone says, "*I don't like this book, it is full of English mistakes and has factual errors.*"

Although there is an opinion there ("*I don't like this book*"), there are things that are not merely an opinion anymore. There are facts. Discard the opinion and take the parts that are factual to the next step.

Step 2: Are the facts true?

Just because someone stated facts, it doesn't follow that they're necessarily true.

Looking at the book example, we can check and test whether it is true or not that the book is full of English mistakes.

If the facts are false, it's not necessarily the person's fault. Maybe they missed something or maybe they did not understand what was going on. Maybe they saw only parts of it. But if the feedback mentions facts and the facts are false, disregard that part of the feedback. That should not affect you.

Even very bad and hurtful comments and feedback, if they are false, should not affect you.

But maybe the facts are true. Maybe the book is full of English mistakes. If so, keep going to step 3.

Step 3: Is there anything you want to or can do about it?

Assuming the facts are true, then you can evaluate whether there is anything you want to or can do about it.

If the book is full of English mistakes, you may want to correct them. And if you do, the feedback was very useful, and had a good result!

Now, maybe the book is not focused on being sold. Maybe it was just an experiment to test whether an artificial intelligence transcription system would work well. And the fact that it is full of mistakes does not matter much, or at all.

So, maybe you will decide to not do anything about it. When you use those three steps to evaluate feedback, you take a lot of the emotion out of it. If the feedback is a fact and it is true and you want to fix it, you can just go and fix it and the feedback was valuable. You will even be very thankful to the person that mentioned it!

But if the feedback is not factual, then whoever gave it is entitled to their own opinion. There's nothing you can do about opinions. If the feedback is a fact, but it's not true, then the person probably just made a mistake. And if the feedback is a fact, it's true, but you did it that way because you wanted to and you wouldn't (or maybe couldn't) do any differently, then it's all according to the plan, and you will just deal with the consequences of the mistakes.

When said like this, it sounds like it is easy to receive negative feedback. It is not.

As we mentioned before, negative feedback is very hard to receive. Hopefully, this process will help you take a little bit of the emotion out of receiving feedback and will help you use unavoidable negative feedback to improve your career.

The interesting thing about this process is that even when negative feedback is given specifically to hurt you, to be mean, and attack you, you can still use it to improve!

Basically, when you hear feedback, pay close attention and separate what is a fact from opinions. What are the facts? What are the opinions?

If it is mean, hurtful feedback but it does mention something true, then you can take some action, fix things, and improve. There is no better response to mean, evil feedback, made to put you down, than using it to grow even more! You will use their negative-intentioned feedback to improve yourself.

This all ties back to taking responsibility for your career. Listening and acting on the feedback you receive is a very mature and responsible thing to do. Not only will you improve yourself, but you will show seniority and trust to everyone around you.

Lastly, be thankful for the person that gave the feedback, even if the feedback was hurtful or negative, because it might not have been their intention, but it will help you to grow and be a lot better in the future.

Interviews

Nikita Koselev

While writing this book, we spoke with Nikita Koselev about his experiences living and working as a developer just outside of London. Nikita shared with us the ways in which his community has supported him. In this interview transcription, Nikita introduces himself and provides some context for his current situation, before delving into the topic of building a community of his own as a support network and the impact it has had on his life.

Q: What led you to get into computer science or to become a developer?

A: Oh, well, two things. One is that I'm into computers and anything to do with them, and finance. And the second thing is food because I'm from an extremely poor background. From the age of 15, my family could not afford to buy yogurts. So, they were buying chocolates 3 months past due, and stuff like that. And my dream was: I will become a software developer, and then I will eat only yogurts because that's the selection of food that developers eat. Well, it lasted for a month, then I had to switch. I like them again now, but there was a long pause in eating yogurts and other niceties. My motivation to become a software developer was income.

Q: How did you train? Did you teach yourself or attend school?

A: I did quite badly in my exams at school. I didn't know I'm autistic, but I found a course that, as I thought at the time, was the closest thing to computer science – power electronics, or something – and it was a huge mistake because it was the one that was the furthest from computer science. So, basically, I was just going to all the computer science courses I could, and I tried to pick up minimal for the energetics so they didn't throw me out too fast. Then, I transitioned to another course, and then to another course. Meanwhile, I was helping people who got good grades in IT, and then I was there. They tried to throw me out of university three times – two times by mistake. Like, oh, we just forgot your paper in the desk drawer – stuff like that; whatever. But one time it was for a valid reason because I switched payment format, so I needed to wait.

Q: How has the community helped you and how did you discover that the community would support you?

A: The community has helped me find purpose in life. I realized that I could work with people and create something good, which helped me form a stronger connection with my team. With medication and help, I began to help the community at work and raise the flag high. I met some amazing people in the community, such as Bruno Souza, who runs the biggest Java group in the world, and he helped me understand that our main values come from sharing. It was at Devoxx UK in London where I met Benjamin Mascall and Sal Kimmich, that I learned how to become a good developer through OpenJDK contributions.

Q: Can you tell us more about Sal Kimmich and his idea of guiding people to make their first open source commit?

A: Sal Kimmich is a person who supports and guides individuals until they make their first open source commit. Once they have accomplished that, he lets them go because the hardest part is done. I thought that this was a great idea, and I decided to create a meetup called "Together with Open Source" to help people who cannot go to universities such as MIT or Oxford but can still do very well in IT. It is especially helpful for people from underrepresented groups and those who face discrimination. In IT, we are judged by our work, and our skin color or gender does not matter. I wanted to mentor people who do not know what they like and build a bridge for them to find something they are passionate about.

Q: How do you help people who do not know what they like to find something they are passionate about?

A: When people come to me and say they want to work in finance and live in London, I start asking them questions to determine whether they really love finance. For example, I ask whether they read the Financial Times to their grandmother and whether they engage in financial dealings. If they do not, I ask them what they do love. If they say they teach other students molecular chemistry, then I can help them learn about finance, but in 20 years, they might be sitting somewhere in London in a small, expensive one-bedroom apartment, disconnected from all their relatives. I want to help people find something they truly love and that gives them purpose.

Q: How does your community involvement help you with your career?

A: Being involved in the community helps me find purpose in life, and it gives me a stronger connection with my team. I no longer have bystander or imposter syndrome, and if something is wrong, I raise the flag. I also help people find something they love, which gives me a sense of accomplishment and purpose. When I was struggling with depression, the community helped me by providing support and finding ways to help me find purpose in life. I realized that if I stand up and work with people, I can create something good and make a difference.

Q: Can you tell us more about how you became a good developer through OpenJDK contributions?

A: OpenJDK contributions helped me become a good developer because they provided me with an opportunity to contribute to the development of Java, one of the most widely used programming languages in the world. Contributing to OpenJDK allowed me to work with some of the smartest people in the industry and learn from them. I did not become a good developer by taking courses; instead, I learned by contributing to OpenJDK, which allowed me to gain practical experience and develop my skills.

Helio Silva

We also had the pleasure of speaking with Helio Silva, a distinguished technical value advisor for Latin America in the observability industry. In this interview, Helio introduces himself and discusses the importance of building a supportive community and the impact it has had on his life and career.

Q: How did you get into this career?

A: It was through a friend. We worked together at another company. Basically, once he remembered he had this opportunity, he called me, "*Hey, there's an opportunity here in the company I'm working for, and I think it is a perfect fit for you. Will you allow me to share your name with the hiring manager so the hiring manager can contact you? Maybe you can talk and it could be good for you as well.*" This was how it happened.

Q: Do you get many jobs like this, or was that the first time? A job where people call you because they think that you are the right person?

A: After becoming senior, I think most of – if not all – the jobs I got, were through recommendations. Let me do a fast count here. The last six jobs I got were through recommendations.

Q: Do you think that when you get a job through a recommendation, it is easier in terms of going through the interviews and getting a good offer?

A: Yes, for sure. When someone posts a position on the web, you already see that people ask for a lot of different things. Sometimes you don't exactly know what the person needs, what the hiring manager needs, or what the company really needs. Sometimes you can identify the technology very easily. If we are talking about a more junior position, such as a simple Java web developer, for example, or a Java frontend developer, you know that the most important thing is the person knowing Java, the person knowing web dev technologies – this type of thing. So, it's easy. But when you are looking for more positions like my position that I used to say this is after senior, it's hard to understand what the position is looking for or what the hiring manager is actually looking for. When someone refers you to a position, they will provide you with extra context. For example, they will say, "*Hey, I am looking for someone that knows Java, but also someone that can manage customer expectations, or someone that has experience with this type of database but also has already led a team in a previous job.*" In this way, you can be more prepared when you talk with the hiring manager, for example, because you know exactly what the person is looking for and you can match what the person is looking for to your experience. So, you will be more prepared, for sure. Also, to add to that, you'll be more secure because you know what the person is looking for.

Q: Does that help in terms of the trust the person has in you before they know you?

A: Yeah. You're saying the person that referred me to have the conversation, to get the job – the person that is actually going to interview you had someone from the organization saying, "*Hey, this guy is great.*" So, when they interview you, they think of you in a better way, right?

Let's say someone referred you – a director, or maybe a manager of another team. If that person thinks that would be good at working in the position that is open, they will say, "*Hey, this person knows everything about – or the most important things – regarding this candidate.*" So, of course, you have an advantage there because it's someone defending you versus a random person on the web that could be a better candidate on paper, or on LinkedIn, but when you work with that person, maybe that's not the case or maybe they're not an easy person to deal with. When someone refers you, you can bet that people are going to think that you're a good person to work with and you are going to fit the company's culture. That is why, in theory, you are ahead of the other competitors, I believe.

Q: Do you think that when you are applying for a position like yours, because of positions that you mentioned here at the beginning, if it's not clear what the position is – because it is not a position such as developer, but a position that's a little bit harder to understand – what it does than just for the description. When you have someone that you like, a friend that knows you and that trusts you, they could even help you understand what the position is all about, right?

A: Usually, those types of more strategic positions are the ones that are hard to find because it's not easy to explain what you're going to be doing, and what your responsibilities will be. It is something where the relationship helps a lot to get. Also, they're challenging roles for companies to hire for because they are not just looking for Java, Python, or another technology; it's much more than that.

Q: The impression that I have is that a position like that also pays more because it is hard to find the right person. It is a more autonomous position where you must know what you are doing. Those positions also pay more. What do you think?

A: Oh, yeah, for sure. And if you think about it, I think it is because of the responsibility. In those types of positions, usually, your boss does not tell you what to do. Usually, you must figure out what's important to your company and customers. Basically, this is what you do. I usually talk with my boss twice per month. Usually, he will ask me, "*Hey, what can I do to help you to do your job?*" He's never going to tell me, "*Hey, I need you to do this, this, and this.*" It is about hiring someone that is smart enough to figure out things that must be done and choosing the person that is going to make the judgment to work. Because the challenge with those positions is that if you're not the right person, you could decide, "*I'm not going to do the work,*" and then the company is going to suffer, and usually, it will take time to figure out that you're not doing what you're supposed to do. That is why it is very hard to hire someone that you can trust at that level is going to make the right assessment of the important things that they must do on a daily basis.

Q: When you get offered a position like that, do you accept it, or do you have to negotiate salary, benefits, and how many hours you will work? How does that work in getting a position like this?

A: Well, usually, as in life, we need to negotiate. For example, I always try to negotiate my salary because it is what makes my dreams possible. That is one of the things that I always try to negotiate. Also, things that you would usually ask for, such as, "*Hey, can this be 100 % remote?*" Or, "*Can this be flexible?*" Usually, you need to ask. One thing that people are going to figure out is that most of the things that you ask for are usually things that people will allow if that is what you need to do good work. For example, a few years ago, I got one job where my ask was, "*Hey, I would like to move from Rio to São Paulo. Would you help me to do this?*" And of course, this was a few years ago when remote work was not a reality. But just for the fact that I asked, my hiring manager at the time said to me, "*Of course, let's make that possible.*" This was one of the things that we agreed on when we signed the offer. Yes, 100 %, you need to take the responsibility of asking for the things that you need to do a good job.

Q: Do you have a story about a friend helping you either get a job or do something important for your career?

A: I have a lot of friends. Usually, when I am going to make a career move, I ask different people for their opinion. Honestly, it's not only about asking people to make the decisions that I need to make. It is more like, "*Hey, let me see this other point of view. Maybe they know something that I don't know about this company.*" I'm going to give you one example. I have already worked for a few start-ups. One day, I was about to make a move to another company. It was a very tiny company. I asked one of my friends, "*Hey, this is an American start-up. It seems like a healthy company. Everybody is so excited about working for this company. So, would you say that this is a good place to go now?*" And then this friend called me – I was texting with him and he picked up the phone and called me and said, "*Hey, man, I would not make this move if I were you because we are going through a recession right now and I really believe that money is going to be more hard and this company is probably going to be acquired or maybe it will go broke in a few months.*"

If your plan is to do an IPO, that is interesting, but it was maybe two or three years. Because my friend – and I really trust him because he has a very high position in another company – said that to me and I was like, "*Okay, so I'll reject this offer,*" which was a great offer. Then, for a few months, I would say that I was thinking, "*Hey, should I... Maybe I made a mistake or...*" But then, one year later, that company was acquired by another big company and you don't hear about them anymore. And it's not that it was bad for them – probably not. But the thing was, I really didn't want to do the full cycle of a start-up and this wasn't the case with that company. So yes, for sure, I will trust my friends. In the end, the judgment is mine, right? But of course, I will talk with people that I believe have the experience to give me good advice. Like this person, who had a particularly good business view and provided me with very insightful advice, for sure, I'm going to ask them if I can. I think Steve Jobs said something like "*everybody wants to help you, you just need to ask.*"

I think one of the things that has helped me a lot in my career was one of the skills that people must learn – how to ask for help. When I say that, it's like, usually, people will come and ask a lot of random things. But I would say that people will try to help you, of course. But if you know what you need and what you need to get from one specific person, this makes it easier for them to help you. For example, I have friends whose opinions I will ask for when I am going to make a career move. I will look to someone with a higher role or position, such as a director or a VP. I will use them if I want to make a career move. If I want to learn a new technology, I have one guy who is a technical leader. Right now, he's a manager. But I will ask him, *"Hey, man, with these technologies, where do you see people struggling more?"* I won't ask a VP, *"Hey, should I learn Spring Boot 3 or should I learn React? Or should I learn this specific Kubernetes thing?"* No, because they're not good at it. They are good at business. They are good at seeing how companies are doing. Also, if my friend is really good at Kubernetes and Java, I'm not going to ask them, *"Hey, can you help me understand whether this company is a good company to land right now?"* You need to about the thing that the person is good at. Make it easy for them to help you. If someone asked me, *"Hey, can you help me to get a good job?"* or *"Can you help me to get my Kubernetes cluster working?"* I'm going to be the person you're going to ask.

Q: Now, just to clarify this last point that you made there. Sometimes it's hard to know what another person knows or does not know. So, how do you ask? Because you said at the beginning that you should ask for specifically what you need. How do you ask? Do you just call the person and say, *"Hey, man, I need this"*? Or, how do you do it? Because sometimes it is hard to ask people to help you, right?

A: One of the things I do is to ask people I already work with. So, as I said, I know the type of things this person would be good at. So basically, usually I share a little bit of background with this person about the thing I'm asking about. Just to give an example, if I'm going to change companies, one of the things that I'll start with is, *"Hey, friend. Have you ever heard about this company? I am looking for a position with them (or maybe I already have an offer from them). I don't know whether you have friends there that you can get good information from for me."* I'm basically trying to figure out whether this company is a good company to land. This is basically the type of thing that I would try to ask a friend to go. You just need to say, *"Hey, I need help with this. Can you help me?"* Then the person will reply with a yes, or maybe not right now.

By doing this, you can better prepare yourself for speaking with the hiring manager. For example, you will know exactly what the person is looking for and can align your experience accordingly. This will make you more prepared and confident. Additionally, it instills a sense of trust in the person because you understand their expectations. So, that's the key.

Q: That's perfect. And does it also help in gaining the trust of someone who doesn't know you yet?

A: Let's say someone who refers you holds a high position such as the director or manager of another team. If they believe you are suitable for the open position, they will vouch for you. It becomes a case of them endorsing your knowledge and expertise in the relevant areas. This gives you an advantage over other candidates who may appear better on paper or LinkedIn but might not be easy to work with. When someone refers you, it implies that you are a good fit for the company's culture. In theory, this puts you ahead of other competitors.

Q: That's awesome. Especially for positions like yours, which are not easily understood from the description alone. In such cases, having a friend who knows you can help clarify what the position entails, right?

A: Exactly. Typically, strategic positions are hard to explain in terms of responsibilities and tasks. Building relationships can be instrumental in gaining a clearer understanding. These roles are also challenging for companies to hire because they require more than just technical skills such as Java or Python; they encompass a broader scope.

Q: Right. It seems like these positions may also offer higher compensation due to their complexity and the difficulty of finding the right person. What are your thoughts on that?

A: Oh, definitely. The higher compensation is often tied to the level of responsibility. In such positions, your boss doesn't dictate what you should do; you need to determine what is important for the company and its customers. It's about hiring someone who is capable of identifying and prioritizing tasks. This requires good judgment and the ability to make the right decisions, as choosing the wrong person can lead to negative consequences for the company.

Q: When you secure a position like this, is it usually straightforward acceptance, or is there room for negotiation regarding salary, benefits, and working hours?

A: Well, negotiation is a common part of the process, similar to other aspects of life. Personally, I always try to negotiate the salary because it allows me to pursue my dreams. It's important to ask for other things as well, such as remote work options or flexible hours. Most requests are usually accommodated if they contribute to better job performance. For instance, in the past, I asked to relocate from Rio to São Paulo for a job, and my manager agreed to make it possible. Taking responsibility for asking what you need is crucial to doing a good job. In addition to money, there are other factors to consider during negotiations. So, yes, negotiation is necessary for various aspects of the job offer.

Q: That's great. It seems like you've received a lot of help and recommendations from friends throughout your career. Do you have any interesting stories about how a friend assisted you in finding a job?

A: When I'm considering a career move, I often seek the opinions of different people. It's not just about relying on others to make decisions for me; it's about gaining different perspectives. Let me share an example. I had worked for a few start-ups when I considered joining another company, a small American start-up in the health industry. I reached out to a friend and asked for their thoughts on whether it was a good move. This friend, who held a high position in another company, called me right away and advised against it. They mentioned that we were going through a recession and believed that the company might face financial challenges or even get acquired.

Their advice turned out to be timely because about a year later, the company was indeed acquired by a larger company and faded from the spotlight. While it may not have been a bad outcome for them, it wasn't aligned with my goal of avoiding the full start-up cycle. Trusting my friend's judgment, considering their business acumen, I declined the offer despite it being attractive. I believe in seeking advice from experienced individuals whom I trust, while ultimately making my own judgment. As Steve Jobs once said, "I believe that everyone wants to help you, you just need to ask."

That's what I do. I ask people in my network for their assistance or advice. I apologize for rambling.

Q: No worries, it's great to hear stories like yours. Do you have any other stories about community involvement, negotiation, or working as a post-senior? Anything else you'd like to share?

A: Certainly. One thing that has greatly benefited my career, and you know this too, Bruno, is learning to ask for help. When I say that, I mean being specific about what you need from someone. People are generally willing to assist, but it's easier for them if you can articulate your request clearly. For instance, when I'm considering a career move, I seek the opinion of friends in higher roles such as directors or VPs. When I want to learn a new technology, I reach out to friends who have expertise in that area. It's about asking the right person for the right help. So, I don't ask a VP about which technology to learn or a tech-savvy friend about the quality of a company as an employer.

To summarize, it's about making it easy for people to help you by asking for assistance in areas where they excel. If someone asks me for help with cooking good meat, I wouldn't be the best person to ask because that's not my strong suit. But if someone wants guidance on finding a good job or troubleshooting a Kubernetes cluster, I'm the right person to turn to. It's about knowing whom to approach for specific matters.

Q: I see. That makes sense. Sometimes it can be challenging to gauge what others know or don't know. So, how do you approach asking for help? Is it a straightforward request, like, "*Hey, I need this,*" or is there more to it? Asking for help can be difficult at times, right?

A: When seeking help, I often approach people I already have a working relationship with. Since I'm familiar with their areas of expertise, it allows me to make targeted requests. Let me give you an example. If I'm considering changing companies, I would reach out to a colleague and say something like, "*Hey, Friend, have you heard about this company? I'm exploring opportunities with them or already have an offer. Do you happen to know anyone there who could provide valuable insights? I'm trying to determine whether this company is a good fit.*" These are the kinds of requests I typically make when seeking assistance. Sometimes, you just need to start by saying, "*Hey, I need help with this. Can you assist me?*" The person will either respond with a yes or let you know if they're currently unavailable due to other commitments.

Summary

In this chapter, we discussed how to take responsibility for your career and how to take action. We shared how to actively ask for help, how to listen and ask good questions, how to have crucial conversations, how to effectively negotiate with other professionals, and how to take feedback in the right way. Using these skills to optimize your support network for growth will enable your technical career to grow and thrive.

In the next chapter, we will share how to acquire the right soft and hard skills deliberately. In your technical career, you will need both soft and hard skills in order to succeed and continue to advance.

4

Acquire the Right Skills
Deliberately

In the previous chapter, we talked about growing your network to support you. We taught you how to take responsibility and take action for your career. We shared how to actively ask for help, how to listen and ask good questions, how to have crucial conversations, how to effectively negotiate with other professionals, and how to accept feedback. In this chapter, we will cover how to acquire the right hard and soft skills deliberately. What really matters for developers are the skills they build in their careers. There are significant differences in acquiring soft and hard skills. Once those differences are understood, it can boost your skill acquisition. This chapter will discuss the differences between hard and soft skills, and how you can practice those skills for the best results in your professional life.

This chapter will cover the following topics:

- Soft versus hard skills – the reality
- The science behind acquiring skills
- Enhancing hard skills
- Improving soft skills
- Combining soft and hard skills for maximum results

Let's begin!

Soft versus hard skills – the reality

Many technical job listings emphasize the need for "soft skills"; these can be skills such as empathy, communication, or critical thinking. In the world we live in today, why do we call them "soft?"

The term "soft skills" dates back to the US military in the 1960s, when "soft skills" entailed anything that did not require the use of machinery. The term has migrated to the corporate world and is often misapplied to colloquially refer to interpersonal skills or emotional IQ. The demand for these skills has risen in recent years. There is an assumption that these skills are easy to develop or are somehow intrinsic to some individuals. The idea that "hard skills" are more important or valuable than "soft skills" is unfortunate and soft skills are often stereotypically associated with women. Employers look for competencies and critical skills and offer training for these soft skills as much as they do for skills that are traditionally taught as hard skills. Skills are really important for our brains. Every time we acquire skills, we change the neural connections in our brains, and we change the relationship between the neurons. We physically change our brains. *The Talent Code*, by Daniel Coyle, is a book that discusses the source of talent. Coyle discovered that talent is not something you are born with but something you develop over the course of your life. Specifically, talent is directly proportional to the amount of myelin (fatty, speed-enhancing nerve insulation) in your brain. The more you work on growing your myelin, the more talented you become. Coyle argues that myelin is the key to extraordinary talent, and you develop it by acquiring skills.

If you look at the top skills reported by the World Economic Forum, you can see that many are in this category. The World Economic Forum also reported that most employers expect workers to acquire or upskill themselves on the job to meet the demand for top skills. Upskilling is the action or process of teaching an employee additional skills.

Top 15 skills for 2025:

- Analytical thinking and innovation
- Active learning and learning strategies
- Complex problem-solving
- Critical thinking and analysis
- Creativity, originality, and initiative
- Leadership and social influence
- Technology use, monitoring, and control
- Technology design and programming
- Resilience, stress tolerance, and flexibility
- Reasoning, problem-solving, and ideation
- Emotional intelligence
- Troubleshooting and user experience
- Service orientation
- Systems analysis and evaluation
- Persuasion and negotiation

Most people try to acquire knowledge. Knowledge is important but it is also important to support knowledge by acquiring skills.

Skill acquisition is a biological process; it is impacted by the growth and changes of biological cells, called neurons. You acquire skills by practicing them deliberately. Therefore, skill acquisition follows three biological rules that we must consider. We call these rules F3.

Fire

The first biological rule is to *fire* on activate neurons. What accelerates neurons is the brain's process of adding myelin to a neuron's axiom. It is the long part of the cell that takes the electrical impulse to other neurons. The faster the neurons transmit electrical pulses, the more sophisticated the skills we can perform.

Because it is a biological process, the brain only adds myelin to neurons that have been activated. That is why the first F stands for *focus on firing the correct neurons.*

Neurons are fired when we do something, not when we read about doing it or watch videos explaining how to do it. That means skills are only acquired when we *do* the skill. For you to acquire a new skill, you must do it, whether it is a physical skill, such as running or jumping, or an intellectual skill, such as solving problems or software development.

Every time you apply and do the skill, you fire the right neurons. The more a neuron is fired, the more the brain envelops it with myelin. More myelin means a faster and more ready-to-be-activated neuron.

A neuron full of myelin can be up to a hundred times faster than a neuron without myelin. A person that can think or act on something 100 times faster than others will be seen as doing something magical.

Force

The second F is *force*.

The brain tries to save energy. It tries to save resources. Because of that, if a neuron already performs at an adequate speed, then there is no reason for the brain to add more myelin to it. So, to become better at each skill, you must force the brain. You must force your neurons beyond their capabilities. That means you need to force your brain to make mistakes.

And that can happen in all kinds of diverse ways. You may need to do something faster, so your brain is not able to catch up. Alternatively, you may need to do something slowly to get your brain to really nail the skill. You may also need to do something more powerfully than you have before.

Forcing your neurons will force the brain to add more myelin and make your neurons faster.

Frequency

The third F is for *frequency*. You have to do something frequently.

It is not enough to force the brain. We must remember that underneath every skill acquisition, we have a biological process that takes time. If we try to force it too much too soon, we are not going to give the brain enough time to add myelin and make the neurons faster.

Conversely, if we space out too much, then we will not force the neurons frequently enough for the brain to consider it necessary to improve. So, the best way is to practice frequently, daily if possible, although some activities might be better done once a week while many activities would be better done a few times a day.

We'll talk about habit creation in a later chapter, but habits are usually created after 66 interactions with something. That could mean about two months or, if you implement a habit three times a day, it could mean about three weeks.

This is what F3 means – Fire the correct neurons, Force it, and do it Frequently.

How do we improve our skills?

Let us think about what skills are important for us to increase our abilities. Most people think of hard skills as technical skills and soft skills as people skills. Although there is some truth to that, it is not a solid definition of hard and soft skills. Some people believe that hard skills or technical skills, because they are *hard*, are difficult, but that is not a solid definition either.

What are hard skills?

We do not call hard skills *hard* because they are difficult. We call them hard because they are precise. Hard skills are skills that need specific precision. Imagine, for example, typing on a keyboard.

You need to be very precise with your finger movements to type fast; the more precisely your fingers move on a keyboard, the faster you type. To be a better typist, what you need to do is improve the precision of your fingers' movement – the faster your brain is able to send signals to your fingers, the faster you're going to be able to move them and type. Typing on the keyboard is a hard skill. Interestingly enough, hard skills are indeed technical.

Many people assume that the use of the word *technical* is because of technology, but hard skills are technical because they involve a specific technique. Getting back to our typing example, there is a technique that, if followed, allows you to type faster and faster.

You start with a resting position for your hands, and you use the little bumps on the keyboards to know exactly where to put your fingers. Then, you learn how to type specific letters with specific fingers. People who can type with 10 fingers and are very precise with their finger movements can type a lot faster than people who type with one or two fingers.

This technique can be improved, and there are all types of different keyboards with different key arrangements, and even separate keyboards for each type of hand. All of these are different techniques and improvements that help you type faster and faster.

To help you type extremely fast, there are some keyboards where you don't move your fingers at all. They rest on the same keys, all the time, reducing the time that you need to move your fingers.

So, you can see that technology can improve the different techniques for you to type on a keyboard faster and faster. The best way for you to improve hard skills is repetition because hard skills are precise skills. The more you practice and repeat, the better you get.

What are soft skills then?

We do not call them soft skills because they are soft and easy. They are called soft because they are malleable. Soft skills are skills that do not require precision but require malleability. They are applied differently in different situations. You can think about soft skills as pattern-matching skills.

When a different situation occurs, there are different things that you can do, different techniques that you can apply, or different technologies that you can use. Soft skills are about experience, about having seen and applied the skills in different situations in the past. That way, you know the best thing to do in the current situation.

That is why we often refer to people's skills as soft skills. When dealing with people, every situation is different. It depends on how the other person is responding, and what your emotions are now. What does this mean? It means what they say and what they do. When we call soft skills *people skills*, we limit them to a specific type. There are many more soft skills that are not people skills.

For example, solving problems is a soft skill. You may need to apply different strategies, different tools, or different mindsets to solve different problems. Solving problems is something that will help you get better at problem-solving. The more problems you solve, the more you will improve your problem-solving skills, although not if you solve the same types of problems repeatedly. You get better at solving problems when you solve diverse types of problems.

The more situations you get exposed to, the better you will be in the future at solving problems in situations you have never encountered before. You may get exposed to different situations and different complications.

The best way to improve soft skills

We improve our soft skills as we improve any skills – by forcing our brains to try new things. We should try new things frequently and focus on activating the neurons.

We have to make mistakes to improve our soft skills. The best way to do that is to apply our skills to different situations. While repetition is also a way to improve soft skills, contrary to hard skills, where we try to repeat the same situation over and over to improve our precision, soft skills are improved by applying them to different situations so that we can better understand the best ways to decide to use the skill.

Software development, which is the main topic of this book, is a soft skill, so improving your soft skills can benefit your career in software development.

Because we often associate hard skills with technology, many people associate software development with hard skills, but soft skill development involves solving different problems in different moments. Soft skill development is very malleable. Software development is a soft skill. The best way for each of us to improve and develop is to apply a skill to multiple different problems.

We need to apply skills to different situations, different technologies, different programming languages, different problems… different everything. You do not get better at developing soft skills by repeating the same thing over and over and being very precise about it.

You get better by applying your skills differently and, of course, combining hard and soft skills. When your skills are applied, they are usually applied in combination unless you are just practicing. Otherwise, you very rarely apply one skill alone.

For any task or activity that you want to do or any problem that you want to solve, you apply several skills at the same time.

When we apply software development, we use our soft skills of problem-solving to solve problems, but we also use our hard skills of typing on a keyboard to type a solution in our **integrated development environment** (IDE). We may need to use our soft skills of asking questions to understand the problem. We also use our hard skills of understanding a language to apply that language to the solution.

As a technical person, you should not be afraid of soft skills. You should shine, polish, and develop them. Many developers ask the question, "*How important is it to know and learn soft skills?*" Since software development is a soft skill, it is not only important but also fundamental. The same techniques you use to improve as software developers can be used to improve other soft skills.

It is not by chance that many developers have other creative abilities, such as music, dancing, or puppet making. Many developers like to solve problems and do puzzles. All these activities are soft skills.

Once you realize this, you may be freer to pursue other soft skills that you might typically shy away from doing. For example, negotiation and public speaking are important soft skills. Developers often shy away from the types of labels we use to describe people with soft skills.

Many technical people avoid people skills because they think they are not good enough, or they think those skills will not help them improve what they do. Because software development is a soft skill, the more we apply creative solutions to other parts of our lives, such as helping our friends, helping our family, or helping our colleagues, the more we can improve our software development.

All these activities create experiences that we can then apply to our software development. Don't shy away from soft skills!

How do we enhance hard skills? Enhancing hard skills requires precision.

The first thing you need to do is to determine which hard skills you want to improve. To do this, you need to understand that if you are trying to improve a hard skill, it requires precision. Hard skills are those skills that need to be executed perfectly every time you do them.

If the skill you want to improve is bad if performed imprecisely and is better done precisely, you know you are dealing with a hard skill.

A few examples of hard skills could be the following:

- Typing on a keyboard
- Writing in a programming language
- Playing the strings of a guitar
- Voice control
- Dance moves
- Karate moves
- Throwing a ball in a hoop
- Passing a ball in a soccer game

All of these are examples of hard skills. If you're able to apply them precisely, you will be very good at them.

The goal of hard skills is to achieve the highest level of precision. Practicing hard skills requires noticing small, very incremental improvements. It requires noticing the small deviance in the precision of perfect movements and creating a practice that allows you to get better and better at repeating the move in this exact, precise way.

All the practice around hard skills involves improving this precision and improving movement. When you practice hard skills, do not just repeat them but also create practices that ingrain the perfect move in your brain.

One great way to practice hard skills is to slow down movements. When you do this, , it is easier to do the movement perfectly, and it is easy to see where you are going wrong. Another important practice of hard skills is to speed up movements – try to do them as fast as you can, which will force mistakes.

Contrary to hard skills, soft skills require different repetitions because soft skills are pattern matching and require different situations for each. You'll get experience. The best way to repeat soft skills is to put yourself in different situations.

A few examples that might make it easy to see some examples of soft skills are the following:

- Public speaking
- Having a conversation with your boss

- Designing a user case study

- Negotiating a promotion

- Conflict resolution

In all those cases, you deal with other people in different situations. To acquire soft skills, you must put yourself in different situations to practice the skills. You must change the variables. With public speaking, for example, you might speak to different audiences – a small group or a large audience. You might speak live or record a video.

It could be in a venue or remotely on Zoom; you could speak using slides or have a conversation with the gathered audience. You might do live coding or just show your slides on the screen. All these factors force you to be a better public speaker. It is a similar case with software development; you can develop a mobile application or a desktop application. You can write things to run on containers or on-premises. You might solve problems using Java, Python, or Perl.

The more different experiences you have, the better you become as a software developer. It is remarkably interesting that solving a problem in your non-preferred language helps you become better in your preferred language.

Key skills to develop

Heather selected her top five skills to develop to excel in your career. These are skills she looks for when hiring and in her community engagement work. You can improve your skills in these areas by practicing them with other people in various scenarios, even beyond your work life, such as in your personal or family life. These skills will help to enhance and improve your life in general, as well as your career:

- **Communication**: In order to be able to progressively enhance other soft skills, you need to be an effective communicator. One of the more important aspects of communication that may seem counterintuitive is listening. You need to listen more than you speak. This can be difficult for many people. Remember to listen or read to understand something, not in preparation to simply respond and put across your point of view. Really try to understand what the other parties are trying to communicate.

- **Collaboration**: You need to be an excellent communicator to collaborate, so you need to put those communication skills to work. Collaboration is also a skill that requires empathy and kindness. Being kind and considering the circumstances of others is challenging for some people, but being cognizant of others and practicing the skill of putting yourself (mentally) in the perspective of others will improve your ability to empathize. When you improve this skill, you will naturally become a better collaborator. Collaboration also makes you a better team player and improves your teamwork skills. This is another highly valued attribute and skill that can be used to hire managers.

- **Leadership**: Leaders are inspiring; of course, they should be in order to excel in their positions. The other aspect of great leaders and people with leadership skills are the aforementioned communication and collaboration skills. Once you have honed these skills, people will want to follow you. Leaders need followers. People will follow others who inspire a vision – one that can be communicated and that others can contribute to in order to participate in that vision. You do not need to be given a management title to be a leader. Look for opportunities to develop a vision and enable others to succeed. These are the traits of a leader.

- **Problem-solving**: You will need to solve problems in any career, but problem-solving is at the heart of software development. Solving problems, and not just technical problems, is a skill that many developers do not continue in other aspects of their careers. Think of every situation that you encounter as an opportunity to solve problems. Bring your communication, collaboration, and leadership style to problem-solving, and step back from the immediate task at hand to see the larger perspective. You will then find that you are equipped to solve any number of challenges coming your way.

- **Conflict resolution**: If you can be relied on to resolve conflicts that will inevitably arise in your career, you will find yourself in high demand. Assuming you have developed the aforementioned four skills, you will put your communication, collaboration, leadership, and problem-solving skills to work to resolve nearly any conflict. Coming to an agreement that will amicably meet the needs of all parties – maybe not completely but at least partially – is possible. Finding common ground where there is agreement can help to resolve the conflicts that arise in software development teams. Being someone who can be relied on with the ability to bring people to a place of commonality is something that will make you valuable to not only management but also your team members.

Combining hard and soft skills for maximum results

Combining soft and hard skills delivers maximum results. Always remember that every skill is a combined activity. It is a combination of multiple skills. There is almost nothing that requires only one skill. There is almost nothing that is all hard skills or all soft skills. You must combine hard skills and soft skills. To learn about a technology, you will need to practice deliberately and incorporate your good habits to repeat and implement the learning. You will need to take action and practice every day in order to develop the skill and establish a habit.

In her career, Heather does quite a bit of hiring and offers recommendations for hiring technical talent. She will often reference a quote by Simon Sinek about the person with the best people skills winning, and she has found in her own experience and those of other hiring managers that when you look for technical talent, or it is time to make a decision about a new role, you will not look for the person with only the best coding skills; you will look for someone who has a combination of superior coding, combined communication, collaboration, and critical thinking skills, as well as emotional IQ or emotional intelligence, and the ability to understand, use, and manage emotions in positive ways. The ideal candidate is someone who will be a positive team member, and the hiring manager will often choose a candidate with a lower level of coding skills in order to have a candidate who can combine coding with soft skills. As Heather says, echoing Simon Sinek, she will choose the one with the people skills every time. The powerful combination of hard and soft skills will give you maximum results in your career. Take the steps to build the practice and habit of acquiring a combination of hard and soft skills in your professional life.

Interview

Arun Gupta

Arun Gupta: Heather, thank you very much. I'm super excited about this opportunity.

My name is Arun Gupta. I am the vice president and general manager of the open ecosystem team at Intel.

A few years ago, if somebody had asked me if I saw myself working at Intel in this job, I would have not even imagined it, and I'm very grateful to all the wonderful people that I've been surrounded with, the impact that the community has had on me over the years, and all the good wishes that I received that got me here.

Now, I'm not discounting all the technical work that I've done over the years with multiple communities. I've been fortunate – over the last several years, I've been paid to come and work for a nice big company, and that is only possible because, essentially, I was doing a lot of work out in the community – blogging, writing, authoring a book, giving keynotes all over the world in more than 50 countries. I think that's been a big part of my career over the last few years.

Although all of that was done in a classical DevRel role, over the years, I've shifted away from DevRel and toward open source strategies. That's the reason I was at Amazon. I was doing DevRel but also creating open source strategies for different service teams at Amazon. There was a lack of knowledge about how open source operates. That was also the reason I was hired at Apple. Apple built an open source program office. Now, at Intel, the open source program office is one part of my team, but I have a bunch of other folks who do DevRel out in the community.

I see myself as a chief storytelling officer – I go out in the world and tell people why open source matters to Intel. It's about understanding what the current landscape of the company is and telling customers out in the real world why and how we do open source. That's the part that I enjoy the most.

Over the years, technical skills have definitely been a big part of it, but equally important are non-technical skills. You need to consider soft interpersonal skills – when you are communicating with somebody, how well are you listening to them? Are you even listening to them, or are you trying to interject with your point without letting them complete their thought? Are you truly being helpful to them?

In an open source world, conflicts happen all the time. On average, we have to do conflict resolution eight times an hour – how should I word this email? Should I send the email now or in 20 minutes? Should I take a break now or in 20 minutes? We do conflict resolution constantly, and when there are other human beings involved, it becomes all the more complex.

How you do conflict resolution in the open source community is important. My approach to it is this – is it a task conflict or a personality conflict? A task conflict is about what and how; a personality conflict is about who. Separating the two is important because it is what allows you to move forward.

Returning to the communication side, you need to be very mindful of when you talk. In the open source, distributed world, there may be childcare, parent care, pet care, and other things going on in someone's life to consider. You may be driving as you're listening to someone on the phone and go through a dead zone where there is no cellphone signal, meaning you might have heard only part of the conversation. You need to make sure your intended impact on the listener and the actual impact on the listener are aligned, so you should be very mindful when you talk.

On the listener's side, you need to truly try to understand, as opposed to interjecting. Once you've listened, you need to paraphrase and reply back, *"This is what it sounds like you're saying."* Don't try to smuggle your point of view into it; just understand the other person's point of view, and then you can put your point of view across. As Stephen Covey says, most people do not listen with the intent to understand but with the intent to reply. Don't try to reply; just try to understand.

The other thing that I often talk about is adaptability. The last three years have taught us how important adaptability is. We lost some loved ones, but on the whole, humanity has survived, and the only reason it's survived is that we adapted. Such pandemics occur once every 100 years. We all bunkered down. Nobody liked it. People had all sorts of different issues, but we didn't die; humanity didn't crash.

That's the exact same thing that happens in technical communities as well. You have a new boss. You have a new tool. Zoom has a new feature. Your internet goes down. Change is the only constant. How do you adapt to these ever-changing conditions? You were using Java; now you've got to understand .NET. Anything could happen. The ability to mark your adaptability quotient is vital.

In terms of the adaptability quotient, what do you look at? You ask the following questions – how can you unlearn and relearn quickly? How do you adapt to failures? How do you recover from failures? Are you genuinely curious about the situations that are given to you? Do you get bogged down or think, *"OK, here is the thing that is not working. I need to get this working"*? Therefore, adaptability is another non-technical skill that is very important.

I used to travel all around the world, and our flights would change schedules all the time. Maybe you can't reach a conference you're supposed to speak at. Maybe you're crossing into a different time zone. How do you handle the circadian rhythm of your body? Change is the only constant, and adapting to that change is what makes you thrive.

We've talked about communication. We've talked about conflict resolution. We've talked about adaptability. The fourth skill that I believe is highly undervalued is kindness and gratitude – kindness to yourself and kindness to others. You cannot be kind to other people without being kind to yourself. And what is kindness? Kindness is an act of helping somebody, or giving a compliment to somebody, without expecting a return.

Say you are walking along the street and realize that somebody dropped something from their backpack – you just go and pick it up and give it back to them. That's kindness. It's humanity as well, but it's kindness too. Say you are waiting in your car at a traffic light. The traffic light goes green, but someone is taking their time to cross. You don't honk at them – you let them cross. Say somebody did a favor for you at work. You were new at work, and they helped you to understand how something worked. That's an act of kindness. That is exactly the element that is missing. We can only be more kind.

Plus, as I said, be kind to yourself. Let's say that in a meeting or a talk, you find you're not performing well. Don't get sulky and bogged down by it so much that it bothers you for the next few days. It's OK to make mistakes. Everybody makes mistakes. Nobody has ever been perfect all the time. Think to yourself, "*OK. You know what? I messed up. Maybe I didn't prepare well, or maybe I should have done things differently.*" Be kind to yourself and then give space and grace to others.

As for gratitude, be thankful for what you get. Often, we say, "*Oh, I wish I did that differently.*" Sure – hindsight is 20/20 – but be grateful for the things that you have, and don't wait for the big moment to happen. Don't think, "*When the release happens, or when the conference is over, then I'll be grateful to the people that helped me achieve them.*"

In my team meetings, we always start with a gratitude check-in: "*What are you grateful for?*" People come up with all kinds of gratitude stories: "*I was trying to do a talk to these people. They were not understanding my point of view. Then, a person stepped in and they conveyed my point of view in a different language, and they understood it. What a wonderful gesture!*" or, "*I was trying to debug some code. I couldn't understand it, and then this person stepped in and they helped me succeed.*" These are both acts of kindness, but being grateful for those acts and explicitly conscious of them is important. That's the fourth skill of being kind and grateful.

Maya Angelou said that people will forget what you did and what you said, but they will never forget how you made them feel. Kindness only makes you happy. It brings more meaningful connections at work. It increases your serotonin, dopamine, and oxytocin. These are the hormones in your brain that give you happiness. And with kindness and gratitude particularly, what goes around comes around, because if I perform an act of kindness that makes you happy, that makes me happy, and then it makes the people who encounter it happy as well. Overall, there's greater happiness.

The fifth skill that I could talk about briefly is mindfulness. That is very important. Mindfulness is living in the present moment without judgment. If you think about it, oftentimes we are not in the present moment. We are often worried about things that have happened in the past or anxious about the future, neither of which is in our control. You can regret the past, but can you change it? No. Is the future in your control? You can be better prepared for it, but it's still not in your control. The current moment, the current breath that you're taking, is the only thing in your control. Neither the past nor the future is in your control. Your response to the past and the future is the only thing that is in your control.

Let me give you an example. You try to fall asleep at night, lying in bed. What goes on in your head? You think about how the day has gone: "*This was good; that wasn't so good.*" Alternatively, you're worried about what's going to happen the next morning: "*Oh, my meeting is coming up and that's going to be difficult.*" Again, you try to live in the past or the future while you try to fall asleep, and then an hour goes by – you're not able to fall asleep. You need to live in the present moment – let go of the past, and let go of the future.

Mindfulness gives you the ability to reduce anxiety. It helps you deal with the current situation. Ajahn Sumedho, a Theravadian monk based out of Thailand, summarized mindfulness in five words. He said, *"Right now, it's like this."* It's not about me or you. It's about the current situation. If you want to be mindful, in a situation that is stressful, think to yourself, *"Right now, it's like this."* Yes, the water should not have been spilled. Yes, you should have done a better job of putting safeguards in place. Right now, it's like this. How do you make progress and move on? Because that gives you a perspective that you can deal with.

All of these skills have been vital for me growing up as a person and being really able to interact that much more impactfully with the Java community, which I've been in for 25 years.

Those are the five skills that are extremely valuable and that we need to focus on. How do you make people feel? Are you being aware? Are you being mindful? Are you able to do conflict resolution? Are you aware of cultural biases, gender biases, and unconscious biases? I think all of those elements are very important if you are a younger developer particularly. Younger developers typically have a lot of imposter syndrome, walking into a room and thinking, *"Oh, my God. This guy has 25 years' experience and is so good. I could never get there. I don't belong here."* Well, he has 25 years' experience, and you have 2 years' experience. In 23 years, you will certainly get there – no question about it.

Don't have imposter syndrome. Be kind to yourself. Just have the courage to ask the right questions, and then that'll help you grow overall. If you continue to live with imposter syndrome, it will never help you grow. My advice to young developers, or indeed people at any stage of their career, is to never have imposter syndrome.

Be fearless, but don't be stupid. There's a fine line between being stupid and fearless, but be fearless. Try to build connections in the community. Forge a network in the community and see how it helps you grow.

Q: Awesome. Can you share a little bit about how getting involved in the community helped your career in the early stages? You developed those skills and realized they were important. How did that impact your career?

A: We used to give JavaOne keynotes. I have keynoted JavaOne for seven consecutive years. In a JavaOne keynote, adaptability is so important. If the system is not working, how do you adapt? You need to do a talk with another speaker. That speaker wants to add their agenda, and you want to add your agenda – how do we resolve that conflict? How do we communicate? How do we adapt?

More importantly, I don't want to be the person who, right after the keynote, just walks out. I never want to work with that person. That's where kindness and mindfulness come in. Giving the JavaOne keynotes opened up a lot of opportunities for me. Being a kind person, being a grateful person, and being able to resolve conflicts in an amicable manner opened up a lot of opportunities because people saw me as a person that they could invite to other conferences. That helped me build a DevRel platform and gain visibility.

Now, similarly, I am part of the CNCF governing board. As the governing board chair, it's very important that I am unbiased and able to talk to all types of people. All five skills I have talked about have been critical for my growth and living a more contented life. Growth and contentment are different things. In your current role, are you satisfied? Are you having fun? Are you happy?

All of these skills have been fundamental. Yes, I've had the technical skills all along, but I can very well imagine that without any of these soft skills, I would not have grown. I would not be here without any of them.

Summary

In this chapter, we talked about learning the correct hard and soft skills deliberately. You should now be able to identify the diverse types of skills, know how to acquire skills reliably, incorporate practices to acquire hard skills as well as soft skills, and also know how to practice these skills in real life.

In the next chapter, we will discuss how to operate outside of your comfort zone.

5

Stepping Outside
Your Comfort Zone

In the previous chapter, we talked about how to acquire the hard and soft skills necessary to advance your career. In this chapter, we will help you learn how to get out of your comfort zone. The most important thing to focus your mind on involves taking action. Learning, improving, and growing are difficult things that require deliberate, focused effort. If you do too little, nothing happens. If you push too much, you give up. This chapter will present strategies for you to keep pushing in a consistent manner. We will give you the specific steps required to force your brain to take action, find the right balance, and acquire consistency in continuing to push yourself outside your comfort zone.

In this chapter, we'll cover the process to do the following:

- Force your brain to take action

- Find the sweet spot

- Be consistent

Let's begin!

Forcing your brain to take action

We have to appreciate the fact that taking action is very difficult. It is difficult for our kids and for our team. It is difficult for us!

Many bosses think that you can force people to act or at least convince them to do it. But forcing – and convincing (a subtle way of forcing) – is counterproductive. When people recognize we are forcing them, they react against it.

Our brains work the same way. Maybe you experimented trying to be your own "boss," thinking you can force yourself to do things. But when you try to corner your brain and be a tyrannical boss with yourself, your brain reacts with fear. You procrastinate. You find excuses and reasons not to do things.

Leaders recognize the fact that forcing is the wrong way and instead inspire people to take action. Inspiring is helping people to decide to act.

That works for us also. Here is a four-step process that you can use to inspire yourself into taking action and achieving your most important goals:

- Step 1 – Create and visualize a great future
- Step 2 – Maximize the current problems
- Step 3 – Build a bridge from here to there
- Step 4 – Plan small actionable steps

Step 1 – Create and visualize a great future

To take action, you need to see a clear and better future, one that you want to be part of, one that you can see yourself living. That's because our brains need a clear image to act upon. The more detailed the future we see, the more invested we will be in trying to achieve it.

The industry knows this very well and uses this to inspire us. You can go to an Apple store and hold and use iPhones, MacBooks, and iPads. You can hold them in your hands and see yourself owning one.

When you go and buy a car, the salesperson invites you for a test drive. You drive the car, and make it your car, long before you make the real decision about acquiring it. When buying a house, the real estate agent walks with you inside a furnished house, and they help you visualize your kids playing in the garden. Those things make our future decisions more real. You can see yourself living in your house, driving your car, and programming on your laptop.

When you *experience* yourself within that "future" life, you are more inclined to take action to make it a reality. You can use those same tactics, but to create and achieve your most important goals.

Imagine how your life will be once you achieve the desired results. See yourself enjoying an event when you are there as a speaker. Visualize your day as a recognized software architect. Create a clear picture of your life when you are working every day on this new technology you want to learn.

Think of yourself in your amazing future! What are you doing? How are you feeling? How do people around you interact with you? How is your family enjoying it? The more detailed you see yourself living in this future, the more you will be inspired to take the needed actions.

You should remember one important thing. Talking with technical people just like you, it is amazing how much we only focus on our careers and professional life! Although this is a book about your career, you will advance much faster and build a better life if you visualize a future for your whole life.

Michael Hyatt, in his book *Your Best Year Ever*, lists 10 areas where you should make plans for your future to help you build the life you want.

Using the following list, write down what would be an *amazing* year for you, in at least three areas of your life. Bonus points if you can imagine how you want to be in all the relevant areas:

- **Spiritual**: How will you connect with the sacred and transcendent? This includes religion, meditation, and mindfulness.
- **Intellectual**: Learning and improving, including books, courses, and training.
- **Emotional**: Taking care of yourself, including dealing with stress, anger management, and self-knowledge.
- **Physical**: Feeling good with your body, including exercise, weight control, hygiene, and health.
- **Marital**: You and your significant other, including time together, and joint projects and activities.
- **Parental**: Focusing on your family, including your parents or your kids, projects, and vacations.
- **Social**: Friends and entertainment, going out, and traveling.
- **Vocational**: Your work and career, including plans to grow, positions, and career dreams.
- **Avocational**: Your hobbies and free time, including sports, side projects, and fun stuff.
- **Financial**: Your money and security, including investments, savings, and side hustles.

Once you have created a vision for your future in some or all of the preceding areas, let us focus on how we can find the sweet spot to find a way to bridge between the vision of our future and the limitations that may prevent us from realizing that future.

Finding opportunities within our limitations – the sweet spot

When you imagine a better life in the previous areas and describe your amazing future, it is normal to not immediately believe it is possible. We limit ourselves, to prevent taking risks or putting ourselves in discomfort.

The way the brain does that in our daily lives is by creating a sense of fear. That is why it is helpful to think far ahead, a year from now. It helps to subdue this fear, so you can think clearly. But this subdued fear does not disappear. It can show up as anxiety, a knot in the stomach.

When you were writing down or imagining your future, did you feel anxiety about some of the things? When you think about committing yourself, do you feel a knot in the stomach, such as negative ideas or the feeling that this is impossible, and you are unable to commit to that future?

Take note of those feelings. They are what we call limiting beliefs – things that you believe about yourself or your life that limit your possibilities. Write them down. Try to put into words what you believe is impossible.

Recognizing the limiting belief is the first step to overcoming it.

Now that you have listed the things that limit you, you can create liberating truths that can help you get past your limiting beliefs. Note that limiting beliefs are real. They are things you believe about the world and about yourself and your situation. Because they are real, you get stuck and cannot overcome them.

The only way to free yourself is by thinking of liberating truths. That is not simply a motivational statement made to convince you! Liberating truths are true statements that you also believe in, but that allow you to move forward.

Here are some examples:

- **Limiting belief**: I don't have the time to do all that. I'll be too busy during the year.
- **Liberating truth**: I can prioritize my activities and reduce time spent on things that are less important, to be able to find some time to focus on the most important dreams and goals. I will be busy, but I can choose to be busy with the right things.
- **Limiting belief**: I don't have the money to do those things.
- **Liberating truth**: I can look for free alternatives, and I can find some extra revenue doing some side job. I can do this because achieving those objectives and goals is the most important thing this year.

Liberating truths put YOU in control of your life. They don't make the problems and fears magically disappear, but they help you see there is something – however small – that you can do about it.

Step 2 – Maximize the current problems

Having a clear vision of your future will help you create the motivation to take action; however, this alone is not enough.

How many times have you created, or seen your friends create, New Year's resolutions? How many of them get dropped or forgotten even before January ends? We create excuses and reasons to not do things that we think are important:

- *I don't have the time*
- *I don't have the money*
- *My boss won't let me do this*
- *My company will never help me*
- *I can't. My wife this, my kids that...*

To help us overcome those excuses, we need another push. We need to see our current reality and realize that staying put is a bad idea. We need to see our current situation and have a clear understanding that we can't continue to live like this. We can't continue to not take action.

What happens if you don't go after your dreams?

If you continue to repeat the thing that's not working?

If you keep on the same loop of not getting what you want?

Recognizing our current situation, our limitations, and our fears is the key to overcoming them. Let's dive into your current situation. Get a pen and some blank paper, or open up a note-taking app.

Spend time thinking and mulling over your past, by answering the following questions:

- *How did you expect the past year to go? Try to think about what you wanted for the past year, and what you expected to happen.*

- *Did you have any plans for the past year?*

- *Were you expecting any breakthroughs or results?*

- *Any New Year's resolutions or lists of activities and dreams? When writing things down, try to register the feelings you have about those dreams. Do you get excited, sad, or uneasy about something?*

- *What were your goals and dreams, if you had any?*

Register any specific goals that you had planned. Note whether they were detailed or vague. Also, make notes on how far you got on each goal.

Also, about your dreams: dreams are usually less specific than goals, but they are also larger and more inspiring. Write down your past dreams and whether you took any specific actions on them.

What about disappointments or regrets? While thinking about your goals and dreams, note the things you got disappointed about and things you regretted. It could be things you regret doing or maybe regret that you missed the opportunity. It can be accomplishments that you expected would be amazing but turned out to be disappointments. It can also be feelings of guilt and self-bashing for not taking action or maybe taking the wrong path.

What do you feel you should have been recognized for but weren't? These can be things you did and no one noticed. Maybe because no one even knows about them, or because they imagine it was luck or their own doing, and don't realize you were behind it.

Sometimes we do things at work or for our families that are very important but invisible, such as when we don't buy something or we work extra hours and save money, making other things possible.

In other moments, someone else gets the credit, maybe by design, such as when you want someone else from the family to get the credit, but sometimes by ignorance or even malice, when someone fails to credit you because they don't know better, or they take the credit.

What are you proud of? List the things you are happy that you did, and that you feel proud to have accomplished. Sometimes we are proud of having given our best, even if we didn't achieve it all!

What are the recurring themes? Now, it is time to look back at your notes. Are there things that kept repeating? Feelings or difficulties that are similar? Reasons for failure or successes that go round and round?

Those repeating themes may be things you need to stop, or maybe the things you need to go ahead and finish:

- *What do you think?*

- *What are the life lessons?*

- *If you could list some lessons that you can take from your life from the past year, what would they be?*

List 10 things you are grateful for! Gratitude is one of the most powerful feelings, and it can push you to your next challenge! List as many things as you can that you are grateful for. Small things, big things. List all you can and take some time to act on this gratitude if possible.

Hidden opportunities! Look back at all you wrote here. Sometimes our biggest opportunities are right in front of our eyes and we don't see them. They are hidden in plain sight.

Are there things you can focus on and get done quickly to get a big win from the start? Do you see repeating patterns that you can either break or benefit from?

Here are some ways that will help you identify hidden opportunities:

- Look for things that you started but didn't finish. Sometimes, it's one step away from good results!

- Think of friends and partners who can help you overcome a problem or a situation.

- Align objectives by asking yourself, are there several points or issues that build on each other?

- Identify repeating issues that, if you fix them, can open lots of possibilities.

- Spend some time looking at everything. What pops out at you?

Step 3 – Build a bridge from here to there

You now have clear dreams and understand you can't stay put. Congratulations! This is more planning than most people do for their lives!

But it is still not enough! One of the reasons it is so hard to take action is that we are very adaptable. No matter how bad the situation is, we adapt and are able to survive.

To prevent our fears from paralyzing us, we need to believe we can go from where we are to where we want to be. We need to believe we can become who we want to become.

For that, we need to build a bridge – a bridge that can take us from where we are right now, to our desired future. A bridge is basically the steps that will take us from our limited problematic situation of today to our amazing life in the future.

Building the bridge

In order to build the bridge, it can be helpful to consider the different areas of your life. Think about a few of these areas listed next and consider what needs to happen in order to get you to your desired vision of the future. What concrete results need to happen in each of those domains? What would need to happen in these domains for you to consider that the year was amazing? Turn your vision into specific things that need to happen for you in a few of the following areas:

- Spiritual
- Intellectual
- Emotional
- Physical
- Marital
- Parental
- Social
- Vocational
- Avocational
- Financial

You can use the specific things that need to happen in these domains to create objectives and actions to take. Now that you have a list of objectives, you need to make them effective. Great goals follow the SMARTER pattern. Evaluate every goal for your year. Make sure they check every point. Having excellent goals will help you achieve them.

SMARTER goal template

Create goals that are SMARTER, as follows:

- **Specific**: Goals have to be specific and focused on a clear result.
- **Measurable**: You must be able to track your progress.
- **Actionable**: Make your goals focused on actions.
- **Risky**: Make them larger, and push yourself to achieve more.
- **Time-keyed**: What's the deadline? That will keep you focused.
- **Exciting**: Make them amazing and fun, so you want to achieve them.
- **Relevant**: Are they aligned with your vision for the future?

Step 4 – Plan small actionable steps

Now you have created goals and objectives, you have an amazing dream for your future! You know you can't stay where you are! You even have a plan! Maybe you are now very motivated to cause a change in your life and take action.

Nothing can stop you now!

Well...maybe...So many people have all of that and still don't get to the other side, and stay stuck.

Why? You see, the issue here is motivation. Motivation can only take you so far. It's a great catalyst for change and can get you started. But real change takes time. And motivation is tiring, and not very useful to keep us going during all the time needed for change to happen. For real change, you need consistency. You have to make sure you have small steps and create the right habits that will get you doing the needed things, long after motivation has run out. That is the only way for you to cross to the other side of the bridge, step by step by step.

Two types of "steps"

There are basically two types of steps that we need to create:

- Steps
- Tactics

Steps are single actions that we do once. Steps will make us move closer to our dreams, and we will tick them off our list as *Done*. Steps are things such as *Create an account on a blog platform*. Once done, we move to the next.

Tactics are strategies, things we do many times until we get results. We focus on doing tactics every day, or every week, to move closer to a goal. Tactics are things such as *Write a blog post for 5 minutes every day*.

Both steps and tactics require that we keep doing things, and keep pushing ourselves to take action every day.

Be consistent

To keep doing things, we will apply the **SCIENCE** of sticking with it. This is explained in detail by Sean D. Young in his book Stick with It: A Scientifically Proven Process for Changing Your Life-for Good. How can you maximize your chances of sticking with it, and how can you get to the end result? It is normal to get lost in the goals along the way. But you can plan and create the conditions that will help you stick with your goals and give them a better chance to succeed. For each of your steps and tactics, apply the S.C.I.E.N.C.E. of sticking with it. The way to use this is for each goal, think of strategies to apply at least three or four of the following ideas. For the most important goals, apply all of them.

STEPLADDERS – small steps

Our brains go into crazy-fear mode every time we try to commit to something that seems to be too big or too dangerous. That causes all kinds of self-sabotage against our plans, such as procrastination, lack of motivation, and fear of success.

The way to prevent that is to plan for small steps. Very small steps. For example, if your goal is to write a book, this may seem impossible or too hard for you.

Some people divide the work into small steps, such as a plan to write just one chapter or one page every day. But even that seems implausible and causes anxiety, so we never start.

The solution is to start even smaller. Commit to writing just a single paragraph or even a single sentence every day. This may seem too small to create any results, but research shows that 80% of the time, once you get started, you will do more than that minimum.

And here is the magic: the hardest part is to start. Reducing fear will allow you to start doing. Once you overcome that fear, the impossible becomes possible!

Create a COMMUNITY

When we have other people doing things with us, we are more likely to pull through. We have increased commitment because we see other people depending on us. We also feel like we are part of a group, which is more fun and increases our motivation. We create accountability within the community.

Think of ways that your goal could be done together with other people. Maybe they are doing similar projects, or everyone is working on the same project. You can plan things such as going with friends to a networking event or creating a joint open source project. It could also be something as simple as joining a challenge on social media, where many people are trying to achieve the same goals.

Doing things together with others also helps with consistency. It is harder to miss a day of running if you know your friend is waiting for you. It is more probable that you will log in to GitHub if you schedule a time for hacking together with a friend.

Now, one little piece of advice. Sometimes we think that more is better. Well, there is a known psychological phenomenon that if there are many people involved, especially if they are strangers, we reduce or even eliminate our need to take action. So, if there are 100 people going to an event, you may think that you don't really need to be there.

So, when creating a community, choose a few people that will actually hold you accountable.

And make sure you hold them accountable too!

Make it IMPORTANT

Motivation is not sustainable in the long run, but it is really important as activation energy to get the process started.

When we are doing something that we feel is important, we stay committed for longer, giving a better chance for the habit to settle in.

Make your goals important. Connect them to the most important things in your life.

Do you want to learn a new programming language? Make it VERY important! Think of the connection that exists between you learning it, you getting a promotion or a raise, and how the extra money will allow your family to go on that amazing trip together.

Connecting your daily activities to larger, more important goals will help you to focus and overcome temptations. But most important, connecting your goals to your larger dreams will give you the motivation to do the other things on this list!

Remember that motivation is a flimsy, expensive activity. Use motivation to get everything else ready to be consistent!

Make it EASY

Life is already complicated enough. Sticking with your goals is very hard, and taking action is unbelievably difficult. Why are you going to complicate matters even more? Don't! Make it as easy as you can. Let's take Bruno as an example.

I wanted to write every day, and for that, I needed to be on my computer. Not only did I have to deal with a lot of distractions, but some days, I was tired, already in bed, or out of the house, with no computer to type on. Sticking with it was hard. I tried to overcome that by typing on my cell phone... even harder! Stop! Why do this to yourself?

I acquired a Bluetooth keyboard. Now, when I need to write, I can just grab the cell phone, and type away. That simple tweak made my writing totally consistent, and I have been writing daily for months now.

This also connects with the small steps. At night, before you go to bed, your brain is not worried that you will go out for a run. So, it will be no problem for you to put the running clothes on the side of the bed. In the morning, when you are sleepy and looking for excuses to not get up to run, the clothes on the side of the bed will make it easier for you to go and run.

Look at what you want to do. Can you make it easy? Can you make it easier to do it than not to do it? That's the way to go; that's planning!

Apply NEUROHACKS

A neurohack is a hack on your brain. Our brains are biologically hardwired to do things in specific ways. If to achieve your goal you need your brain to function differently than it does, it will turn into a tug-of-war. Guess who wins every time? Yep, your biological brain. So, you need to understand how the brain works and do things in a way it is willing to do. Get your brain on your side!

All the items on this list are already working with your brain, such as stepladders (so your brain doesn't freak out) or making it easy (so it's easier to do than not).

One extra neurohack you can implement is getting your brain to *want* to do things. The common-sense idea tells us that the way our brains work is like this: *I think that I want to do something, so I go and do it.*

Although this is what most people believe, this is not true. We are habit-driven creatures: our brains prefer to keep doing what we already do, and will resist anything we want that's different.

The truth is that our brains function like this: *Since I do this thing, I must be someone that does this, so, I'll continue to do it.*

If you try to do something different, your brain will resist. On the other hand, if you try to do something you already do, your brain will go along with it.

The neurohack is to understand that this is how our brain works and, instead of fighting with your brain and getting upset, just let it continue to believe it has the situation under control. Do you want to do something that's important for you, and you don't like it, or procrastinate on it? Start small, very small. So small, your brain doesn't really consider it a threat, because it is nothing at all.

It's almost not doing it. (So, it's almost as if nothing changed!) Then, keep this "a little more than not doing" for a few days. That will become your new normal. Your brain will catch up, and will start functioning as if it always wanted to do that! This is the basis of the saying "fake it till you make it": look at someone that you admire or someone that you aspire to be more like, and start doing what they do.

Want to be a great runner? What do great runners do? Run every day? Do the same. Start small (maybe just 1 min of running), but do the same and run every day.

Want to become a great developer? What do great developers do? Do they code every day? So, you start writing code every day, even if just for a few minutes or just a few lines of code.

Soon enough, writing code every day is the new norm, and your brain will miss doing it! That's when you become who you want to become!

CAPTIVATING – make it rewarding

Another thing that our brains love is to receive a reward! That's why it's so easy to get into addictive habits such as smoking or looking at the phone every time it beeps.

Our brains love the rewards of those activities, even when they are detrimental to our health, our productivity, our job, or even our sanity. We can use the love of rewards to our advantage.

When you plan something, look for ways to add captivating elements to it:

- Can you make it fun?
- Can you turn it into a game?

- Can you add a reward to the end of it?

- Can you just be playful and imagine something?

Let's explore some ideas:

- **Make it fun**: Plan to do it with friends or in a place you like. Invite your significant other to join you so you can work together, or at least side by side. Put on some great music that you love.

- **Turn it into a game**: Try to beat yourself. Use a Pomodoro timer, and try to finish before it dings. Create a personal score, rules, and points. There are even apps that add gamification to our daily lives.

- **Add a reward to the end of it**: Promise yourself a good reward, such as an ice cream or 30 minutes of a video game. It can be simply doing something you love: going for a walk, jumping in the pool, adding a few pieces to a jigsaw puzzle, giving a hug, and commemorating with someone you love.

- **Be playful and imagine something**: Just imagining can do wonders to make it fun! Imagine you have to finish this to be able to close the bridge before hordes of orcs will gain access to the castle. Imagine you are running from zombies, and you just have to do one more lap to get to safety. Oh! The path is blocked! One more lap and you can reach the helicopter!

Sounds silly?

But it is fun! And it works! Your brain will happily go along with it, and you will accomplish a lot more and feel a lot better!

ENGRAINED – create routines

And last, but definitely not least, you have to do it over and over.

That does not sound like fun, but done together with everything we said so far, it can be!

Here are a few things that can be very helpful:

- Do it at the same time every day. Not necessarily at the same time in hours or minutes, but after a common activity, such as right after you open your laptop for the first time, or when you finish pouring your coffee.

- Set a timer or a reminder on your phone.

- Use a habit-tracking tool to remind you to do it.

- Force yourself to do it for a few minutes every day.

Do it after something else you already do, such as after brushing your teeth.

One that is used very frequently, which is both a game and an everyday thing, is Jerry Seinfeld's so-called *Productivity Strategy*. It is easy: mark on a calendar with an X every day you do the activity/habit. The idea that you can't break the chain of Xs will help you try a little harder. And you will try to beat it every day, making an instant game.

The best performers in the world make daily practice its own reward. Just doing it every day becomes the reward you are looking for. That spirals into greatness.

Make your move!

You have a fantastic dream for your future, and you are clear about where you want to get.

You understand your current situation, and how bad it is to stay here – for you and for the people around you. Doing nothing is not an option.

You have a bridge! You have a plan that is actionable, it is realistic, but it is also exciting and challenging. You know it will take effort, but you can do this!

Last, but not least, you mapped out small steps. They are small enough to prevent your brain from going nuts with fear but are sure enough to get you across this bridge.

Here are Scott, Thiago, and Nikita's views on the topic.

Scott Wierschem

Bruno Souza asked me to help with the Java Community Keynote at JavaOne. This was my first JavaOne, so I was very intimidated being around all of these industry leaders. It turns out I have a real skill for developing a story and arranging a skit. It was a big hit and I've been asked back to help with the Java Community Keynote every year since, and I've gotten to meet industry leaders, all because I stepped outside my comfort zone.

Thiago Bomfim

I worked for 5 years in the same company (Mirante Tecnologia, which became Singular) – an amazing company where I learned a lot – but I think I was in my comfort zone. I was facing new challenges, but nothing that made me afraid.

Furthermore, I received a proposal to go abroad, and I accepted it. It was not easy, but I learned a lot – I'm still learning – and with this opportunity and with my mentor, I became able to grow faster in my career and receive better opportunities.

This is my story of how I got outside my comfort zone, and how it helped me to grow more in my professional career and personal life.

Nikita Koselev

I spent five years working at the same company, an exceptional organization from which I gained significant knowledge. However, I came to realize that I had become too accustomed to my routine and was not facing any truly intimidating challenges.

Then, an overseas opportunity presented itself, which I ultimately embraced despite its difficulties. This decision has been a continuous learning experience for me, and thanks to this chance and my mentor's guidance, I've managed to accelerate my career growth and access improved prospects.

In essence, my journey, like Thiago, involves stepping beyond the familiar and into the unknown, which has greatly contributed to my advancement in both my professional journey and personal life.

Final lessons

In this section, we'll go through some final lessons before concluding the chapter.

Embrace failure

The thing to know about stepping outside of your comfort zone is that as you grow and evolve, so will your comfort zone. As you step outside of it and become comfortable with things that made you uncomfortable in the past, your comfort zone will extend into that area. You will need to continue to journey to go further and step outside of your comfort zone again. As Heather likes to say, get comfortable being uncomfortable. This will allow you to grow. And you may be afraid, but it is okay to have some discomfort when you overcome your fears. To quote Aristotle, *"He who has overcome his fears will truly be free."*

When you embark on a journey to overcome your fears and step outside of your comfort zone, there will be failures. You can learn to embrace failure and learn from each failure, as each failure will bring you things on the other side of that failure – lessons learned, wisdom, and knowledge. And failure is often a part of the process of stepping outside of your comfort zone. It is only through trying new things that you will achieve the things you want, on the other side of fear and potential, dare we say, promised failures along the way. Embrace the journey, process, and lifestyle of continuously stepping outside of your comfort zone. Just as we talked about continuous learning, we believe in continuous growth in your career path.

Along the way, there will be resistance in the form of many things or excuses, and most commonly, procrastination. We get in our own way with procrastination.

Procrastination is when we delay, put off, or avoid doing something. Most people face this at some point in their lives, even when there are negative consequences to doing so.

How to avoid procrastination

There are significant benefits to embracing discomfort, and as you embrace this activity in your life, think about the role of your mindset in overcoming challenges. The ideas we are talking about fall into a growth mindset. A growth mindset centers on the belief that you can improve your talents and skills over time. The opposite is a fixed mindset or a set of limiting beliefs that you cannot learn and improve your capacity over time. In addition to a growth mindset, the other mind shift that can be significant in advancing your career is the power of now. In the New York Times best-selling book *The Power of Now*, Eckhart Tolle talks about living fully in the present. This concept, the power of now, is a powerful one. One of the most prominent quotes of this book is "*Realize deeply that the present moment is all you ever have. Make the Now the primary focus of your life.*" If you focus on the present and act with immediacy in the present, you will be able to grow and advance continuously in your life. This is easier for some people than others. It has been studied and found that people who are highly conscientious do not procrastinate as much as others. Even if you are not highly conscientious, there are steps you can take to limit the amount of procrastination in your life.

In the paper by Schrager S, Sadowski E., *Getting more done: Strategies to increase scholarly productivity, J Grad Med Educ*. 2016;8(1):10-13. doi:10.4300/JGME-D-15-00165.1, there are several tips laid out for overcoming procrastination. These tips include developing a schedule, planning, and improving time-management skills:

- **Make a plan**: To help keep you on track, create a schedule, action items, and lists with completion dates

- **Chunking**: Break down the items into smaller and more manageable steps to avoid large tasks that may be overwhelming

- **Watch for warnings or triggers**: Pay attention to thoughts of procrastination and if you feel tempted to procrastinate, proactively spend some time working toward your plan

- **Distraction**: Think about and eliminate sources of distraction such as social media scrolling (aimless time scrolling through your news feeds or timelines), watching television, and so on

- **Celebrate small wins**: Congratulate and reward yourself when you accomplish a task you have planned on time

If you bring the power of now to your life with a growth mindset and reduce procrastination, there is no limit to the things you will be able to achieve on your career path. Opportunities will open and present themselves to you. It is your responsibility to be ready to welcome them and achieve your career goals and dreams.

Interview

Scott Wierschem

Q: Scott, can you quickly introduce yourself?

A: My name is Scott Wierschem. I've been doing software development for about 40 years. I've been doing Java development for 20 years.

My forte is working on legacy systems: old crusty code that most people are afraid to dig into. I like to find ways to get in there and make it maintainable.

I have a project I call the Keep Calm and Refactor project. It's a mentoring program to help developers who have got some experience but need help to become better at handling legacy software development, as that's really what most of us are going to be working on for most of our careers. If you can be good at that, you will have a much more enjoyable career in software development. That's what lights my fire these days.

Q: That's awesome. One of the things that you do is help developers not only deal with legacy code but actually to become better developers. You practice the skills and technologies with them in depth.

A: Yes, I help them to understand the value of the fundamentals. Test-driven development is one of those skills that are hard to develop, and so I work with developers to help them develop that skill so that they can then take it to their regular work and become better developers who are constantly looking for ways to do better work and make work more enjoyable. We enjoy work more if we're really exercising and developing our skills.

Q: Do you think working outside your comfort zone is important for developers to improve their skills?

A: It's essential. You can't improve your skill set if you keep doing the same old stuff. If you go back and look at code that you wrote a year ago and you're not embarrassed, then you've not developed as a software developer. If you're going to stay within tried-and-true things that you're familiar with, you're not going to learn new things.

For instance, in Java, I know people who still don't know how to do lambda programming. That's been out since Java 8. It's the same with streams. This is stuff that's been around for many years but some people just don't understand it yet. You're really limiting what you can do. You're not taking advantage of how to make your software development better by learning the latest features of the language that you work with every day. You need to go through the pain of feeling, "*I'm not familiar with this. I feel like an idiot trying to figure it out.*" And then, you spend the time and you learn how to do it, and realize, "*Oh, yeah. This was so easy. Why was I thinking it was so hard?*" Well, because it was hard! What you did was hard, but you worked on it every day, sometimes for years. It's OK to struggle with something that's new because that's how you become better at what you're doing.

Q: But it's also scary to put yourself in a position where, as you said, you feel like an idiot and you don't know what to do. That's very scary.

A: It's especially scary if you're going to do it on your production work; that's not the way that you do it. What you should do is do the scary stuff where you feel like an idiot someplace else – on an open source project or some tutorial that you're working on at home.

You have to invest in your career in your time. You can't necessarily expect your employer to do that for you. You can go to conferences and learn about stuff. You can buy books, work through tutorials, and have friends who can help you, but you have to spend some extra time doing it and not expect your employer to train you.

There are some employers who will help you learn new things, but you can't expect that. You can't just say, "*Well, if they're not going to train me, then forget it. I'm not going to learn.*" It's your career. You've got to take control of your career.

I like to tell people a story about the woman who cuts my hair. She was cutting my hair once and someone came in one time selling scissors for cutting hair, and she said, "*Oh, yeah. Those are the cheap ones. They're only 200 dollars.*" I said, "*What?*" It turns out that she goes to barber conferences to get the nice shears for cutting hair, and they're about 500 dollars – for a pair of scissors! And we're whining about spending 150 dollars for an IntelliJ license. Get over yourself! I pay her 15 dollars to cut my hair. I get paid more than 30 bucks an hour. I should be able to afford the tools that I use and the training that I need to keep myself up to date. She doesn't have her employer sending her to barber conferences. She sends herself to barber conferences and she pays outrageous sums of money for these tools, and she has to pay to keep them sharp. You've got to pay for the tools you use and the licenses for the tools that you use. You've got to support the online open source projects that you're a fan of. Living your life for free is a loser's way to approach your career.

Q: And in the same way that she needs to keep her tools sharp, you also need to keep your tools sharp.

A: Absolutely. In the same way that she goes to conferences, learns new techniques, and subscribes to magazines to see different hairstyles and keep up with what people are interested in, I've got to make sure I keep up with the latest technologies, techniques, and best practices in my industry. That's just what a professional does, and it's up to me. It's not up to somebody else to make sure that I learn it. Nobody cares about my career more than me. Not even my mom cares about my career more than I care about my career!

Q: Do you have any stories of how working outside your comfort zone actually helped you in your career? Is there anything that you can remember that happened to you that shows the value of working outside a comfort zone?

A: At some point, I realized that I liked working on legacy systems and that I wanted to do that. So, I talked to you, Bruno, and you gave me some advice on how I can find other people who are doing this sort of thing and make it a part of my career.

I discovered that there's a community that meets on a regular basis to discuss things with respect to working on legacy code, and I met the author of a tool called Approval Tests. I met him and he talked about this cool tool that he has. I started playing with it and found that it's an exceptionally useful tool. I've become a big fan of it.

At first, I struggled with it for months, trying to figure out how it worked – I knew that I wasn't using it right. Finally, a year or two later, I was able to catch up with him again. I told him how frustrated I was trying to use it because I knew that it had all kinds of great features, but I couldn't figure out how to do it right. He said, *"You know what? I need to improve the documentation on that, and you are in the ideal situation to help me with that."*

Now, I have been meeting with him for two hours every week, working on improving the documentation. I bring my ignorance and he brings his experience, and we're able to help each other. I'm able to help him make the documentation better, and he's helped me to understand the product better and vastly improve my software development skills through pairing with him to make changes to the application to improve it so that we can make the documentation work better.

This is one of those 10x developers. He charges maybe $800 an hour for his consulting fees. He's a very in-demand guy, and I get two hours of his time once a week. That has been absolutely amazing in helping me to advance my career.

Q: That's great. What's his name?

A: His name is Llewellyn Falco, and he wrote the Approval Tests open source tool.

Q: Cool. Do you have any advice to help people become better developers and improve their skills? Is there any advice that you want to give the people reading the book who are trying to improve themselves?

A: There are a thousand things I could say.

The first thing that comes to my mind is that if you take ownership of the work that you do so that you take pride in making sure that what you turn in every day is of the highest quality, that will make all the difference. It will make you want to learn more about how to do things better. It changes how you approach everything that you do so that you start to care about the little things, such as spaces versus tabs. This affects how the team works together. It's something that we all need to work together and communicate. Are we going to adopt a test-driven approach? How are we going to do our unit testing? We need to agree on how we're going to do this, and we all need to make sure that we're doing it in a way that's effective for our team, for the product, and, most importantly, for the users. If I write something that's really fun and cool to work on but nobody uses it, it doesn't matter – I'm still going to lose my job. You need to create value and take ownership of making sure that everything that you do every day creates value for your employer and for the end user.

Q: Nice. You mentioned that you love to do legacy code and that you actually help people understand legacy code. There is a perception in the industry that legacy code is bad – that it is old technology that won't help your career. Why do you think working with legacy code is important for developers?

A: Well, first off, there's a lot more legacy code out there than there is new code. And frankly, once you've been working on something for a week or even a couple of days, it's already started to turn into legacy code. Like I said, if you go back and look at code that you wrote a year ago and you're not embarrassed, then you're not growing, and you should be growing every day.

One of the big advantages of legacy code is that it is already creating value for the company. The company is making money from it, and so it's a critical piece of the company's profitability. It's important that it keeps working well and that you are able to enhance it in some way.

Netscape was far and away the best browser in the industry, and they decided that the code was too ugly. They said, "*We're going to go and rewrite this sucker from scratch.*" That became the Mozilla project, which is now far behind Google Chrome. Now, the industry – even Edge – has decided to build on the engine for Google Chrome. That is what everybody's using. Why did Netscape lose that edge? Because they decided, "*Oh, we're going to throw away all the learning we had over the years, start from scratch, and make all those mistakes again.*" That's a really expensive way to go.

Being able to maintain legacy code and work with legacy code adds a tremendous amount of value to your skill set, and if you can find ways to make it interesting, then you will have much more enjoyment in your career. There isn't a whole lot of greenfield software development out there, where you get to go and make all the decisions for how everything works. Generally, someone else has already decided what the database is that you're going to use. Someone has already decided what language you're going to use. Someone's already decided on your framework and your libraries. Sometimes, even the IDE is forced on you. If you can find ways to work within the parameters that are given, add value, and make things interesting and fun, then you'll have much more joy in your career, you'll be much more effective in the work that you do, and you'll be able to bring a lot more value to the table. People will notice.

Q: Cool.

A: We only do refactoring if we're maintaining existing code or adding new code, which is all the time when you're doing test-driven development: red, green, refactor. That's adding new code. When you're going in to fix a bug, you're effectively refactoring something to correct a problem. When you're enhancing an existing system, you're going to have to go and refactor it in some way so that you can plug in the new functionality.

So, yes: refactoring – we use it all the time! That's why I call my project Keep Calm and Refactor, because refactoring is a critical skill set. You can never completely master it, but there are always new ways for you to enhance your skills. That's what I like to help people do.

Q: Cool. Let me go back to working outside the comfort zone. I know that you have a great talk about reading code. That's such a basic skill for developers. Can you work outside your comfort zone when reading code, which seems like such a basic, easy thing to do?

A: Reading my own code is easy because I wrote it and I know what I was thinking when I wrote it – unless I wrote it a few months ago or a year ago, in which case I go back and say, "*What was I thinking?*"

But when I'm looking at someone else's code and I'm trying to understand it, I often don't understand what they were thinking. I'll say, "*That's a stupid thing to do. I'm going to go do it the right way.*" But you can develop the skill of going in and reading others' code, understanding how it's doing what it's doing, and getting into the mindset of the developer, who may no longer be around. You can develop that skill and think, "*OK. This looks like a design pattern, and so this is the design pattern they were putting in place,*" or, "*This is a function that they needed to implement to make sure that these other pieces all work properly. We had to have this initialization step put in place in a particular way to make sure that it would all follow correctly.*"

Being able to do that quickly and effectively makes you a more effective developer and makes you much more valuable because you can quickly get into some unfamiliar code and understand how it works. You can go and make a change or instruct someone else on how to make the change properly. You can do code reviews and say, "*OK. These are areas that are going to be potentially problematic and we need to look at. Let's find ways that we can make that a little bit better before it gets pushed into the production code.*"

Reading code is a skill that we really need to work on and develop. It's something that we just don't do because it is hard and – for the most part – not enjoyable unless you can find a way to make it fun. The way that you make something fun is to start to develop a skill in that area, and then, when you exercise that skill and develop it in some small way, that's what makes things fun. It's fun because I'm learning how to implement an algorithm in a slightly different and better way than I did the last time I tried to do this, or I'm learning a new tool or a new feature that makes it much more interesting to do what it is I'm trying to do. That's what makes software development so much fun. It's because we're constantly learning a little bit more, and you can do the same thing with reading code.

I get excited about this because it's a skill that is neglected, but as you start to develop the skill, it really can be a lot of fun. It's neglected because it's hard and not fun, just like learning object-oriented development was hard when you first learned it. You just don't remember how hard it was. Functional coding was hard when you first learned it. You just don't remember how hard it was. Everything we do was hard when we were first learning it, but you've got to get comfortable with being uncomfortable and realize, "*If I learn a little bit every day, eventually, things are going to start falling into place.*"

Summary

This chapter has been all about getting out of your comfort zone. You have learned the four steps to taking action, the correct way to work out of the comfort zone, strategies for being consistent, and the science behind consistency, as well as the most important aspect of consistency. These skills and strategies will enable you to be able to continue to expand your skills in your technical career.

This concludes *Part 1* of the book on learning and practicing technical skills. In *Part 2*, we will focus on the next set of skills that will help you to advance your technical career, one that is often overlooked. You will learn how to get involved and how to participate in the community. In the next chapter, we will start with how to become a team player by embracing communities.

Part 2
Get Involved: Participate
in the Community

Although developing your technical skills is a great step, to have an amazing career, you need to go beyond the technical. Software development is a team effort, and being able to work together with others is a requested skill that puts you at the next level. *If you want to go fast, go alone. If you want to go farther, go together* (an African proverb). Building a career is playing the long game. We are not here for the fast, short sprint, but long-term unique results.

This part will prepare you for the long run.

The following chapters are included in this part:

- *Chapter 6, Become a Team Player by Embracing Communities*
- *Chapter 7, Focus Your Growth by Giving and Receiving Mentoring*
- *Chapter 8, Be Part of a Larger Group: Meeting People at User Groups and Meetups*
- *Chapter 9, Grow Your Network Using Social Media*
- *Chapter 10, Build, Lasting Relationships*

6
Become a Team Player by Embracing Communities

Although being technically fluent is a great step, to have an amazing career, you need to go beyond the technical. Software development is a team effort and being able to work together with others is a required skill that puts you at the next level. There's an African proverb that goes like this: *If you want to go fast, go alone. If you want to go farther, go together.* Your career development is a long game. We are not here for a fast, short sprint but for the long-term results. This part of the book will prepare you for the long run.

Software development is a team effort. It is one of the most multidisciplinary jobs and requires many different professionals. Because of all that, developer communities are not only the place to meet and network with other developers and keep up to date with the latest innovations in technology but also the place to practice collaboration, communication, and teamwork skills.

In this chapter, we will discuss the value of communities. We'll cover the following main topic in the chapter:

- The value of communities
- Identifying communities of relevance to your career
- Participating in communities to increase your networking
- Building internal communities
- Leading external communities

In this chapter, we will help you to identify communities that are relevant to your career. By the end of this chapter, you will have learned how to participate in communities to grow your network and improve your networking. You will even learn how to build communities of your own, whether they are internal or external communities. And finally, you will understand how you can lead communities, wherever they may be – internal, external, virtual, or in person.

The value of communities

A community is a group of people gathered over a common interest either in person or virtually. Community is inherently about people. People connecting with each other provides an opportunity for us to exercise and deepen our humanity. Technology is also about people. People use and create technology. Technical careers are about technology, and they are equally about people. Technical communities also provide opportunities to increase our technical proficiencies and expand our network and leadership skills.

It is timeless wisdom that by working together we can achieve more, and a community provides leaders with connections and opportunities that cannot be achieved in isolation. In Heather's presentations, she often draws on the idea that you can participate as an individual, but by working together, as a team, you can achieve more. This is the essence of community and the power that it provides. If you want to succeed and advance in your technical career, you will need more than the technology and skills we identified in *Part 1* of this book; you will need other people working in collaboration.

Identifying communities of relevance to your career

You know that both of us are passionate about Java technology. This is the technology we have chosen to build our careers around – or Java chose us. One thing is certain, and that is: Java moves our world. Once you determine the technology you are passionate about, you need to spend time understanding how that technology is utilized and how it is developed and evolved.

For example, we know that Java helps you to stay safely and securely connected with your friends and family. Think of any industry or technology and you'll see Java – from banking, health, commerce, gaming, insurance, and education to quantum computing, artificial intelligence, blockchain, and many more. It is everywhere. As a trusted ecosystem, Java has adapted to changing developer and business needs and continues to be relevant and popular. Java continues to be at the top of the rankings of programming languages used by companies and developers. For example, the TIOBE Programming Community index is an indicator of the popularity of programming languages. The index is updated once a month. The ratings are based on the number of skilled engineers worldwide, courses, and third-party vendors. Popular search engines such as Google, Bing, Yahoo!, Wikipedia, Amazon, YouTube, and Baidu are used to calculate the ratings. It is important to note that the TIOBE index is not about the *best* programming language or the language in which *most lines of code* have been written. The index can be used to check whether your programming skills are still up to date or to make a strategic decision about what programming language should be adopted when starting to build a new software system.

Where in the index is your technology of choice used and how is it used? Once you understand this, think about how and on what platform the technology evolves.

As you know, GitHub is where most developers worldwide collaborate to write source code. GitHub publishes results on the projects being developed there in the GitHub survey results. You can also look at reports for future trends. RedMonk, a popular industry analyst, tracks programming language usage.

The results are a product of combining GitHub activity and contributions with Stack Overflow discussions to come up with a correlation between use and discussions. We know that Java continues to be popular in current and future adoption trends.

It is important to know where your technology is in these trend reports. This is useful to help you not only decide about new technologies, as we discussed in *Part 1* of the book, but also identify the communities that will continue to be popular and worthy of your time investment. If you see your community performing well in these areas, you can safely plan to invest time.

Once you have identified **technologies** that you are using and that are also performing well in developer usage and trends, start to investigate how those technologies are developed. Are they developed by a single company or a consortium of companies? Are they developed in an open source project? Who maintains the technology and what is the process for evolving it?

With respect to Java, part of its success can be attributed to how the language has evolved and how the developer community is collaboratively involved in the evolution. The **Java Community Process** (**JCP**) program is the process by which the international Java community standardizes and ratifies the specifications for Java technologies. The JCP program ensures high-quality specifications are developed using an inclusive, consensus-based approach. Specifications ratified by the JCP program must be accompanied by a reference implementation (to prove the specification can be implemented), and a technology compatibility kit (a suite of tests, tools, and documentation that is used to test implementations for compliance with the specification).

Experience in the Java ecosystems has shown that the best way to produce a technology specification is to use an open and inclusive process to co-develop a specification and implementation, informed by a group of industry experts with a variety of viewpoints. This also includes giving the community and the public opportunities to review and comment and a strong technical lead to ensure technical goals and integration with other relevant specifications and user expectations.

The JCP program is overseen by an **Executive Committee** (**EC**) representing a cross-section of both major stakeholders and other members of the Java community that is responsible for approving the passage of specifications through the JCP program's various stages and for reconciling discrepancies between specifications and their associated test suites. Every year, the membership of the JCP program elects the members of the JCP EC.

After being introduced in 1999, the JCP program has continued to evolve over time using the process itself to bring significant benefits to the community and to specifically focus on transparency, streamlining the JCP program and broadening its membership. With many changes in the Java community, the continuation of the JCP program remains constant. Anyone can apply to join and participate in the JCP program – either as a corporation or non-profit (full member), Java User Group (partner member), or individual (associate member). The stability of the JCP program and participation from community members ensures the continued success of the Java platform and its future. Standards enable the execution of technical strategies and the JCP program enables the collaboration of companies and participation from the developer community.

How has your identified technology evolved, and does it have processes you can identify? This can be a great starting point for figuring out which communities make sense for your career.

Join a group that resembles a place where technology evolves – it is like being a citizen of the technology.

Joining is the first step after you have identified a community. Sometimes there may be a process or recommendation required in order to join, but we will cover that in the next section about participation. After you join the community or communities you have identified, you will then be able to determine other communities that you can participate in, and also build and lead those communities.

Participating in communities

Once you have identified communities, it is time to start participating. You cannot reap the benefits of a community by being silent and only observing within the community. To enjoy the benefits, you need to participate and contribute. You identified and joined the community – that is awesome.

Congratulations! That is only the beginning. Now comes the more challenging aspect of figuring out how to participate. This can be daunting and overwhelming at times. In all our combined years of experience, all of us have experienced some form of imposter syndrome. It might be easier to just call it part of the human condition! Imposter syndrome is the persistent belief that our own accomplishments or our own success are not due to our skills or efforts but given to us through some sort of mistake and that, at some point, we may be found to be an inexperienced fraud who does not belong. This can also sometimes lead to anxiety about being placed in certain situations (such as a community of peers).

Since both of us spend time talking to developers from all over the world, we have observed that when the discussion gets to participation in and contributions to a community, the response is often something such as *I am not good enough, I am not experienced enough, My feedback is not important*, or *My opinion does not matter*.

Nothing could be further from the truth! In order for technologies to be successful, architects and maintainers need real-world developer feedback. They need this feedback from people just like you – people with diverse backgrounds use cases and experiences, and levels of experience. As we mentioned, the **Java Community Process** (**JCP**) is the organization that defines the Java specification standards. The largest companies in the world are part of it and collaborate to evolve Java technology. The Executive Committee has representatives from corporations, open source and non-profit groups, Java User Groups, and individual developers. At the meeting, we had top developers such as Brian Goetz (the Java language architect), Mark Little (Red Hat, representing IBM), Mala Gupta (JetBrains), Martijn Verburg (Microsoft, representing the London Java Community), Chandra Guntur (NYJavaSIG, representing BNY Mellon), Ivar Grimstad (Eclipse Foundation), Simon Ritter (Azul), Miro Wengner (Mission Control developer), and so many other amazing people. Remember what we said about impostor syndrome? The feeling that you don't deserve to be where you are? That's the feeling that we get in the EC meetings.

When you look at such a group, full of Java Champions, developer advocates, distinguished engineers, CTOs, and open source developers, it is amazingly easy to believe it is impossible to participate – impossible to "be there."

Now, if you want to grow beyond senior-level positions, getting involved with such a group will give you several skills that are important for the next steps in your technical career. Not to mention the visibility and networking that can really push your career to the next level! Does even thinking about being part of such a group trigger all your impostor syndrome neurons?

One thing is sure: it poses a dilemma. Do you acquire the skills to be part of groups like this? Or, does being part of groups like this allow you to acquire the skills? As with almost everything in our careers, it is not an *either-or*. It is actually both. You *BOTH* acquire the skills to be part of groups like this *AND* being part of groups like this helps you to acquire the skills. In your career, things build on top of what you did in the past.

Your career is a spiral, not a straight line. One thing that especially amazes me is that when you look back at the JCP meetings, you see so many of the members being part of them. Some participated in Java specifications. Others helped with the open source implementations of those specs or joined special JCP working groups. Some were elected to be a part of the JCP Executive Committee or won JCP awards. You can see how the dilemma worked for them. They built the skills. Being part of it builds their skills. And they are still building their skills. Skills are like this – you are always improving them! And participating in communities helps you improve.

Along with imposter syndrome, there is online criticism or disapproval. This can be difficult to accept and sometimes it can be personal. There are a variety of tactics for handling these and you can see one example by Ann Friedman on her website: *The Disapproval Matrix*: `https://www.annfriedman.com/the-disapproval-matrix`.

Heather often advises developers who want to get involved and participate in communities to follow five steps:

1. In the community, you can help each other and work together. Identify the project you want to work on. Think about either a project you are working on or a project that is in an area you want to work in. Maybe there is a project that has a dependency on one of your projects. Have you ever heard the phrase *scratch your itch*? Think about an area that can help you to alleviate that "itch" in your career or solve a problem you are currently facing.

2. Join the mailing list of the project and browse the archives to get familiar with it.

3. Express your interest in participating either on social media or by subscribing to the mailing list. Download draft releases or first access builds – run your applications against them and then discuss them and provide comments. If you need sponsorship or mentorship to get involved in a community, this is often one of the best ways to demonstrate your interest and potential

value to be in the community. For example, the Java language and platform evolve in OpenJDK and as part of the Quality Group, and there is also the Quality Outreach group. These are great places to get started to be able to contribute as a beginner.

4. You can support **Free and Open Source** (**FOSS**) Java projects and keep up to date with the latest release of Java. There are over 100 projects currently participating in testing new Java versions, Two examples of projects participating that have found new contributors via this program are Apache Maven and Eclipse Collections.

Communicate to identify tasks

Remember to communicate with leaders and maintainers and other community members or contributors. Participation in a community is a two-way street – it is vital to communicate your experiences and collaborate on the next steps.

If you do not have direct access to communication, you can communicate with leaders on public discussions and issue trackers.

Take action

Once you decide on the next steps, commit and take action to contribute. Follow through on your commitments. This will help to strengthen your relationships and build trust in the community. Here are some suggestions that we often hear from project leaders or contributors:

- Share ideas and feedback and comment on lists and public issue trackers.
- Read early versions and share feedback on specifications and documentation.
- Download and provide feedback on early access (reference) implementations.
- Try writing sample applications using early builds of (reference) implementations.
- Write or speak about technology and encourage others to participate. Translate it into your native language.
- Evangelize the JSR – via social media, blogging, or lightning talks.
- Help with documentation.

Contribute the actions to others

It is important to share your feedback and follow up to share your agreed-upon contributions. Always remember that the leaders of a project make the final decision on incorporating feedback or contributions. For projects that are further along, new feature requests may not be considered for the current release, but they may be considered for future releases. For projects in the early stages, new features may be accepted if they are within the existing scope. Multiple individuals and groups can and *should* collaborate on a particular project. There is always plenty of work and going through the material multiple times only makes it that much better. When communicating with maintainers, contributors, or expert group members on mailing lists, include a recognizable tag in the subject line and when filing issues/bugs, and always use the same recognizable tag so that it is easy to track your progress and contributions.

Have fun

It is easy to realize at this point that you are having fun in this process of getting involved in the community. What may have seemed daunting at first, is now second nature and you are enjoying the relationships and results of your efforts. At this point, take the time to take the following steps.

- Sharing your results and having fun in the process is a key component of participation in a community!

- Update your GitHub, CV or resume, and LinkedIn profile to include your community participation and contributions. Be specific about your contributions and list the names of the projects and how you have participated or contributed.

- This is real-world experience that will be valuable to your growth in your career. You can add skills you have developed, especially the types of skills we discussed in the previous chapter on hard and soft skills.

- Share your experiences with colleagues and on social media as well. This is an opportunity to shape your social media participation and build your following. We will discuss this in more detail in a later chapter on social media.

- Sharing on social media helps both to provide exposure to the project and to your personal career and accomplishments.

Those are the basic steps to participating and contributing to a community. Follow your interests and needs, communicate, do your research, participate, contribute, and share by communicating your results and having fun.

You can grow organically from there, to continue to expand and deepen your relationships in the community and grow your influence.

As you continue to participate and contribute, you will observe your skills are evolving and your network is expanding.

This is the topic of the next section.

Participating in communities to increase your networking

When you take the initiative to be part of a community, you are also part of the solution. You will acquire knowledge and learn from experts, and gain early access to the latest and greatest technologies.

This will allow you to get your projects into production faster and allow you to put your suggestions and requirements for projects forward.

You will build your resume by adding experience and skill development. This also helps you to grow as a developer, increasing your practice of communication, collaboration, negotiation, and teamwork skills.

In turn, this will increase professional visibility through your CV, articles, workshops, and presentations. When you participate, you grow your reputation and your network.

It can be altruistic to make technologies better – technologies that solve real-world problems – based on real-world experience.

Most of all, being part of a community is *fun*.

Building communities

Once you have experience participating in communities and you have seen your network grow exponentially, the natural evolution and inclination may be to build a community. Whether or not you decide to build communities of your own, these techniques can be applied to your advanced participation in communities and to further strengthen and provide feedback to community leaders.

These suggestions can be utilized if your community is an internal corporate community for employees or if your community is external to your employer. In today's climate, communities happen in a multitude of environments – internal, external, virtual, or in-person.

You can adapt techniques to fit your particular community.

When you are ready to initiate a community, take the time to define a strategy and target audience. It is often tempting to dig right in and start taking action when the motivation strikes to build a community; however, it will be helpful to define a strategy and parameters and to be able to qualify your target community members.

This will also help guide the participants in your community.

Next will be building the components to launch and manage the technical community and associated technologies.

Some tasks include a definition of technical community values, establishing the legal foundation of the technical community; the definition of member personas of the community; the definition of how to lead, manage, and engage the community; and the launch of the technical community with an operational plan to maintain the community.

As you plan, build, and grow your community, these are important values and points to keep in mind:

- Listening to community members is key. Creating a mechanism for your community members to give you feedback is required. Receiving feedback is not the end; you must then take it, discuss it, and act on it in an iterative way. This seems easier than it is!

- Invite people to join your community. As people join your community, give them easy pathways to bridge the chasm from "interested in joining" to being a full-fledged member of the community.

- Make sure that you are actively communicating with your community. Not everyone is going to see the changes and understand what you are doing (for example, leadership, architecture, or license choices). In this case, explaining the "why" will go a long way to keeping your community engaged.

- It is rare to have one size fit all for members. Think about how to make it easy for different types of people to contribute (whether it's different membership categories or different activities). It is easy to assume that it's an open community or an open source project, so everyone just contributes. There will be different people who want different things.

- As you evolve, stay true to your values. Always be conscious of these values. Be deliberate in the changes you make. Stay true to the values of the community and communicate.

- As you look at evolving the governance structure, look at the governance structure as a living and breathing thing. Keep up with the needs of the community members. This should be a constant, ongoing consideration.

These are the core guiding principles to keep in mind as you build your community. Now let's talk about leading communities.

Leading communities

Once you have built your community, you will need to lead your community. Or, perhaps you are part of an existing community and you have been invited to assume a leadership role in the community. It is recommended, to ensure the longevity of communities, that you have a leadership pipeline.

If you want to be a leader of an existing community, tell the current leadership. This is an opportunity to grow your leadership abilities. There are some tips that will help you understand how you can lead communities, wherever they may be – internal, external, virtual, or in person. Always remember that most community projects receive far fewer contributions than they would like.

Think of the 80/20 rule. In many aspects of life, 80% of the work is done by 20% of the people. Often, communities are volunteers or additional projects for individuals, so when life or work becomes hectic or overwhelming, the community can languish. A healthy community will have a leadership team to prepare for these circumstances and a pipeline of emerging leaders to pull into the leadership team over time. Some communities even build in term limits or elections to ensure the health of the community in the long term.

When you are leading a community, choose the right technology and people for your team. The technology platform should fit the needs of your vision for the community. This is not something that you want to be constantly updated or changed.

It should provide mechanisms for feedback, communication, and transparency. Can the public and members of the community view information on the project, download and view drafts, view schedules, view and contribute comments on issue trackers, and view and provide feedback on mailing or discussion lists?

The community's leadership reflects your values and principles. Define the values and principles of your community and regularly reflect to ensure that the leaders of the community are a representation of those values and principles.

Consider drawing from the community to champion these values by providing a designation of recognition, such as influencers, champions, experts, or ambassadors.

Select the right people to champion your community. Provide them with a designation and a process for engaging, along with tangible benefits for engaging and participating. You will need to engage diverse types of community members from varying geographies, different sizes of companies and organizations, nonprofits, educational institutions, students, and so on.

You can start with a target that fits the community you are building, but as you lead the community, be thoughtful about how you will continue to remain vibrant and relevant.

In the Java community, for example, there is an initiative started within the JCP to bring up the next generation of Java developers to ensure that the technology continues to be popular and taught as a language of choice to younger or more junior developers and students.

Consider the overall lifespan and health of your community members as you grow and lead them over time. Are there levels of recognition that can be provided or ways to highlight their current status and tenure in the community? How can they build on their participation and contributions to the community over time?

Finally, select the right online community features to build your membership – to lead and keep a community engaged, you need regular content and material that is relevant and a regular cadence of contact with your community, either through online or in-person meetings.

Select the cadence and format that works best for your members. Communities should meet at regular, expected times – whether that is daily, weekly, monthly, bi-monthly, or even annually. Look for ways to build connections between regular meetings through other forums such as message boards, mailing lists, social media, Slack, or your website.

Some communities meet every week and some meet once a month or less frequently. Experiment to find the frequency that works for you and the format that works best for you. Incorporate different elements into your online or in-person meetings – formal presentations, informal presentations, networking, job referrals, hack days, and outreach to other communities.

Challenges of participating in communities

Of course, as with anything you endeavor to do in life, there are some challenges and potential drawbacks to participating in communities. While we wholeheartedly believe that these challenges are overwhelmingly worth the reward, we will provide some guidance for you to consider as you approach your engagement in communities. There are sometimes choices and challenges you will face as you begin to participate in a community, such as the time involved and balancing your community involvement with work responsibilities. You can determine the time commitments you make to community engagements, but it is important to balance those commitments with your work and personal or family obligations. There is immense value in participating in communities, but you need to be mindful to meet your obligations in your work and personal life to achieve results and rewards. Another challenge that can arise is actually a positive that you may recall from earlier in the book and involves conflict resolution. When you collaborate and engage, working together, conflicts inevitably arise. In order to be successful, you need to be skillful in successfully managing and resolving conflicts within communities. Develop your communication skills and learn how to work together with other people to bring any potential conflicts to an amicable resolution.

Building strategies for managing time and setting priorities will help you to eliminate the potential for time management difficulties. The first thing to do is to evaluate where you are spending your time. Document how much time you are spending on the different areas of your life and identify the priorities. Determine whether there are priority areas where you are not spending enough time. Avoid multitasking. Studies have shown that your brain is not meant to do more than one thing at a time. You can do more than one thing at a time, but it is not efficient and you will waste valuable time. Your brain spends energy switching between the different tasks and priorities. Focus on one thing at a time. You can use application features to focus such as "do not disturb" and set calendar appointments in your schedule to block out time for specific activities, comparing them to your priorities and evaluating how you are spending your time on the different areas of your life.

You can plan in advance to develop strategies for conflict resolution. First of all, recognize and acknowledge the conflict. Ask questions and listen to all parties to understand the problem or issue at hand – this is where your communication skills will be critical. Discuss and clarify the issue to come up with possible solutions, and do this in a relaxed and neutral environment without distractions, for example, outside of work or the community gathering place. Listen and communicate with all parties, and look for solutions that give each person a favorable part of the solution to resolve the conflict. Agree and communicate on the best solution and discuss how each person will give and take to come up with a solution that is best for the community at large.

Again, community engagement is a powerful way to influence the direction of your career in a positive way, especially if you are prepared with some of the skills we have taught you in this book.

Interview

Edwin Derks

Q: Welcome, Edwin Derks, who is a Java Champion. One of the most impactful things in his career was becoming a Java Champion.

Edwin, tell us a little bit about yourself in terms of where you work and your career journey.

A: I am a consultant at Team Rockstars IT in the Netherlands – it's a consulting company of about 500 people – and I have a Java developer background.

I started professionally developing in 2007, but over the years, I have grown all the way from Java developer to architect, and now I work more as a consultant because, with every step, I tend to find out that I'm more of a problem solver and a manager than a developer per se, but this technical package that I have is really useful for finding the right solutions to the big problems companies have in IT. I'm making myself useful with consulting, mostly, but also inspiring and coaching colleagues to become experts in their field.

Q: Very exciting. That's quite a career journey you've had. Can you tell us about a moment when your career started to accelerate and advance?

A: The first one was the moment I started to do open source development.

Up until I started to go to conferences and talk to people about open source development, I thought, "OK. I'm a developer. I need to develop and get knowledge, but mainly develop." I had heard about open source development but never thought it was something for me, but then I was convinced by someone that I still have a lot of contact with today – Emily Jiang from the MicroProfile community. She said, "OK. Edwin, you have to own this, because you can do this and that." I said, "OK. I will try that."

I've now met so many new people that I've learned from, not only around me in the Netherlands but also from all over the world. I've gained so much new knowledge, just by joining an open source project. It's really, really valuable. Open source is not just about development – it's about a community that you can learn from and inspire, and that's really the thing for me.

That thing ultimately saw me included among the Java Champions because, apparently, I had something to share with people. Now I am a Java Champion, which gives me more leverage and a label to also inspire other people to do this stuff. Being an advocate of open source, I think this is not only important for one's own self-education but also for people around you, and that's what being part of a thriving community with these people is all about.

Q: Definitely. What were some of your early contributions? You say you joined the community and started contributing to open source. What were some of the first things that you did when you joined? Tell us about some of your first contributions. Did you change the whole project?

A: A lot of people want to contribute to open source. They think, "I need to contribute. I need to be amazing. I need to be able to change the whole project. Otherwise, I have nothing to contribute." That was the perception that I had.

I just started by joining mailing lists and seeing what was there. I started joining meetings to be able to hear what people were talking about, and then, slowly but surely, I got into some pull requests for documentation and a little bit of code, participating in the process of releasing stuff. Gradually understanding what was going to be needed or done in a certain community gave me the confidence that I needed. I was not leaping too far but instead going with the flow, trying to find my place there.

Everybody can contribute, even if it is just giving your opinion on something. If you are using a technology and it's a resource, you have the ability to shape the future of the technology because you have a voice. If you don't use your voice, you're not going to get the feature that you might want in that technology. It's a safe environment to just ask for what you want. If you cannot make the feature yourself, maybe other people will develop it for you. But maybe you want to contribute: "Oh, I have just built this feature. Do you want it?" If it's a good feature, it gets accepted and you have provided something yourself.

You can do all kinds of stuff. It's not just that you need to provide code; just being there is valuable.

Q: Also, as you're in the community, you're building trust and becoming known, increasing the chances that when you have something to contribute, it's going to be accepted. You talked about becoming a Java Champion – how has being a Java Champion impacted your career?

A: Being a Java Champion, you get a label, and then you can do stuff with it. You can also decide not to do stuff with it. It is a label that you can use to inspire others and to grow yourself so that people really recognize you and say, "You are now one of the recognized people because you bring something good to our community." That is how I like to use my Java Champion label: to inspire others to overcome hurdles such as thinking they're not worthy. You have something to contribute. You become a champion just by doing the right thing, even if you are not a Java Champion. Being about to tell people that I am proud of them, that they are doing things that I think are good, makes me proud myself. That's what makes me valuable as a Java Champion: inspiring others.

Q: It is a great accomplishment that you have become a Java Champion.

One interesting thing that you said in your story is that "Java Champion" is a label. How do you think you became a Java Champion and how can other people do the same?

A: Everybody has their own story, and no Java Champion is the same. Not every Java Champion knows everything about Java. We all have our thing.

I have my thing with my years of experience in the Java EE/Jakarta EE/MicroProfile development ecosystem because I'm consistently advocating for people to use the technology for certain purposes and be persistently visible on the mailing list, in sessions, and in meetings. Just be there: participating, trying to help others out, evolving certain technologies, and building a community. Everything comes down to persistence. Make sure that you're seen and that you provide something, and then everything will figure itself out.

Q: This leads a little bit into mentoring. You talk about what you've enjoyed about being a Java Champion, and how having that distinction and honor is inspiring to other people: that is like mentoring them in a certain way. Are there any examples that you want to share of where you've been able to influence others?

A: I am glad you asked.

I have a company that wants to find new staff, to grow, and also do our projects. Our company is also a culture and a community. There have been several times that I have been asked by a recruiter, "Can you participate in this conversation? The person in question is a Java developer but they want to know more about Java, and you are the Java Champion. Can you help inspire this?" Coming into these conversations and being a champion, sometimes people look up to you. But when I get into a conversation and the level goes back to where we are both people, and I have a lot of experience that I want to share, we have beautiful conversations where someone who wants to grow in their career looks up to me and asks, "Can you help me?" I say, "Yes. Certainly. I want to – if possible – mentor you and give you directions on how you can become the best of yourself."

Those are the moments when I can really use my Java Champion status to do inspirational stuff.

Q: You touched on how it's not just the mentee but also the mentor who gets something out of it. You, in the mentor role, are also getting something out of it. It can even be like peer-to-peer coaching/ mentoring. There isn't just one type of mentoring. The mentoring experience can benefit anyone in their career.

A: That's an example.

As a mentor, I don't know everything. I have learned from mentoring people because everybody is different. I learn every day just by being in the community, being around people, and learning from them.

Q: Bazlur has a question.

We all enjoy working all the time because we tend to do things that we love. That's a hallmark of a software developer because we are able to work on things that we love to work on. But how do you find balance between work and life?

A: Sometimes, I really ask myself, "How do I do all this stuff?" Because I also have a wife and three little kids at home, and sometimes, they have to do without me for a week.

Finding balance is about giving and taking within the environment that you have. I have a really good understanding with my wife about what I can do and cannot do, and with my employer about what I can do and cannot do. Within these limits, I just do whatever I think is good because work is my hobby, and my hobby is my work.

So, I just like doing what I do on a daily basis, and if I can make that work within the boundaries that I have, it turns out to be the right thing. You need to find balance with the people in your life.

Q: You said it was very important for you to mentor other people. Have you ever been mentored by others?

A: I'm glad you asked.

I have been inspired by other people, and not only by people from the community: I have a wife who believes in me. I have a manager who believes in me and who pushes me to conferences all the time because he believes in me. I also look up to people in the community and try to learn from them. I'm not the center of the universe. I learn from other people as well.

I'm really grateful for the people that I learned from and that shared their experience and feedback with me. I'm glad to hear that I'm doing things wrong because I can then fix things, and that's not always a given – it's a gift that you receive. Sometimes, it's a little bit of a scary situation to give feedback to people that are not doing well, but sometimes it is the right thing to do to tell someone, "Hey, maybe you should do this instead of that – I hope it turns out to be the right thing." Feedback, inspiration: it all comes together in the right balance.

Summary

In this chapter, we have helped you to understand the need for community in technical careers, identify the type of community to become involved with related to your interests, how to participate and contribute to communities and increase internal visibility and results through communities, how communities can help you grow, and how to participate in communities to not only grow but improve your network.

You have learned how to build communities of your own, and how you can lead communities wherever they may be – internal, external, virtual, or in person.

Now we will focus on another aspect of critical importance for your career growth. To advance your technical career, you will also need to spend time giving and receiving mentoring. Mentoring is the topic of the next chapter.

7
Focus Your Growth by Giving and Receiving Mentoring

Once you are part of a community, the value of helping others and of being helped becomes clear. We cannot become our best alone. Giving and receiving mentoring is an awesome way to connect more deeply with peers. This chapter will show you how to do it.

In this chapter, we will explain a couple of concepts vital to understanding the role mentoring has in your career. These concepts are that it takes a village to build a developer, and mentoring is not a one-way street. You will also learn how to be selective and intentional in your mentoring relationships, how to find a mentor, and how to be a good mentor.

The main topics of this chapter are the following:

- It takes a village to build a developer

- Mentoring is not a one-way street

- Being selective and intentional

- Finding a good mentor

- Being a good mentor

By the end of the chapter, you will understand the need for mentorship and peer coaching, be able to identify the types of mentors and coaches, and know what is needed in mentor relationships (to give and get), how to be intentional in interactions with mentors, how to find mentors, and how to mentor other people.

It takes a village to make a developer since software development is a soft skill that you practice by doing, and you do it better when you do it with others who are better than you. Software development is not only about training and learning, although those things are important – it is also about experience. Developers usually learn on the job. That is not ideal because mistakes are costly. Mentoring can help fill this gap.

Remember: software development is a soft skill. As we said earlier, soft skills are skills that need to be practiced in real life. Software development needs to be practiced by doing software development. And as we talked about before, software development is a team activity that is better done with other developers. An important corollary of that is that software development is not only better when practiced together but also when learned together with other people, specifically with other developers. You learn and practice soft skills better when you are working together with people that know more than you or are better than you.

You become better at software development by practicing with other developers as part of a team. When you practice and learn with other developers, you will learn from them because you work together to collectively improve your software development skills and your communication, teamwork, and collaboration abilities. Many developers you work with will know more than you or be better than you, and that is a good thing. This provides an even greater opportunity for you to improve your skills.

Some learning and practicing can be done through training. That is why the training industry around software development is so big and powerful. Training is important to learn new skills and new technologies, and to simply get started. But to really dive deep into software development, there is no substitute for real-life work. That is why most developers learn on the job, working on real projects in a real team.

A big challenge of on-the-job learning is the risk. Mistakes are too costly for the company, the project, and the team. Worst of all, they are especially costly for the individual. When you make mistakes, you can damage your reputation, feel incompetent, and even feel like an imposter. Mentoring can fill this gap between improving through training and growing through real-life experience, on the job. Building relationships with mentors can supplement your learning and add to your "village" on your journey to becoming a better developer.

Different types of mentoring

There are many types of mentoring, from sporadic advice and Q&A sessions to a more hands-on, daily approach. But they all center around the mentor being part of the mentee experience, be it by listening and understanding the situation and provoking thought and mentality changes, providing advice and guidance, helping with course correction, or helping with avoidance and recovery from mistakes.

In mentoring, we learn from each other. Whether it is peer to peer, pair programming, community activities, or formal mentoring, we learn by working together. Mentoring gives us access to people that have more knowledge or experience and can give us the information, training, and skills that we need to succeed.

Making the decision to work with a mentor gives you a chance to create relationships with other developers that can help you or may need your help. Mentoring builds friendships, connections, and communities. Mentoring is also the best way to transfer experience from you, as a more experienced developer, to less experienced ones. Mentors bring their expertise and share their knowledge, their successes, and their failures. A mentor helps you to achieve results faster and to fail less.

Not only will mentors help you achieve results with fewer failures, but mentors will also help you see clearly. They can point out situations, identify problems, and foresee difficulties. With their questions and advice, mentors can help you get the clarity that you need to advance and acquire the right skills.

Mentors help you avoid risky pitfalls, so you can learn with a lower risk of damaging your career. Mistakes are indeed part of skill acquisition; it is expected that you make mistakes to become better. But when you make mistakes that are too damaging, they can delay improvements. Mentors help you avoid those risky mistakes.

Mentors also improve your networking and help you be part of something. Mentors that are already connected and involved with other developers, communities, and companies can make their network available to mentees, increasing the effectiveness of networking and reducing the time it takes for you to get results.

Working with your mentor will allow you to meet other developers, especially more experienced developers, helping you acquire skills faster. A mentor may also help you reach out to less experienced developers, so you can also be a mentor to other people. Mentoring other people also helps you to improve your own skills! The more you teach and explain, the more you understand your own experience. Oftentimes, a more junior developer can help you to see things in a different way and expand your own understanding of the current environment.

Mentoring is not a one-way street

Since mentoring is so important, we may imagine that, as developers, we need to be mentored. Often, we forget that we can also mentor. The relationship formed between mentee and mentor can be an amazing one. When you do things with your mentor, it will form a stronger bond in your relationship. You can plan personal or virtual events with your mentor – take a walk or have a walking meeting, have a coffee, enjoy a meal together, or watch a movie together.

When searching for a mentor, it is easy to imagine that they will help us, but mentorship is a two-way street. A reality of career evolution is that helping others helps you too. When your mentor is working with you and helping you advance, you are helping your mentor improve their own skills. Mentoring is a required skill for leadership! Because of the mutual benefits, the relationship between mentor and mentee can become strong and fruitful.

Friends have fun together, but that is only part of a friendship. Friends are people that do meaningful things together. When you work with your mentor to advance your career and skills, you are doing meaningful work together. That creates a strong bond in your relationship.

So, what are some of the benefits of mentoring for you? There are two sets of benefits that we must consider: the benefits of being a mentee and of becoming a mentor. As a mentee, you have access to expertise. Being able to access expertise from people that have done what you want to do accelerates your results, and you make fewer mistakes in achieving your results. Here are some more benefits of mentoring:

- **Access to private information**: Working with a mentor will give you access to information that is not easy to come by, from stories of success and failures to behind-the-scenes knowledge of how things happen and even personal insights and tricks. Those are not usually published or easy to come by from others.

- **Access to people and networks**: Having a good network of peers is fundamental to our career. It improves our knowledge and reputation and gives us access to opportunities. Because a mentor-mentee relationship becomes one of trust, a mentor can help you by introducing you to people but also recommending and vouching for you. Imagine having access to people that you would not easily have access to and having privileged access from the start!

- **Opportunities**: The best opportunities in the job market are offered to those people that we trust and who have a great reputation. When we build a relationship with our mentor, that is a relationship that is built on trust. Your mentor can help you get opportunities that you may originally not have access to because of the trust bond that exists between you.

With all of that, it is easy to think that mentorship is something where the mentor makes all of the effort, but that is not true. Mentoring is not a one-way street. When working with your mentor, you also help your mentor grow. One of the best ways to improve is to apply your experience to different situations. And by asking questions, discussing different experiences, and having a distinct perspective, you also help your mentor think about different situations that they have not had previous experience with. Your mentor will grow by helping you overcome obstacles and by having to delve deep into their own knowledge to help you with yours. Also, being a mentor will help you with skills such as leadership, communication, empathy, and listening. Many people start mentoring others to grow in those skills also.

With that, here are a couple of the benefits of being a mentor that you should consider:

- **Helping people**: Every time you help people, you grow. You understand your own skills and identify your limitations. Facing your own issues so you can help others face their issues is a fantastic way to improve specific skills.

- **Reputation**: When people that you are helping grow and succeed, your reputation in the market also grows. You build trust in your industry.

Now that you understand some of the benefits for mentors and mentees, let's discuss how to decide on the right mentor relationships for you.

Be selective and intentional

Although mentoring is a great tool for improvement and growth, it is not only a "feel-good" activity where you do it because it is fun and you will feel great about it (although it can be a lot of fun at times). Mentoring is challenging work for both sides, and it requires a big effort in time and commitment. You should use it to improve in specific areas.

It is easy to consider mentoring as just a conversation or to build a relationship with your mentor and confuse it with friendship, but being mentored is hard. A good mentor will push your limits so you can succeed faster and grow further. That is stressful, and often, your mentor will possibly end up annoying you with tough questions and criticism, making you see the truth that you are trying to ignore (or hide even from yourself).

A good mentor will push you to do things you are not comfortable with – things that are outside of your comfort zone. One of the hardest parts of mentorship is when it forces you to deal with your failures. It is not comfortable to be reminded that you failed or to confront the reasons why that happened. It can be especially hard because, most times, you fail because of your own issues, such as procrastination, lack of focus, lack of attention, carelessness, and other internal reasons. You may want to blame others, the circumstances, and things outside of your control. Your mentor will challenge that and force you to confront your own shortcomings.

This will help you grow where you need most, but that is not easy. Invariably, it will create some level of attrition between you and your mentor that you both will have to navigate, and that is not comfortable either. That is why it is so important to search for a mentor that you trust, that can guide and inspire you to be on track, even when things are hard and uncomfortable.

And because attrition will happen, your mentor needs to be empathetic to your situation. Many times, a mentor may be judgmental or point bluntly at your mistakes and difficulties. That may cause hard feelings and make your progress slower. A strong trust in your mentor will help you overcome even those obstacles.

Being honest, open, and direct with your mentor will help you both to achieve a level of understanding and comprehension, and working together will help you both in communication and growth. That is one reason why, when you are looking for a mentor, you should be selective and try to find one that you can have good conversations with and with whom you have mutual trust. Look for a mentor that you can trust to be really interested in the positive attributes and skills you have to offer. Once you have selected a mentor, make yourself available to your mentor, and be willing to not only receive advice from your mentor but also to help your mentor with their work and initiatives when possible.

How to select a mentor

Write out your goals for your career and make sure they are SMARTER. This will help you to understand where you have gaps in achieving your goals and help you to see where you could use mentorship. Some examples are to develop new skills, expand your network in a specific industry sector, or build confidence to have some difficult conversations. Once your goals are outlined and you have identified your gaps, think about how a mentor could help you to achieve your goals. Create a specific plan or description of how they could help you, whether it is working on a certain project, introducing you to their network, or coaching you on how to have a particular conversation that is hindering your success. Next, you can start to search your network. Consider people you have met at events or conferences, through current or previous roles, from your academic career, or even second-degree connections.

Look for someone who fits the description or has the skills you are looking for to achieve your goals. Oftentimes, people think that you need to find someone who is exactly like you to be a mentor. This can be comfortable, and often it is a good match; however, you can learn from and be challenged more by people who are different from you, whether that is in gender, race, cultural background, or anything else. Look for a way to create diversity in your network. This will help you to grow in your career and embrace different points of view.

Finding a good mentor

Mentors can be found in many places, among your friends, work colleagues, people in the industry, teachers, and many more possibilities. There are the steps to finding a good mentor:

- Be clear on what you want to accomplish

- Look for someone that has done what you are trying to do

- Look for someone that you trust or admire

- Look for someone that is willing to build a relationship with you

Let's look at these steps in detail:

Step 1 – be clear on what you want to accomplish

Because mentorship is better if you are trying to grow or improve a specific situation, it is important that you are incredibly clear about what you want to accomplish. Finding a mentor that will help you achieve what you want will make the entire process a lot more interesting for you both. Go after your big dreams and find a mentor that will help you accomplish a specific thing that you want and create the motivation for you to face the challenges and difficulties around mentorship. Be clear about your main goals and search for a mentor that can help you achieve those.

Step 2 – look for someone that has done what you are trying to do

There is a substantial difference between mentoring and coaching. A coach will help you think about your own problems and figure out your own solutions. A mentor, however, will bring their experiences to guide you toward your goals, and because of that, it is better that you work with a mentor that has done what you are trying to do. That way, your mentor will help you achieve what you really want based on firsthand experiences. Notice that a mentor does not have to have achieved exactly your dream. The mentor should have experience and results in similar skills, areas, and achievements to the ones you are aiming for.

Step 3 – look for someone that you trust or admire

Mentoring is demanding work. You will clash with your mentor multiple times because you are trying to overcome your own failures and limitations, and your mentor will be pushing you to do it. It will be easier if you trust your mentor and if you have some level of admiration. If not, you will be questioning all the time whether your mentor can really help you or not or whether your mentor is really the person that is right for you. If this is the case, then you will not do what needs to be done, so it is better to search for another mentor.

Step 4 – look for someone that is willing to build a relationship with you

Mentorships are all about relationships. A mentor that is not willing to work with you will not help you. It goes both ways. Look for someone that you are willing to have a relationship with. As an example, if your mentor is someone that goes to places that you don't want to go, deals with people that you don't want to deal with, or does things that you don't want to be part of, there is a big chance that you're not going to be able to build a relationship with that mentor.

Once you have found what you are looking for in a mentor, it is time to make the ask. From our experience, this is often one of the most uncomfortable parts of mentoring relationships. It can be awkward. It can be especially challenging to find the courage to be vulnerable and ask the question. We offer two approaches for you to consider at that moment:

- **Let it grow organically**

  Our advice for this approach is to start small with little commitment – send a short email asking for a brief meeting and take time getting to know a little bit more about them to see whether you think they are a good fit. Ask if you can get their advice on a situation or challenge, and then express your appreciation for their time. Ask if you can follow up with them again in a specified amount of time and thank them for their willingness to meet with you. Follow up for another meeting, and keep it simple with a follow-up based on your last conversation. If they agree to meet with you again, suggest that you would like to expand on your conversation from your last meeting and then suggest another topic you would like to discuss with them. This can become a segue into a more long-term relationship. Heather has used this approach successfully in the past to initiate a mentoring relationship in a more informal mentorship process.

- **The direct approach**

  There are also times when you want a more formal relationship and commitment. Keep in mind that this is more responsibility for you and your potential mentor. You should also take the time to get to know your prospective mentor in this situation and be prepared to listen more than you speak to get to know more about them. If you feel it is a good fit, and you are ready to dedicate the time that will be required for a productive mentor relationship, ask simply and sincerely whether they are willing to mentor you for a specified amount of time. Share with them and express your appreciation for their expertise and be specific about what you are looking to achieve and how you think they can help you achieve it. Heather has found that six months is an ideal amount of time for most desired outcomes. Once you achieve the goals you specified in advance, you can then follow on with another goal or continue with your mentor relationship if both parties desire. Express your thanks and appreciation for their consideration, whether they accept or decline. Be mindful that formal mentorship is a big time commitment that not everyone will be willing to invest time in developing.

- Use SMART goals:

  Specific

  Fully describe in concrete language the desired outcome. Describe what is to be accomplished.

  Measurable

  Make sure your goal is quantifiable or measurable in some way. Describe how you will know you've achieved your objective.

  Attainable

  Create stretch, yet achievable goals. To assess attainability, have a conversation about practicality as well as the resources and support needed.

  Relevant

  Relevant to your group's objectives and mission.

  Time-bound

  What is the time frame for achieving the goal?

  Answer the question: "*By when will I achieve the desired end result?*" (Note: large goals may include milestone dates.)

Being intentional

Mentoring should help you grow in a specific area and direction. It is not a catch-all activity. It is important to be clear on why you are looking for a mentor. Here are a few ideas for you to consider and build clarity on:

- **Achieve a goal or dream that you have**: Many times, we have great dreams that we might think are impossible, that will take too long, or that we do not see a way to achieve. A mentor can accelerate or shortcut your path to achieving those dreams. Search for a mentor that has achieved similar things to what you dream about and that has dreams that align with yours. Look for a mentor that has skills you admire or has accomplished something you want to achieve.

- **Be recognized as someone that you aspire to be**: A mentor can also help you become and be recognized as someone that you want to be, such as an expert in your field. Be clear with yourself about who you want to become. That could be a specific position or gaining recognition in the market. Recognition is one of the most important things for our careers, and a mentor can help you to be recognized for the things that you have done by the people it is important to be recognized by.

- **Improve or acquire skills**: A mentor can also help you improve or acquire one or more skills that you know you need. Helping you accelerate the acquisition of skills is one of the best results that a mentor can bring to your career. Skill acquisition, especially soft skills, is not only arduous work, but if done alone, it becomes even harder. Working with someone that has the skill and that can point you to the right path can help you advance faster. Look for mentors that have the skills you need and dream of having. As we talked about in other chapters, skills require doing, so your mentor should have done it and mastered the skill, or have close contact with people that have mastered it, so they can help you do the same. Look for mentors that are recognized for the skills you want and need to improve.

- **Overcome obstacles**: One of the most critical areas a mentor can help you with is overcoming obstacles or limits that you have been dealing with. It is extremely easy in our careers to reach a wall – a place or situation where you believe you cannot go further. Although those hard-to-conquer obstacles offer exciting potential for growth, they are very frustrating and can lead to you giving up and believing it is not possible, especially when you do not know why you cannot overcome the obstacle. A mentor may have faced similar obstacles in the past and overcome them. That way, you can understand what is really preventing you from doing the same.

- **Identify limits**: Mentors can also identify limits that we do not see. They can guide us to skills, knowledge, and people that we might not even know exist. They enable you to do things that you thought were impossible and help with your understanding of markets and situations. On our path to growth, it is normal to not know where we are going. You do not know the environment, the landscape, or the people. Because of that, you imagine that some things are impossible, or you believe you need to take long routes to get to your desired destination. Often, this is just a misunderstanding of reality because you have never experienced it. And that builds a mentality trap, where you cannot fathom what is possible. Because your mentor has experienced that situation, they understand what is going on and can help you see the real path.

Once you are working with a mentor, be intentional and make the best of it. Next, we will give you a few tips and tricks for you and your mentor to get the best results and enjoy the process.

Create a plan

When Heather was mentoring a junior developer at Andela in Nigeria, she used a document template they had created to guide their discussions. It was a simple Word table document that contained the goals and skills to focus on in the mentoring relationship. Heather found this kept their conversations focused on the end results and the purpose of their interactions. This is a best practice for intentional mentorship. Create a document outlining what you will accomplish in your mentoring relationship – use it as a working document each time that you meet. It will help add clarity for you and for your mentor by helping share the goal of the relationship and being accountable for the results. It can also guide you to create an agenda for each meeting. You can share your goals and milestones and be accountable, going prepared for your conversations. This document will also be useful in helping you to measure progress toward your mentorship goals. And always send a thank-you note after every meeting to express your appreciation and capture any action items.

Go deep into discussions

Go deep into discussions so you really understand how your mentor thinks and makes decisions. You can mimic what your mentor does and apply it to your life as fast as possible, bring back results and failures to discuss, and then apply the advice again, and fix and adjust things, to build a feedback loop.

Going deep will allow you to really understand how your mentor thinks and makes decisions – this helps you to develop skills such as empathy and emotional intelligence. Knowledge can be easily acquired through books and tutorials, but the way other people think is extremely hard to learn. Mentorship works best in that situation.

Paying close attention to how your mentor thinks and understanding the reasons behind your mentor's decisions, suggestions, and ideas will help you think like your mentor. We call those "mental representations" – the way your mentor sees the world and represents the things in their mind is what makes them who they are. Understanding how your mentor thinks and the mental representations they have helps you build your own mental representations and eventually make decisions like your mentor.

Mimic what your mentor does so you can do the same. Have you ever heard the expression *"Fake it to make it"* or another incarnation, *"Fake it till you become it"*? If you do the things that your mentor does, it will help you become like your mentor. Pay close attention to the things your mentor does with you and with other mentees or for themselves and in their own career. As much as possible, mimic what they are doing in your career.

Apply lessons in your life as fast as possible

Mentorship will help you grow faster, but for that, you have to apply things as fast as possible. When your mentor suggests something to you, try to experiment with it as soon as possible. Apply the suggestions in small situations, as an experiment in side projects, and apply them to other parts of your life. The sooner you experiment with something, the sooner you are going to have something to discuss with your mentor. This will help you to develop more truth in your relationship. For a mentor, it is frustrating to repeat the same thing repeatedly for lengthy periods of time without any response from the mentee. No matter whether it is done correctly or not, trying things out will give you results and make the mentoring more valuable and interesting for both of you.

Bring back results

It is important to bring back results or failures to discuss with your mentor. Once you apply things, you'll make mistakes, and you'll have good and bad results. Bring results back to your mentor, so you can discuss them together and see why the failure or success happened. Create open communication and dialogue in this process. Your mentor will be incredibly pleased to hear about your successful results, but they will be even more interested in learning how you tried to apply things and how that failed to work. That discussion can be very fruitful for you both. By figuring out ways to overcome obstacles created in your situation, you help your mentor.

Reply and try again once you get some feedback, re-apply it, fix what you tried, try again, and adjust what you did. Then bring your results back again. This is how results are achieved.

Be the best mentee for your mentor

A good mentee will pay close attention and will work on the things that need to be worked on. A good mentee will do things to get closer to the mentor and will want to do things with the mentor... as much as possible, of course! You want to be appropriate and respectful, not overly demanding of your mentor. Strive to be the best mentee to your mentor by doing the things suggested, applying the things you need to apply, and asking questions. Also, be helpful to your mentor. Help your mentor achieve things they want and work on their projects as well. The closer the relationship that you build with your mentor, the more results you are going to have in your own life. And once your mentorship arrangement comes to a close, you should continue to say thanks every so often when you think of them. This goes both ways – when you have given and received mentorship, sending a note of thanks and appreciation can deepen the trust and connection in your relationship and recall memories of your time together.

Being a good mentor – you can mentor people too!

Now that you know how to be mentored and once you have gained some experience in this process and built a mentor relationship, think about how you could mentor other people. There are some guidelines to keep in mind when you are ready to start mentoring people.

Here are five things to consider while mentoring people:

- Build experience: mentors do best when they have done it
- Be one step ahead of your mentees
- Listen, listen, listen
- Mentors are not coaches: help direct their efforts
- Mentors are not teachers: help them do it in real life

Mentoring is not only great for the mentee. It is also helpful for the mentor. When you teach, you better understand what you are teaching, and that helps you deepen your knowledge of the things that you are good at. When you mentor others, you are trying to help them do what you have already done. It motivates you to keep growing toward your own goals. A mentor also strives to be one step ahead of their mentees, which will push them to try things out and gain experience in things that they intend to do. Finally, when you mentor people, you become a trusted advisor.

That is a great position to be in. It creates recognition not only for your mentees but for everyone around you. When people see you helping others to achieve success, they recognize you as a leader and as someone that has experience and is successful. Since mentoring is such a powerful thing for your own career too, let us look at the preceding list in more detail.

Step one – build experience

Mentors do best when they help people achieve things that they have done themselves. Although it is not necessary to have done exactly what your mentees want to do, having real-world experience in similar situations is extremely important to help them overcome their obstacles. As a good mentor, try to implement things in your own career. When you learn about new ideas, methods, and tools useful to your mentees, try to experiment with them. Work them into your life and career. See if you can get tangible results. Because of your experience, you may be able to get results faster than your mentees would or figure out shortcuts that can help them.

Not only will you grow and advance yourself, but you will be able to guide your mentees toward implementing the same ideas and tools in their careers. That is especially important for skills. The two most important things as a mentor are to help your mentees with mindset and skill sets. Work on building new skills yourself. Experiment with new ways to apply your existing skills. Overcome your own difficulties in building new skills. All of these will help you and your career by helping you improve your current skill set and will also make you a better guide for your mentees.

Step two – try to be one step ahead of your mentees

When mentoring people, your experience will help you see ahead of time the obstacles, difficulties, and necessities that they are soon going to face. You can then be ready to be one step ahead of them. When you see they will need a skill that you do not have yet, build it for yourself. When you realize they are going to need tools or experience, or an example, you can find the tools, create some real-world experience for yourself, and use that as an example of what is possible.

Apply the tools or experience and be ready to help your mentees when they arrive at the problem. Being one step ahead will not only help your mentees to achieve results faster, but it will help you to keep growing. An effective way to be one step ahead of your mentees is to have a mentor yourself. Working with people even more experienced than you can help you understand, grow, and be ready to help your mentees when they need it. You can also apply the lessons you learn from your mentors and translate them to your mentees at the exact stage they are in their careers.

Step three – listen, listen, listen

It is amazingly easy to believe that as a mentor, it is your job to solve all the problems or to tell people what to do all the time. That is not the case. As a mentor, you need to understand your mentees' problems and help them think like you so they can solve their problems in a comparable way to how you would solve them. This mindset change you will provoke in your mentees will help them think at the same level as someone more experienced, so they can solve problems better and better. This can have a profound impact on your mentees' lives.

The best way to do this is to listen and not speak. Listen to what they are going through. Listen to how they are thinking about things. Listen to what challenges they are facing. Listen to what solutions they are proposing. That way, when you offer advice or guidance, you can start from their perspective and from the specific situation your mentees are going through at that time. To be an amazing mentor, practice listening and ask questions. Try to understand exactly what is going on. Dig deep into how your mentees are thinking about the situation. Producing a suggestion or some advice too early may negatively impact your mentee's ability to think for themselves and to learn to think as you do.

Step four – mentors are not coaches – help direct them

When we mention the importance of listening, it is easy to go all the way to the opposite side and believe that you are not supposed to offer any advice. That is, for instance, how a coach operates. A coach is someone that helps people to solve their own problems by themselves. Coaches are encouraged to never give their opinion, so people can come to their own conclusions and own solutions.

That is why a coach can be helpful even when they do not have experience. A coach helps their coachees use their own experience to solve situations. This is all good and fine – there is a place for coaches, and sometimes you can even use this strategy with your mentees. Again, mentors are not coaches. Mentors have experience in the goals you are trying to achieve. They have done it. You have done what your mentees want to do! Because you have the experience, you know the path. You see the challenges. You know people that can help. You know the tricks and the pitfalls. And if all of those things can help your mentee to solve challenges faster and better, you should guide them.

Guide your mentees to their desired outcome, so they can achieve the things that they want to achieve by using your experience. That does not mean forcing something upon them; it means listening to their current situation and giving advice based on your stories and your results. You can tell stories. You can ask questions. You can suggest experiments. You can introduce people or point them to resources. There are many ways to guide your mentees to their outcomes without forcing them. But at the same time, participate actively in their success!

Step five – mentors are not instructors – help them do it in real life

Another common pitfall for mentors is to believe that they are instructors – that their job is to teach the mentee how to do things. The mentor helps with the mentees' mentality and skills. And those things only work if you help your mentee to apply things in real life. Instead of considering mentorship as a moment to instruct people, use your mentorship time to evaluate what has been tried and to analyze the obstacles, the problems, and the difficulties so you can help your mentee take one more step or try one more thing. You should help them move closer to their goal, and that will only happen if they do it themselves. Work with your mentees to get them to act and apply things to their lives and careers. Use your examples and experience to motivate them to take concrete steps.

Considering all those five steps, mentorship is about helping your mentee to act, so they can achieve results and success in things and skills that you have had similar experiences with in the past. Use your experience, your life stories, challenges, and the difficulties that you have had in the past to help your mentees re-evaluate how they think and take action about their own problems and difficulties. Help them implement a plan that will take them where they want to be. Along the way, while you are helping them, use mentoring to help you move forward in your own goals and results. The best mentors are the ones that keep growing and evolving and keep achieving even better, stronger results in their own careers. When you grow, you can help your mentees to do the same.

We would like to share with you the experience of Elder Moraes, working at Red Hat as an example.

Interview

Elder Moraes

Q: Can you tell us where you work now?

A: Currently, I work at Red Hat, having moved there from Oracle in early 2020 at the beginning of the pandemic. My role at Red Hat involves leading the Red Hat developers for Latin America, where I work with the Latin community, delivering Spanish content and talks.

Q: Do you speak Spanish?

A: Yes, I do. When I was interviewed for my current role, my boss asked me if I could speak Spanish, and I had to learn. It was not too difficult as Spanish is a close language to Portuguese, which is my native language.

Q: How did you first get involved with the Java community?

A: In around 2015, I discovered a group in Brazil that was discussing Java on IRC called SouJava. I contacted the group, and a year later, I was working with Bruno Souza when he asked me to help promote the release of Java EE 8. We ended up conducting a series of interviews with prominent figures in the Java community, which brought me to author a book about Java EE. SouJava's initial recognition of my initiative set me on a path that led to my current role. I passionately believe in the power of community, especially in the Java ecosystem, where people are open to new members, making it helpful for one's career.

Q: Can you recall your first encounter with Bruno, and how did you two meet?

A: Oh, I cannot remember [laughter]. It has been so long, but we kept in touch through phone calls and emails for months. We had not met in person until a developer conference, JavaOne Brazil, where we were scheduled to give a talk together. We had never met before, so it was like meeting an acquaintance for the first time. After that talk, Bruno and I gave dozens of talks together. Every experience we had with the community convinced me of the power of connecting with people who share similar interests and passions.

Q: I heard that you have a mentoring program. Can you tell us more about it?

A: Yes, I do have a small mentoring program, and it is because I am the result of having a mentor myself, who happens to be Bruno. I believe in the power of having a mentor because it can save you a lot of time. As someone once said, a mentor is someone who is just a few steps ahead of you and can reach out their hand to guide you. When you have a mentor, you can avoid making mistakes that they have already made, and they can offer advice on what to do and what not to do. In my case, having Bruno as my mentor helped me to grow my career significantly faster than if I were doing it alone.

Q: What inspired you to start your own mentoring program?

A: A few years ago, as I started to achieve some results in my career, people started coming to me with questions like, "What should I do next?" or "How can I prepare for an interview?" I realized that I could use my experience to help others who were in the same position that I once was. That's why I decided to create a small group where I could mentor people more closely. It has been a fun and rewarding experience, and I am still learning from it.

Q: What do you think are the benefits of mentoring, both for the mentor and the mentee?

A: The benefits of mentoring are numerous. As a mentee, you can learn from someone who has more experience and knowledge than you, which can help you to grow and develop faster than if you were doing it alone. As a mentor, you can give back to the community by sharing your knowledge and experience. Also, mentoring can help you to reflect on your own experiences and learn from them. Ultimately, both the mentor and the mentee can benefit from the relationship by learning from each other.

Q: Can you share some advice for those who want to start mentoring others?

A: My advice for those who want to start mentoring others is to be patient and understanding. Every mentee is different, and you need to adapt your mentoring style to their needs. Also, be open to learning from your mentee because they can offer fresh perspectives and ideas. Finally, be willing to share your experience and knowledge generously, as that is the primary purpose of mentoring. Remember, when you are mentoring, you always learn something along the way – mentor or mentee. That is the point of mentoring.

Q: Can you tell us about a success story from your mentoring group?

A: Yes, there is one guy named Maximilian, or Max for short, who I am very proud of. He had 20 years of experience but felt stuck in his career. When he came to me, I answered every question he had with advice based on my own experiences. As a mentor, it is important to share your knowledge and get involved with the community. Max started to do this, and in the two years that we have been working together, he has become a developer advocate for a big company in Brazil that is related to a big bank. He never thought he would be able to do this kind of job, but by working together and becoming closer, he saw that not only was it possible, but he also had the skills to do it. Seeing people achieve their potential through mentoring is amazing.

Q: How did you help Max achieve his goals?

A: I answered every question Max had with advice based on my own experiences. I also encouraged him to get involved with the community, lead initiatives, and build relationships. By doing these things, Max was able to see the possibilities that were available to him and develop the skills he needed to achieve his goals. I supported him every step of the way and helped him to believe in himself.

Q: What do you think is the most important quality for a mentor to have?

A: I think the most important quality for a mentor to have is the ability to listen. You need to be able to listen to your mentee's concerns and questions in order to provide relevant and helpful advice. You also need to be patient and supportive and be willing to provide guidance even when it's difficult. It's also important to be knowledgeable in your field and to be able to share that knowledge with others.

Q: How can someone become a mentor?

A: To become a mentor, you should have expertise and experience in a particular field or industry. You should also be willing to share your knowledge and help others achieve their goals. It is important to have good communication skills and be able to listen to your mentee's concerns and questions. You can start by volunteering to mentor someone in your workplace or community or by joining a mentoring program or organization. Networking is also important, as it can help you connect with potential mentees.

Q: What advice would you give to someone who is looking for a mentor?

A: If you are looking for a mentor, start by identifying someone who has expertise and experience in your field or industry. Look for someone who is willing to share their knowledge and provide guidance. You should also consider the person's communication skills and whether you feel comfortable talking to them. Do not be afraid to reach out to people and ask if they would be willing to mentor you. You can also look for mentoring programs or organizations that match mentors with mentees.

Summary

In this chapter, you learned about the need for mentorship and peer coaching. You can now identify the types of mentors and coaches you require, what is needed in mentoring relationships (giving and getting), how to be intentional in your interactions with mentors, how to find mentors, and how to mentor other people.

Next, we will discuss how to operate in larger groups and how to interact with people via meetups and user group meetings.

8

Be Part of a Larger Group – Meeting People at User Groups and Meetups

The power of community participation is not an abstract one where our careers magically start growing just because we spend time with people we already know. You must actively look for and engage with peers, and reach out to a larger group. That is when the benefits of community participation kick in and help you to advance your career. This chapter will discuss some of the most vibrant and accessible communities for you to engage with in your area of interest.

In the chapter, we discuss user group meetings as places where real developers meet. We will expand on how to find a community near you, how to make the most of your participation, the benefits of getting involved, how to deepen your participation, and the results you can expect from attending user group meetings.

We'll discuss these main topics in the chapter:

- Where real developers meet
- Finding a community near you
- Making the most of your participation
- The benefits of getting involved
- Deepening your participation and your results
- Starting your own user group

By the end of the chapter, you will understand what user groups and meetups are. You will be able to find a community that you can connect to and join, participate in user groups with purpose, be clear on the objectives of your participation, and be able to take action to increase your involvement toward leadership of the group.

Where real developers meet

Software development, especially in the modern era, is a group activity. The days of the single developer working alone in their garage are long gone. Not only that, but as we said in a previous chapter, software development is a soft skill. That means it's much easier for you to learn and improve your software development skills while working with other developers, particularly ones that are better than you.

One aspect related to communities is networking. Meeting your peers is an important and frequently discussed element of career growth. We must point out that communities and networking are not the same. Networking is the sum of people that you know and interact with.

People in your personal and professional networks can come from all kinds of places: your family, friends, and work. They may or may not know and interact with each other. The commonality they have is their relationship with you.

Communities, on the other hand, are centered around common goals and interests. That can be a technology, a project, a specific objective, or even participation in something, such as an event, project, or activity. This is also networking in a way, but communities are focused on promoting relationships between the participants. In your own personal network, you probably know people from the multiple communities that you participate in. So, although not exactly the same thing, networking and communities go hand in hand.

With that in mind, communities of software developers are places and spaces where developers with things in common meet, usually around learning, using, or improving a shared product or technology. Being part of a community like this lets you network with peers that have similar interests and objectives as you.

As Adam Grants describes in his book *Give and Take*, networking can give you an edge in your career. Adam explains the research behind having access to a larger network that gives you access to knowledge, experience, and influence. Since communities and networking go hand in hand, the same benefits are provided, and enhanced, by being part of a community.

These are some of the benefits that networking and being part of a community can deliver:

- **Access to knowledge**: As part of a community, you have access to confidential information, meaning information that is not easily or publicly accessible, such as details about projects, problems encountered, job opportunities, and more, that people from the community know about and will share with you because you are part of the group.

- **Access to diversity of skills**: In your community, you will come across and be able to benefit from a diverse set of skills. Members have different experiences, work on distinct types of projects, use a variety of tools and technologies, and have gone through unique difficulties. All these build skills and expertise. Being part of the group, and being able to learn all this information from people and reach out to them when you need help, allows you to advance your own skills faster and more easily.

- **Influence and power**: Each of us has some level of influence in our companies and the projects that we participate in. Knowing and having access to people in the industry gives you a little influence through them. As an example, when someone from your community knows and trusts you, and suggests you, let us say, for a job, that is you having a power that you would not have alone.

Adam Grant mentions the research that shows that those people who build large networks, that is, participate in communities, tend to be evaluated more highly in their job performance, are promoted faster, and end up earning more money than people that don't build their networks. This is a result of the knowledge, experience, and influence that you have access to by being part of a community.

Knowing this, it is not a surprise that developers that get involved with communities grow their careers at a faster pace, often to levels that those who do not participate can never achieve.

That is not to say that community participation is a utilitarian process. Those that think they can just turn up and enjoy the benefits usually do not. This is because it requires trust, and that in turn requires involvement and giving. Just wanting to be involved is not enough; you need to do it in a way that benefits both the community and your career.

So, let's take a look at what it takes to get involved with communities in a way that will get you growing. First, a quick primer on what communities are all about. Many developer communities are called **user groups**. Developers like you may flinch at the word "users", but user groups are groups of users of a specific technology or product. In the case of development technologies such as programming languages and programming tools, the users of those tools are developers. You.

Technology or development-focused user groups are groups of developers that use a specific technology or product. And because we use the same tech, product, or tool, we have similar problems. User group communities, then, are the place where we can come together, discuss problems we are going through, evaluate solutions, and share experiences – in general, solve our problems together. It is a place, be it physical or virtual, where we can meet and work with people that are better than us.

It is also a good place to discuss the future of our technology of choice since an important part of user communities is the objective of advancing the technology. Users of technology are the ones who really understand where things need to improve and what the difficulties or challenges are that prevent the technology from being adopted more widely.

Precisely because of those discussions, user communities attract the participation of vendors. A smart vendor will connect with those communities to figure out how users are benefiting from their products, how they can improve things, and even how they can increase their sales. With this coming together of the users and vendors of a technology, user communities tend to become extremely important and valuable. Not only do they tend to help improve the technology and spread knowledge about its usage; they are also pivotal in bringing in new users to the technology.

User communities are often a place that receives beginners and introduces them to the technology in question. They provide things such as tutorials, step-by-step guides, and other beginner-focused content. This helps bring newcomers up to speed in learning about new technologies.

Being a port of entry, many make the mistake of believing that user communities are composed only of beginners. That could not be farther from the truth. The people that participate in those communities grow as professionals together. The connections and friendships made in those communities often last for years. Professionals that build their careers on a technology or product end up growing and achieving a large reputation in those networks.

Communities, especially those that have existed for a long time, are usually built of a significant percentage of professionals that bring benefits to and benefit from relationships and networking. Communities are a congregation of beginners, experienced professionals, and vendors. All work together in one way or another to spread knowledge, advance technology, bring newcomers up to speed, discuss problems and solutions to move forward, and analyze difficult problems and solutions that are faced by many.

There are several ways that a community like this can be organized. In the Java world, for example, developers are usually organized around Java User Groups (JUGs). But almost every technology has its own user groups, meetups, discussion forums, mailing lists, online groups, Facebook groups, Discord servers, Slack channels, or other forms of organizing and bringing the community together.

As a developer, one thing that you can do to really grow your career is to get involved with a community that is close to you, either physically, or in terms of technology. Use that to increase your network, and with that grow your access to knowledge, experience, and influence.

Finding a community near you

There is no doubt that in-person meetings are better for networking. When you meet with people face to face, it is easier to build friendships. You have more opportunities to discuss things. You have even more possibilities for meeting new people.

That is why the best way to participate, delivering greater results to you and to the community, is by getting involved with a local community located physically near you. That said, online meetings are clearly more convenient. You can participate in online meetings from anywhere, without problems of transportation, and less time and money needing to be spent. Especially with the increase in sophistication of online conferencing tools and other remote technologies, meeting online has become the preferred way of doing things, and many communities now provide ways for you to participate fully online.

The problem with online participation is that it's usually harder for you to meet people and have parallel conversations, which dramatically reduces your opportunities for networking and ends up restricting your participation to that of only a receiver of content. In an in-person meeting, both before and after the main presentation, you have the chance to meet people and have small-talk. You can learn about projects, activities, and job opportunities in more informal, one-to-one conversations like this.

Online meetings, however, are usually centered around the main presentation and lose a lot of that parallel networking. That said, if you participate in the organization work of the community, you will probably have the same level of access to people, either online or in person. Online communities also try to replicate in-person activities by running online forums, Telegram groups, Discord servers, or Slack channels. That way, members and participants can have those parallel conversations and meet people, even outside the meetings and presentations.

That brings us to the question of where you could look to find a community, either near you physically or close to your interests. Of course, the first place you should look is a search engine. A quick search for your location and the name of your chosen technology, perhaps also adding the words `community`, `user group`, or `forum`, will usually lead you to someone or something around you if it exists. Also consider the following:

- **Meetup.com** is a good starting point. It's more focused on in-person talks, and the site has little support for building the community itself, so it is more of a directory where you can find information about upcoming meetings.

- **Discord and Slack** are chat platforms for synchronous or asynchronous conversation, and are universally used by developers. They allow communities to organize themselves in their own space. Searching for either a Discord server or a Slack channel that focuses on the technology you're interested in is an effective way to get involved in a community.

- **Facebook** also has some strong group features that allow many communities to be formed. By and large, Facebook communities are organized by less technical people and are preferred by groups and communities not related to technology, but many developers-focused communities do meet in Facebook groups.

- Eventbrite.

- Twitter Spaces.

- LinkedIn Groups.

- Mentoring groups.

- Informal or formal groups at your company with colleagues.

- Online discussion groups such as Stack Overflow, Reddit, and Quora.

- **groups.io** provides mailing list solutions, allowing communities to organize themselves using email. You can find thousands of different communities here.

Don't forget to look at the site of your preferred technology. Many of those sites will list communities, places, and future meetings that you can participate in. Even if you can't find anything near you, getting involved with any of those communities, even if only online, will give you insights into certain places and meetings that you might not easily find information about otherwise.

One caveat that we have to point out when looking for communities is the fact that most communities are organized by volunteers with little time on their hands. It is not uncommon that communities have very outdated sites or communication channels. If you see a website or a social media account that seems to be inactive or with very old posts, that does not necessarily mean that the community itself is not active and no longer meeting. We suggest that you reach out to whatever contacts you can find to determine the real situation.

Making the most of your participation

With participation, the first level is of course being present, even if just to watch and follow the content. You, as with most people, may start participating in communities because you see valuable content: presentations, articles, blog posts, or any content that can help you evolve. Even on the first level of just watching, you can derive much greater results if you make a little bit of extra effort.

First, *participate live* as much as possible. Even if you're watching a fully online community where everything is recorded, try to be there live. That way, you can properly interact with other people, with the organizers and speakers of the community, and you have the option to ask questions.

So, make a special effort to *ask questions*. This helps the wider community, increasing the interaction between the speakers and the audience, and even between the participants. It also helps the organizers to see that their efforts are working! When you ask questions, you help the speaker create content specific to the situation you are experiencing. It turns that generic presentation into something that really helps you in your career goals.

Another effortless way that you can participate, even if you are only online, is by *promoting the event and the speaker*. Every community strives to grow and that usually happens by word of mouth. So, the more you promote the events, the better it's going to be for everyone in the community as a whole.

You can do this by sharing future events on your social media and inviting your colleagues from work to watch and participate with you. You can also take pictures and screenshots of the speaker while they are presenting and share that. All of this helps attract a larger audience to the content. Even after the presentation is finished, you can share the recordings on social media, along with the lessons you learned, or you could provide that information directly to your friends and projects. All of this helps the community be more visible and draw more people to future activities.

Participate in person if you can. As we mentioned before, in-person participation is much better and much more useful for you, but it also provides more value to the community too. Pictures of an auditorium full of people; speakers interacting with developers in person; many developers visiting offices. All of these help the community to be seen as more effective and important.

Not only do you win by having better networking opportunities but also in the future the community will attract even more interesting speakers and vendors, giveaways, and of course, larger audiences. Everyone wins. No matter whether online or in person, *help the group however you can*. Promote the events, invite friends, take pictures, offer a meeting place at your company, suggest that your company sponsors the community, and register for paid community events and activities. All of these are small things that can be done that increase the value of the community and expand the benefits that the community provides to everyone.

You should also offer to help. When you start helping the community, you start moving from just participating to helping the organizers. Organizers get the most value from the community because they have the possibility of stronger, deeper interactions with speakers and vendors. Organizers have more access to opportunities and have the benefits of networking on a much larger scale. Of course, organizers also put in more work.

The task of organizing communities is usually volunteer work done by people that see the value of doing it. But at the same time, it does usually impact their personal and family time. That's why when you are willing to help, it is always useful. When community organizers can share the load with multiple people, each person has to put in less time themselves, the community can do more, and the whole group benefits from greater results.

When offering to help, don't try to just do the things that you want to do. Those already involved in organizing the community will have ideas on how the community should be run, what its goals are, and what needs to be done in the future. Start by listening. What do the existing organizers want to do? See whether there are things that you can help with.

That may involve doing some tasks that are not extremely rewarding, nor very visible, especially in the beginning. Trivial things such as arranging the chairs at an in-person meeting before the event starts, tidying up the room once the event finishes, and receiving people at the door may seem of little importance but are actually very important. *Someone* has to do it, and if you volunteer for it, you help free up the organizers to focus on the speakers and vendors.

Help like this is extremely appreciated precisely because it is not glamorous and needs to be done. When you are willing to help in ways like this, you will be seen as a giver who is interested in helping and will gain the trust of the organizers. With that, you will quickly advance to more interesting activities. On the other hand, if you just want to be involved to gain benefits and help with visible things, you will be seen as a taker, and you will not be accepted into the inner circle.

One more thing that is important to consider is that organizers usually do not have the time to think about activities or help you get more involved. If you just wait for the organizers to remember that you are there to help, it might never happen. Also, consider that sometimes, people do not want to help, but want to sound helpful, so they just say *"if you need help, call me"*, because they know no one will have time to call.

So, the suggestion is that you show up and do whatever you can. That will remind people that you are there to help if there is anything else that can be done.

A couple of things you can do without waiting for anyone to tell you anything is to arrive a few minutes early and see whether there is anything you can do. Also, especially if it's your first time at a meeting, make sure to stay afterward, help tidy things up, and help close the place.

Often in-person events offer a hybrid option, so you can offer to facilitate participation from online participants. Utilize the chat function and encourage online participants to answer questions to increase engagement early in the event. Ask questions such as, *where are you located? Is this your first event or are you a regular attender?* As the event progresses, prompt them to offer their impressions or ask questions of the speaker to keep them engaged and involved in the conversations.

You may need to do this multiple times until organizers can think of something that you can help with. Many people have started their community participation by being there frequently, and then suddenly becoming the person to help when one of the organizers could not come, or someone left for a vacation.

The benefits of getting involved

Doing non-glamorous activities that are not directly related to software development may even take you away from watching the presentation, as well as taking time from your family or your studies... That sounds like a recipe for disaster and not something that will benefit your career...

But in reality, let us remind ourselves what communities can bring us. As we pointed out at the beginning of this chapter, participation in communities gives us access to knowledge, experience, and influence. That translates into you being evaluated more highly, promoted faster, and eventually earning more money.

Those are tangible career benefits. More than any of that, participation in communities will bring you friendship, help, and support. Also, you are going to be able to help and support others, increasing your leadership and mentoring skills. All of those are extremely positive benefits for your career.

Now for the most closely guarded secret: people that spend time organizing and building the community get not only slightly better, but hundreds of times, even several orders of magnitude, better results than people that just participate. Those that organize the community are more visible, have a better reputation, meet better contacts, make friends with more important people, have more access to vendors and speakers, and much more. Join communities so you can help others, and in many ways, help yourself too.

Deepening your participation and your results

Here are some steps for you to participate in communities the right way and get the best results:

1. **Search for communities near you** where you can participate in person and help solve local problems. Bonus points if you can find communities that align with your long-term career goals.

2. **Listen**. Join the Discord server, Slack channel, Telegram group, mailing list, or whatever communication channel the community has. Understand what the organizers need and what the community is trying to do. Also, help newcomers to feel at ease.

3. **Make yourself available for help**. Introduce yourself to the organizers and offer help. Make sure to be there if they ever need you.

4. **Do things that need to be done, even before anything is asked of you**. Do things that are obviously needed. Answer questions from newbies on the list. Promote the community's presentations and activities on your social media accounts. Take pictures and share them with others. Clean up and tidy the place before you leave. All of those are things that need to be done and that no one needs to ask you to do!

5. Gently **remind people** that you are there to help. Make it easy for the organizers to ask for help. Even organizers are wary of asking people to do things… So, remind them that you are there to help with anything that's needed. You may need to do this multiple times, and you may need to gently insert yourself into some activities.

6. **Show up**. Be consistent and participate frequently. Say hello to people in the chat. Ask questions to speakers. Participate in activities, both online and in person. Joining a community is a long-term strategy, not something that works if you only show up sometimes.

7. **Think about the members**, not only about yourself. Leaders are those who think about others. Watch for what both other participants and organizers need and figure out how you can help them.

8. **Share** the community's activities, the difficulties you have, and the results of going to the talks that you've had. Share what you learned from the speakers. Expand the reach of the community by sharing whatever you can with whomever you can, be it social media, friends, or work colleagues.

9. **Grow the community**. Bring people to participate. Invite friends to come join you. Promote the community inside your company. Share with managers the benefits you got from participating. Invite experienced people in your company to join and share their experiences.

10. **Deepen relationships in the community**. As much as you need to grow the community, you also need to grow the relationships you have made inside the community. Look for ways to continue to build on your connections in your user group space. Share updates and look for ways to deepen relationships by showing your consideration and looking for opportunities to share experiences together. You will inevitably have conflicts in your community and part of deepening relationships is finding ways to resolve those conflicts. By managing disagreements, inevitably you grow your emotional intelligence and build your conflict resolution skills. Being able to sustain your community and develop relationships rests on being able to manage disagreements and resolve conflicts.

These are some of the ways you can participate more fully in user group activities to get the most out of your attendance at the events. It is important to attend events, but you will reap even more benefits from your attendance if you engage more deeply and meaningfully in some way. Remember to find a balance between community, work, and family or personal time.

Starting your own user group community

Sometimes, you may be located somewhere where there is no existing user group covering your area of expertise. The following are some steps you can take as best practices to start your own user group when this is the case. Consider partnering with an existing user group before you decide to undertake this initiative, but there are times when a new user group is warranted, depending on your area.

Here's how to go about it:

- Register a domain name with your user group initials.
- Set up a collaborative website, preferably a wiki. Available options to consider include Confluence, GitHub, Eventbrite, Meetup, XWiki, or Drupal, among others.
- Set up a newsletter that people can easily subscribe to.
- Make sure to send out the newsletter on a regular basis.
- Reach out to potential sponsors in your area, making sure to include the visitor stats of your website to encourage them to sponsor your site.
- Run events on a regular basis, such as once a month or every two months.
- Publish content on your site regularly (RSS feeds are a nice way to get some content).
- Invite and set up a steering committee of different people, and meet and schedule your events.
- Once the group takes form, think about setting up a non-profit organization.
- Consider asking for a membership fee to cover the logistics costs. You'll need this once the JUG gets bigger.
- Keep events as neutral and technical as possible, so the JUG members get value.
- Consider recording your events (via video or just audio) and publishing them online.
- Take pictures of your events to display your passion to potential JUG members and sponsors. Publish these – promote on social media.

Having a clear objective

Community participation is a special career activity, and takes time and effort over the long term. The only way for your participation to succeed in the long run is if it aligns with your career objectives. You should not try to participate in communities just for short-term, selfish benefits. That seldom works.

The more clarity you have on how your community participation aligns with your long-term goals – with what you want to achieve for yourself in your career – the more you can align what you do and the community you participate in. This will give you all the more reason to be helpful, participate, and be consistent, even when required to put your own personal time into it. Ultimately, this clear objective allows you to grow in your career.

Whether your objective for attending user group events is to learn more about a technology, develop your leadership skills, network with more people, find a mentor, find a job opportunity, or just to have, you will be more likely to find success if you have established a clear objective or set of objectives in joining or attending the specific user group events or meetings you select.

We would like to share with you the experience of Rodrigo Graciano working at BNY Mellon as an example.

Interview

Rodrigo Graciano

Q: Can you share a career story related to user group participation?

A: Absolutely: my story revolves around how I was able to help someone advance in their career thanks to the **JUG**. This individual joined one of the Java SIG meetings, the New York Java SIG meetings, during the Covid-19 pandemic when we were holding them online. If it wasn't for the pandemic, he would have never got in touch with us, but sometimes good things come from bad situations. He asked for help on how to learn Java and I provided him with a list of sources, videos, and people to follow. After some time, he disappeared, but then a few months later, he reached out to me again saying that he had a job interview for a Java developer position. I offered to help him prepare, and we spent an hour on Zoom going over interview questions. He had studied hard and was very dedicated, even attending the call at 2 or 3 A.M. his time from his clay house in Cameroon with minimal furniture. He eventually passed the interview and secured the job, and now he has moved to Portugal and is already giving back by teaching others Java. This experience showed me how the community can come together to help others and how even small actions can have a huge impact on someone's life.

Q: Can you tell us about your experience with the Java User Group?

A: My career can be split into two periods: before and after being part of a Java User Group. At first, I didn't know about the different groups, such as Java Champions, Ground Breakers, and ACE Directors. I was intimidated by these groups, and I thought I wasn't smart enough to be close to them. But when I joined the Java User Group, I started to have contact with all these people, and they helped me at every step of the way, providing feedback and support. They even helped me prepare for my first talk.

Q: Who are some of the notable people in the Java User Group?

A: There are many smart people in the Java User Group, including Jeanne, who wrote many of the certification books that I used before, Barry, who has taught Java for many years, and Frank, who co-led JSR 381, Visual Recognition Specification, in the **Java Community Process (JCP)** program.

Q: How did the Java User Group help you gain confidence in speaking at conferences?

A: The Java User Group helped me gain confidence in speaking at conferences by connecting me with well-known Java speakers such as Mark Heckler, Josh Long, James Gosling, and Brian Goetz. Jeanne also helped me prepare for my first talk by reviewing my deck and giving me feedback. She even reviewed my presentation in Portuguese and gave me tips to improve it.

Q: Can you tell us about your recent speaking engagements?

A: This year, I gave talks at DevNexus and JavaOne, which was an amazing experience. It's important to stop and be grateful for our efforts and congratulate ourselves for our achievements.

Summary

In this chapter, we learned how to become a part of a larger group, especially by meeting people in user groups. You now understand what user groups and meetups are, how to find a community that you can connect to, join, and participate in with purpose, along with developing clear objectives for your participation and taking action to increase your involvement toward leadership of the group.

In the next chapter, we will explore how to grow your network using social media. We will discuss the basics of social media for technical career development, personal versus professional social media usage, building your online presence, reaching out to people, and having meaningful conversations.

9

Grow Your Network through Social Media

Like most things in life, social media has its pros and cons. Maybe you find yourself getting lost in a sea of topics and discussions, using social media to procrastinate. This is a bad use of the tool. It is possible to use social media to expand your network, connect with people, and engage in meaningful conversations. This chapter will show how social media can be an asset in your career.

In this chapter, we will cover the basics of social media for technical career development, personal versus professional social media usage, and how to build your online presence, reach out to people, and have meaningful conversations.

You will learn how to use social media to advance your career, how to create a professional profile, how to adjust your social media experience for professional benefit, how to meet people and get involved in the online community, and finally, how to initiate and participate in career-advancing conversations.

The following are the main topics we'll be covering in this chapter:

- Basics of social media for technical career development
- Personal versus professional social media usage
- Building your online presence
- Reaching out to people
- Having meaningful conversations

Let's get started.

Learning how to use social media to develop your technical career

Since the early days of the internet, there has been some form of social interaction and dialog. Social media can be said to be a collection of interactive technologies or media that aid in the creation of information, ideas, and dialog, and that facilitates the sharing and distribution of them based on different interests. They can be shared electronically in social communities or as part of social networks. There is a wide variety of social media services currently available, but new ones are added on an ongoing basis, and there are those that fall out of favor over time. While in the early days of social media, interactions were text-based, in the days of Web 2.0 and Web 3.0, social media can be said to comprise text-based content and/or a combination of multimedia content, such as photographs, videos, or memes. This content is generated by a user and intended to be interactive on web-based applications or mobile applications. The interaction and the data that is generated are the value and uniqueness of social media.

Whatever platform you chose, users have the ability to create profiles for that website, service, or application, encouraging the creation of an online community or social network by connections made through the user profile – connecting to either another individual or another group. Social media encourages and enhances social networks and/or social connections. As users of social media, you can create, share, discuss, and participate in online discussions. People do this for many purposes, such as research and discovery, documenting memories, self-promotion, forming friendships or professional connections, exploring new ideas, and learning new things. The forms can include micro-blogs, blogs, podcasts, video games, and photo and video sharing. Some of the most popular social media websites are Facebook, Twitter, LinkedIn, TikTok, Instagram, WeChat, Baidu, Weibo, YouTube, Quora, Telegram, WhatsApp, Signal, Line, Pinterest, Reddit, Twitch, Slack, Discord, Mastodon, Twitch, and Snapchat. There are an increasing number of social media platforms being introduced currently, and it can be overwhelming to think about participating in so many social media platforms.

For technical career development, you will need to select some social media to focus your attention and efforts. Depending on your location and the role/stage of your career, this will vary. You can start by asking and observing where some of your peers participate. For example, use one or two platforms for messaging and groups, such as WhatsApp and Slack; one or two for more general posting, sharing, and engagement, such as Twitter and Mastodon; and then one or two to consume video content, on platforms such as YouTube and Discord (live streaming).

Here are some of the most popular social media platforms:

- **X (formerly Twitter)**: A microblogging platform where tech professionals share concise updates, the latest trends, and insights related to the tech world. Experts use Twitter (X) to engage in real-time discussions, follow thought leaders, and stay updated on rapid industry developments. The platform's fast-paced nature facilitates quick information sharing and fosters connections within the tech community.

- **LinkedIn**: A platform tailored for tech professionals to showcase their professional accomplishments, connect with industry peers, and network with potential employers. Tech experts use it to share industry insights, collaborate on projects, and seek job opportunities. The platform's emphasis on professional achievements makes it a hub for job searches, discussions on emerging technologies, and career advancements.

- **Facebook (Meta)**: Facebook is one of the most popular social media networks in history. In the tech world, it is used primarily to connect with friends and family, in a more informal way. While not exclusively for tech professionals, Facebook is the largest social network to date. Many use Facebook to connect with colleagues, share tech-related articles, and engage in industry groups. It's a platform to discuss tech trends, attend virtual events, and network within tech circles. Professionals also use it to maintain a more personal connection with peers, colleagues, and their families.

- **Mastodon**: Tech professionals interested in decentralized social media turn to Mastodon. They create accounts on instances tailored to tech topics, share tech news, and participate in discussions without centralized control. Mastodon's open source nature appeals to those who value privacy and seek alternative social media platforms within the tech sphere.

Discussion forums and Q&A

Here's a list of some popular forums:

- **Stack Overflow**: An online Q&A platform where tech professionals ask and answer coding and programming-related questions. Tech experts use Stack Overflow to seek solutions to coding challenges, share their expertise by helping others, and expand their knowledge across various programming languages and frameworks. It's a vital resource for troubleshooting and continuous learning within the tech field.

- **Reddit**: Tech professionals turn to Reddit to participate in specialized communities (subreddits) dedicated to specific tech topics. They seek advice, share insights, and discuss the latest advancements. Reddit provides a platform for in-depth discussions, problem-solving, and knowledge exchange among tech enthusiasts and experts in a variety of niches.

- **Reddit's programming subreddits**: It's worth highlighting that there are numerous programming-related subreddits (such as r/programming, r/webdev, r/python, and r/java) where tech professionals can engage in discussions specific to programming languages, frameworks, and software development.

- **Quora**: Tech professionals turn to Quora to ask and answer in-depth questions related to programming, tech trends, and industry insights. They share their expertise, provide detailed explanations, and engage in discussions to help others solve tech-related problems. Quora offers a platform to share knowledge and build a reputation within the tech community.

Video, streaming, and images

Here's a list of popular video streaming platforms:

- **YouTube**: As the premiere video and streaming platform, YouTube is used to create educational content, tutorials, and in-depth tech reviews. Professionals share their expertise in programming languages, software development, and hardware innovations. The platform allows tech experts to engage with a broader audience, demonstrate complex concepts visually, host interviews and discussions, and establish themselves as authoritative voices in the field.

- **Twitch**: Initially used by gamers, Twitch appeals to tech professionals who utilize the platform to live-stream coding sessions, tech talks, and software development tutorials. They engage with an interactive audience, answer questions in real time, and share their screen to demonstrate coding techniques. Twitch offers a dynamic platform for tech experts to connect with fellow developers and learners.

- **Instagram**: A platform focused on pictures, images, and videos, Instagram is leveraged by tech professionals to showcase their creative side and highlight projects, designs, and innovations. Through visual storytelling, they give followers a glimpse into their tech journey, behind-the-scenes processes, and tech-related hobbies. The platform offers a unique way for tech experts to blend their personal interests with their professional identity.

- **TikTok**: Although still considered a platform for entertainment, TikTok is used by professionals to create short, engaging videos to showcase coding challenges, tech hacks, and innovative projects. They simplify complex concepts into bite-sized content, catering to a younger audience interested in tech. The platform offers a playful way to share insights, collaborate on coding trends, and inspire the next generation of tech enthusiasts.

- **Pinterest**: A visual platform, focused on discovering visual assets, Pinterest is a place where tech professionals can curate boards to visually showcase coding tips, design inspirations, and tech-related tutorials. They use the platform to gather and organize ideas, making it a valuable resource for planning projects and staying creative within the tech realm.

Chat and direct messaging

Following is the list of some popular direct messaging channels:

- **Slack**: A communication platform heavily used inside large companies and technology communities, Slack is the go-to platform for professional team communication, project management, and collaboration. You can organize channels for specific tech topics, share code snippets, and discuss software development in real time. Slack streamlines work conversations and facilitates efficient communication among tech teams.

- **Discord**: Because of its extensive community-building features, the possibility to create large communities for free, and also its early usage by gaming communities, Discord attracts tech professionals who want to create servers for coding communities, workshops, and tech events.

They engage in voice chats, share resources, and collaborate on coding projects. Discord's versatile features make it a hub for both casual discussions and focused tech-related interactions.

- **WhatsApp**: Because of its direct connection with the user's cellphone number, Meta's WhatsApp became almost a full replacement for SMS. Tech professionals on WhatsApp create groups to collaborate with colleagues, share quick updates, and discuss project developments. It's a platform for real-time communication, allowing tech experts to stay connected and informed about work-related matters. The app's widespread adoption makes it an essential tool for both casual and professional discussions.

- **Telegram**: Tech professionals use Telegram for group chats and channels dedicated to specific tech topics. They collaborate, share resources, and discuss coding challenges. Telegram's security features also make it a suitable platform to share sensitive information and discuss confidential tech projects.

- **Signal**: Signal is favored by tech professionals for its strong emphasis on privacy and security. They use it for confidential discussions, sharing sensitive information, and collaborating on projects that require a secure communication channel. Signal's encryption features make it a go-to choice for tech experts who prioritize safeguarding their conversations and data.

- **Line**: Line serves as a communication and collaboration tool for tech professionals, especially in Asian countries. They use it for business chats, sharing project updates, and collaborating on coding tasks. Line's diverse features, including stickers and video calls, cater to both professional and casual conversations within tech circles.

Blogging and articles

Here are a couple of popular blogging sites:

- **Medium**: Tech professionals use Medium to publish articles, tutorials, and in-depth insights on various tech topics. It's a platform for showcasing expertise, sharing knowledge, and engaging with a broader audience interested in tech trends and innovations.

- **Dev.to**: A community platform specifically designed for developers, Dev.to allows tech professionals to share their coding experiences, best practices, and tips. It fosters discussions around programming languages, tools, and industry challenges.

Specialized communities

Here are some specialized communities you need to know:

- **GitHub**: A developer-centric platform where tech professionals collaborate on coding projects, contribute to open source software, and showcase their coding skills. Tech experts utilize GitHub to collaborate on software development, track changes in code, and demonstrate their expertise through repositories. It serves as a virtual résumé for programmers and fosters community-driven development.

- **Meetup**: While primarily an event platform, Meetup is important for tech professionals to find local tech meetups, workshops, and networking events. It's a great way to connect with fellow tech enthusiasts in person and stay updated on tech-related activities in their area.

- **HackerRank**: While not a traditional social media platform, HackerRank serves as a platform for tech professionals to practice coding challenges, participate in coding competitions, and assess their skills. It's a way for tech experts to hone their coding abilities and benchmark themselves against their peers.

- **Snapchat**: While less common in professional contexts, some tech professionals use Snapchat to offer quick glimpses into their tech-related activities, such as attending tech events or showcasing coding challenges. Snapchat's ephemeral nature lends itself to sharing informal updates and behind-the-scenes moments within the tech community.

Locality-focused communities

Here are a couple of locality-focused communities:

- **WeChat**: Widely used in China, WeChat serves as a multifunctional app where tech professionals connect with colleagues, share industry news, and discuss tech developments. They form professional networks through WeChat groups, exchange business cards digitally, and stay informed about the rapidly evolving tech landscape in the region.

- **Weibo**: Tech professionals in China leverage Weibo, a microblogging platform similar to Twitter, to share quick updates, tech insights, and industry news. They use it to engage with a wide audience, including both tech enthusiasts and the general public. Weibo fosters discussions, enables knowledge sharing, and helps tech experts stay connected within the Chinese tech community.

- **XING**: Particularly popular in Europe, XING is a professional networking platform similar to LinkedIn, where tech professionals can connect with peers, join tech-focused groups, and explore job opportunities within the European tech landscape..

Whatever platform they choose, users have the ability to create profiles for that website, service, or application, and the creation of an online community or social network is encouraged by making connections through the user profile – connecting to either another individual or another group. Social media encourages and enhances social networks and/or social connections. As a user of social media, you can create, share, discuss, and participate in online discussions. People do this for many purposes, such as research and discovery, documenting memories, self-promoting, forming friendships or professional connections, exploring new ideas, or learning new things. The formats this can take include micro-blogs, blogs, podcasts, video games, or photo and video sharing. Some of the most popular social media websites are Facebook, Twitter/X, LinkedIn, TikTok, Instagram, WeChat, Baidu, Weibo, YouTube, Quora, Telegram, WhatsApp, Signal, Line, Pinterest, Reddit, Twitch, Slack, Discord, Mastodon, Twitch, and Snapchat.

There are an increasing number of social media platforms being introduced currently, and it can be overwhelming to think of participating in so many social media platforms.

For technical career development, you will need to select a social media platform to focus your attention and efforts. Depending on your location and your role/the stage of your career, this will vary. You can start by asking and observing where some of your peers are participating. For example, use 1-2 platforms for messaging and groups, such as WhatsApp and Slack, 1-2 for more general posting, sharing, and engagement, such as Twitter and Mastodon, and then 1-2 for consuming video content on platforms such as YouTube and Discord (live-streaming).

Personal versus professional social media usage

You may have many interests and hobbies. Most people do. Consider maintaining separate accounts for personal and professional interests, especially if you have interests that are distinct from your technical professional career, such as politics.

While it is important to show a well-rounded perspective of yourself and some insight into your personality, your professional social media accounts should focus primarily on your professional interests. Since most employers will check your social media account, and they are often listed on your professional profiles, you should aim to keep your social media image and reputation on a career-oriented plane. You can add any personal accounts you would like to be consulted in the description or biography portion of your profile as an option to learn more about your personal hobbies and interests.

Building your online presence

Consider your brand when you build your online presence. Your brand is how others perceive you. One of Heather's first lessons in her career was that perception is reality. Have you ever heard that phrase? How you are perceived is the reality of your brand. Your brand should reflect the reality of the way you show up in the real world and online in the virtual world. You don't need to display perfection. It is important to be authentic when you build your online personality and presence. Consistency is also essential in building your presence. You will need to remain true to your brand on social media in order to be successful. That doesn't mean that you cannot evolve and grow; that is normal.

Create your profile using your brand. This will be key in building your online presence. Your brand should be meaningful and memorable, but also adaptable. Think about your skills and experiences, values, ideals, and principles that are important to you.

There are some elements to think about as you formulate your brand. The elements to consider include your target audience, strengths, skills, values, goals, and vision for the future. Also consider the areas where you are lacking and need to fill in. To get a clear picture of your gap areas, collect feedback from people who support you in your career aspirations. One of the first exercises you can do in forming your brand is to create a headline or tagline for your social media profiles. Your profile should be a reflection of your personal brand and what you can uniquely offer to your audience. Your profile tells audiences what they can expect from you in terms of content and interactions on this social media platform.

Add visual elements

Social media accounts with visuals enable richer and deeper engagement from followers and potential followers. Start by considering visuals for your profile avatar and your profile's background image. Almost all social media platforms provide the ability to include a profile and a background photograph. You should upload a photo that captures your face and shoulders. Having your shoulders visible in a photo has been shown to build more trust. This type of photograph is often called a headshot. For your background image, choose something that relates to your professional profile and ensure that it works well when displayed together with your headshot. It could be a location or related to an area of interest you have in technology, for example. Select a high-quality photograph for both your headshot and your background photograph. Profiles will look different depending on the social media network or service you are using.

Your profiles will include slightly different elements, depending on the social media platform. The following are a few examples for your reference:

- **LinkedIn**: About section and title – use a tagline or keywords

- **Twitter**: Bio, tagline, keywords, location, and URL

- **Facebook**: Bio section

- **Blogs**: Bio section and social media channels

Think of a simple and concise headline for your profile. You should use a similar headline or bio across various social media vehicles. The profile should have a concise description, including a photo and your real name. For your description, think about your purpose and your brand. Take the following example:

I help x (audience, people) to achieve or improve x so that they can x

GitHub is often referred to as a resume or CV for technical professionals. You should definitely ensure you have a GitHub account. Include your username and also any repositories that you contribute to your social media bio.

Virtual reality/the metaverse is a growing area to watch. As you participate in this realm, remember to keep your online personality in this area consistent with the rest of your platforms.

Creating content

Think about how you express your brand in writing and conversation. Determine keywords and hashtags that are relevant to you and your career. Ask questions, comment, and repost/share posts related to these areas.

Select keywords and hashtags that you want to incorporate for posting and engaging with content. For instance, if you are a Java developer, you would want to focus on keywords and hashtags relevant to your area of expertise, such as machine learning, artificial intelligence, microservices, big data, developers, careers, language features, and Java releases. Incorporate these keywords and hashtags into your posts and utilize multiple hashtags per post.

Think about the areas of content and topics that you want to generate content for. You should designate core and related topics and ensure you spend the majority of your time and posts on your core topics. For a few suggestions, refer to the following list:

- Core topics: Things you spend the majority of your time doing
- Related topics: Things you spend 30-40% of your time doing
- Your open source project
- Volunteering activities
- Reading (blogs, books)
- Events
- Hobbies

Maintain a list of keywords, hashtags, and topics that you would like to post content on and ensure you are continually giving your audience this content.

Now that you have a guide for the topics you should post, start to think about ways to capture attention and engagement by asking questions and sharing stories in your content. Some popular types of content include the following:

- Lists
- How to ...
- Learn ...
- Steps to ...
- Tips and tricks
- Tutorials
- Articles
- Videos
- Events
- Quizzes
- Polls
- Challenges
- Discussions
- Technical content – docs or code samples

Think about your content in storytelling terms. German novelist and playwright Gustav Freytag developed a model for dramatic structure, later named **Freytag's Pyramid**. It is based on the classical five-act play and includes the following element:

1. **Introduction**: This is the beginning of the story and incorporates expository information, such as the setting and characters, as well as any backstory information on the characters. This introduces the key elements of the story as well as an inciting incident that puts the plot into action.

2. **Turning point/progressive complication/rising action**: Once the inciting incident occurs, rising action and complications start to happen. This can bring us to the high point of the story.

3. **Climax**: This rising action results in the high point or climax of the story. The main character faces obstacles, potentially a villain character in the story arc.

4. **Falling action**: Following the climax, there is a falling action or uncertainty around the outcome of the story.

5. **Resolution**: The resolution brings the close of the story, and completes any unanswered questions or issues with the characters.

The following is a simplified example:

- **Inciting incident**: I walk into work on a rainy day.

- **Turning point/progressive complication**: There are multiple projects being worked on throughout the office. Some of the services go down.

- **Climax**: Customers are panicking and calling support.

- **Falling action**: I resolve the issue for a top client.

- **Resolution**: This catches the attention of management who note my excellent performance under pressure.

You can also modify this format with a couple of other variations on the method:

Variation #1

1. Hook
2. Context
3. Challenge
4. Conflict
5. Resolution
6. Transition
7. Lessons

Variation #2

1. Hook

2. Context

3. Problem/solution

4. Solution #1

5. Solution #2

6. Lessons

Now that you have some content for your social media feed, think about creating a regular cadence for posting the content. You should aim to post at least five times a week, and possibly more frequently, up to a few times a day. You can schedule your content using a social media calendar or tools. Consider dedicating one day a week to planning your posts for the week. This approach can be effective to ensure that you are not spending too much time on social media channels. While social media can be an effective tool to advance your career, you want to be certain to balance the time you are spending on it with your development work. Scheduling and planning out your posts for the week can assist in limiting the time you spend and avoiding the dreaded doom scrolling, that is, endlessly scrolling through your timeline or media feed(s).

Reaching out to people

In order to achieve that "network effect" of social media, you need to build your social connections and network on the selected social media channels. In order to do that, you need to continue to be authentic and allow your audience to know, like, and trust you. This can be achieved by teaching, inspiring, and connecting with them. People respond to positive people who support them, lift them up, and inspire them. Inspired people inspire people, as the saying goes. How do you start to do this? You need to share yourself. Show your face and let your audience get to know you and about you in the content that you post. If your content is consistent with your profile, people know that they can trust you, which puts you in a prime position to start reaching out to build your network on social media.

Similarly, as with the topic and keywords you identified to utilize in your content, identify your ideal followers or audience in these areas. You can use your keywords and hashtags to identify the people you would like to connect with in these areas. Make a list of the top 10-20 people and/or corporate accounts that you would like to connect with. Follow them and comment on their posts. Look for ways to engage with them on a regular basis and have meaningful conversations. Consider when you have some value to offer them to send them a private message or **direct message** (**DM**). You can give them compliments, offer solutions, and answer their questions. Follow people who are influential in your space. You should share the content you create, tagging these people. The key is to engage with these people and accounts. Ask more questions and go into details. You can also ask a repeat version of a question you posted in the comments on their posts. We advised you to tell stories when creating your content. You can also share stories and examples as you engage with people in your network on their social media feeds. Share things from your life and your career or business. This makes you more relatable, but also more interesting.

If you want to experience more engagement, be more engaged! Continue conversations in comments and be willing to offer your advice and expertise. Building relationships takes time, but you can effectively build relationships over social media. You must be authentic and consistent. And above all, focus on true connections, not on numbers.

Think about incorporating calls to action and links in your posts, as well as more videos, photographs, and infographics. You can also investigate tools to help improve the quality of your media content or to manage your content. Some of these tools are Prequel, InShot, Facetune, FaceApp, Canva, Feedly, RiteTag, Hootsuite, and TweetDeck. Consider how you can use these tools to track your network activity and engagement to build your network and connect with more people.

There can be potential challenges with social media, such as managing your time and avoiding regrets. Time management is key in all your career endeavors. Just like any other activity, you need to balance the time you invest. Social media is a valuable tool, but you need to manage the time you devote to spending on social media. Schedule it into your day, at a time that works best for you, and monitor your use and time to ensure that you are allowing time for your other priorities and responsibilities. Since you have immediate and constant access to social media through your phone or other devices at any time, it is an activity that warrants close monitoring regarding the time spent using it. Set time limits and boundaries.

One other thing to keep in mind with your use of social media is that the internet has a long memory. Once you have said something on the internet, it lasts forever. It is best to act with caution in your social media posts, as well as your likes and shares, comments, and retweets. Keep your professional brand and goals for social media in mind as you post and determine which posts are appropriate to like or share. Those decisions will be considered by the public as endorsements or reflections on your brand.

Finally, when you are reaching out to people online, keep in mind networking etiquette and best practices. Let people know how they can help you but be careful not to place pressure on them. A good first step is to ask questions and gather information. Respect that other people have their own time limits and boundaries. Reciprocate when someone offers to make a connection for you or a reference. Share knowledge with people and be free with your praise and compliments. Remember to stay connected after an initial introduction or conversation and always send a thank you.

Interviews

Mary Grygleski

Q: Hi, Mary. How are you today? I'm so happy you're going to be sharing with us a little bit about your career. Why don't we start with you telling us your full name and what you're doing now in your career, and how you got started in your career as a developer?

A: My name is Mary Grygleski. I'm currently the developer advocate for the streaming team at DataStax.

DataStax is a company that primarily does Apache Cassandra and open source stuff. Then, two years ago, they started also incorporating Apache Pulsar to support more new features, such as event streaming, so I got hired for the streaming team.

I'm a developer advocate, so I go out and do outreach work: doing presentations, going to conferences, and contributing to books such as this one. There are a lot of virtual conferences and outreach opportunities, and I enjoy it a lot.

As for how I got here, it's actually very interesting. I didn't start out as a developer advocate. I was a math and computer science major many years ago, and at that time, computer science was still new. Oracle was just starting to become popular and the SQL standard was just starting, so that tells you how old I am! All those things were starting to brew, so I was thinking, "Oh, I just want to be a programmer." I didn't know about the internet yet; I liked the more lower-level-compiler/operating-system-type work. I thought I would try to work there, but it wasn't as easy to find jobs in those areas.

I started off as a developer programmer for a chemical company, in the IT department, and that's how I started my work. I was working on older stuff, such as Fortran and a very old, pre-relational database. Eventually, I got more C and Unix work in the 1990s. That's when Java was also born, and so I became interested in that too. I joined Sybase because they were a way into doing enterprise-level Java. I was mostly a development engineer there.

I did not think I would become a speaker. I was more of a typical nerd: head down, coding, working with fancy algorithms. But eventually, it just started to get to me. After 15 years of working like that, I wanted to do something different, but I was not quite sure what it was.

And then, at the time, I was also in the middle of moving with my family. I moved to Chicago, and there weren't as many product engineering jobs there. I got into doing a bit more application-level engineering and application development work, and then I worked at the Chicago Mercantile Exchange on the financial use of Java. That gave me a new appreciation of things, learning about the user side.

So, long story short, I was following this path and I felt like something was missing. In the meantime too, I attended a couple of conferences. Conferences were beginning to become a thing. Of course, JavaOne started, which I went to an early version of – it was exciting. I realized I really liked something but didn't quite know what it was.

Fast forward to the early 2010s, and it was time to take the plunge. I saw that user groups were becoming a thing. I joined the Chicago Java user group, and I started attending a lot. At the time, Freddy was the president, and he said, "Oh, why don't you come and help?" I said, "OK. Why not?" I attended every single meetup; I never missed it. I like talking with people, getting to know them, and finding out what's going on. I found myself learning a lot that way, just by interacting with people, and that's how I got involved with CJUG.

Eventually, Freddy moved away and I became president. To this day, I'm the president – I didn't even imagine that happening! And because of my involvement with CJUG, I also got opportunities. Because of my interaction with the community, people began to know who I was. CJUG used to have lightning talks by members, and I remember the first time I thought of doing it. I was really nervous; preparing for a five-minute talk took me two weeks! But that was the start of my speaking career. Once you've got over that hump, you realize, "Oh, it isn't so bad."

I started doing a bit more community talking. IBM was forming the Java advocacy team at the time, and because of my involvement in the community, people started to know me, which meant I got the opportunity to become a Java developer advocate at IBM.

That's how I started my career as a developer advocate. After five years, I'm still an advocate, I'm traveling a lot, and I absolutely love it. It's all down to the community and talking with people. I just find I have this need, even though I'm still an engineer in some ways. I would like to be by myself, thinking of things and solving problems, but I also really like interacting with people. It gives me another level of appreciation. It's something I really enjoy: talking and meeting with people.

Q: Being a developer advocate, like you said, combines those two. You're a developer and you also talk about it, so you developed all the skills that are required.

How has using social media helped you in your career? What are some examples of things that have helped you to open new relationships in your career through participating on social media? How do you use social media?

A: Currently, I have social media. I use Twitter; a lot of the Java community uses Twitter too to communicate about what's going on in Java. I think it's good, because you start to see the names of people if they are more vocal. You start to see people and people start to see you, and you can be tagged by people. That's important too. You can be the best out there, but if nobody knows you, it doesn't mean much. You need social media to advertise yourself, to make yourself known. It's not about boasting. As a professional, you need to make yourself known, because the more people know you, the more trust you build with people that are following you or looking for somebody like you.

As a developer advocate, I advertise all the product capabilities my company has. In some ways, it's part of my work; I need to rely on social media. Through that medium, I can essentially bring messages to the world, so that is very important.

I also have a Twitch stream, although I have to admit these days I'm traveling too much to consistently do many streams. But I have to say, with the pandemic, during those two or three years of not being able to travel, I developed my skills too because initially, I had never really streamed before. Through trial and error, I started to learn how to do it.

Because of my Twitch stream, people started following me – they are quite loyal too. I also set up a Discord server so I can then communicate with people outside Twitch. I met people from Norway, India, Malaysia… everybody was following me – it was amazing. Then, I was in Oslo for JavaZone, and a guy from Twitch came out to see me, even though he was busy. That was amazing, to meet him in person.

It's interesting to get to know people and learn what their world is like. That's what I like to do: it's not just about me when I meet people. As a developer advocate, I'm building up developer relations. That's how you build a relationship: you let people know you, and then you have a common interest. I didn't just meet the guy in Norway, but another person in Lithuania also. We got to meet in Vilnius, and these days he asks me whether I can help him with stuff and for mentoring.

It's amazing. It feels like there is a ripple effect after you meet with people all over the world. You realize their problems, their aspirations: everything is just the same. But the thing is, it's nice to share, so you can then help people.

Q: You gave two great examples of using Twitter for your job but also to establish trust, which is something that we talked about earlier in the book: that's important to advance your career. You also mentioned looking for opportunities during the pandemic and using Twitch to expand your network and communicate via Discord.

Do you have any tips for time management? Sometimes people can get easily distracted with social media. Do you have any tools or techniques that you've used to balance social media with other things that you need to do in your career, such as development work or writing presentations?

A: It is all about constant context-switching.

To borrow computer terms, I'm in an operating system where I find myself having to context switch all the time. It is a challenge; it's not easy. I could be writing proposals for a conference six or nine months ahead of time, and then there are also proposals for talks that I'm planning to do that need writing. Then there are things that I need to do for tomorrow's conference!

I don't know whether there are any tips, but one thing is true: there's just no time for regrets. When I was an engineer, I used to think, "Oh, I didn't do this well," and then I would just lament over the thing I didn't do well: that consumes energy and time. But these days, because everything happens so fast, I have to keep doing something and just look ahead, which I actually enjoy thoroughly; I find I don't even pay any attention to regrets. I have no regrets, basically. If I make mistakes, I make mistakes. I just keep going. I think that might be the best way.

I just have my goals. Every day, I know what I need to do. I write down a list of things I need to do – interviews, streaming on Twitch, presentations, flight reservations. I know what I need to do, and then I go through them.

It does take up a lot of time. Sometimes I need to do some things over the weekend as well, but that's just part of the job. Because of how passionate I am about doing what I do, I don't even mind.

So, the point is that there is no time to regret and look back. Just keep going. I developed this skill, and it's great because there's really no point in regretting things. Whatever you do every day, it's a joy. Just embrace it, whether good or bad. The more you embrace it, the better you get at it. That is just part of life – it extends beyond just being a developer advocate.

Maybe it's not for everybody, but for me it certainly works. I find myself being a better person because of it. I don't regret things now. If I make mistakes, I just say, "OK." My skin is getting thicker and I don't really worry. Let other people criticize me. That's my way of handling it.

Q: That makes sense. I read something about that just a couple of days ago. I was talking about lamenting things that may have happened in the past: you're the only one who's thinking about it – no one else even remembers, most likely. You're only taking up more of your time thinking about what you shouldn't have done or should have done. Keep moving forward. Amazing advice.

Congratulations on your career success, and thank you so much for sharing your story.

A: Thank you, Heather.

Trisha Gee

Q: Welcome, Trisha Gee. Thanks for agreeing to be in the book.

A: I'm Trisha, currently working at Gradle, a Java Champion and lead developer advocate – or developer evangelist. These titles are all a bit fluffy, aren't they?

I got into programming when I was quite young – 9 or 10 – like a lot of people do, but I did take a very classical route. I'm from the UK, and I did computer science at A level, which is from 16 to 18, and then I did a computer science degree: computer science and artificial intelligence.

That was a fairly classical way to get into a programming-type role. I was very lucky in that I went to university from 1997 to 2001; they were teaching Java, and we were the first year to learn it. So, we got really lucky. I'd already done a bit of programming before then. I did Pascal at school, and I did Basic before then. Then I did an internship at Ford while I was at university, and we did a little bit of ASP and VB and things like that. But really, it was when I got into Java at university that I thought, "Oh, right. This feels like something I can get. I understand how it works."

When I left university in 2001, there were lots and lots of roles in Java: JSP was a new thing, servlets were a new thing, and the web was a fairly new thing. I'd been doing web stuff when I worked at Ford in my internship. So, looking back, it was fairly easy to fall into a Java job. It wasn't because it was 2001: it was during the dotcom crash, and things were a bit tricky. The thing that really helped me out was having an undergraduate internship, as well as a computer science degree and a working background in writing web apps in Java and ASP.

One thing eased my passage: my dad is a careers teacher, and he said that when you come out of university, there are going to be a lot of people who have the same qualifications as you, and you have to stand out from the crowd and get in the door for those first few roles. An internship or sponsored student program is a good way to get hands-on experience in a real-world organization. Then, you can use that to open doors to everything you could possibly want. In 2001, when the crash was happening, it was really important that I had 18 months of actual work experience and my degree to go out and find myself that first job.

As for those first few jobs, in the early noughties, a lot of what we had was web development-type roles. I did a bunch of stuff with JSP, servlets, Java backends, and a bit of JavaScript on the frontend too in Netscape and Internet Explorer. (Nobody uses any of those things anymore!)

The thing that's interesting to tell juniors is that your first few roles are not necessarily indicative of what all jobs in the industry are like. My advice to junior developers is that you've got to have a bit of a Pokémon mindset. You've got to catch them all. You've got to get out there, get your skills, and get skills on your CV. Try taking up jobs that you might not ordinarily be super excited about because what you're trying to do is build up a skill base and learn about what you do and don't enjoy. Learn what different types of companies are like; learn how different teams work. You need to understand that working in a place where you feel uncomfortable doesn't necessarily mean that the whole industry is not for you. There are different domains, different technologies, and different types of roles. I know a bunch of people who went from development into technical writing, business analysis, technical leadership, and architecture. You don't know what's going to suit you until you've had a taste of everything, which is one of the reasons why I jumped around quite a lot in the early few years of my career.

Q: Ace. Obviously, you've been successful, and that's great advice at the beginning: building up your skill set.

Tell us a little bit about how you started once you were into your career, the first few times you got involved in the community, and when you felt like being involved in the technical community made an impact on your career.

A: The community was one of those huge level-up things.

I've played computer games forever, and when you've played a bunch of computer games, you realize that you can just keep plodding along doing what you're supposed to do, but what you're really looking for is those magic coins that give you that extra ability, help you get more experience, and help you to move on. For me, the community was one of those things. You can be perfectly successful in your career without these things – without community and so forth – by being good at your job, finding the right niche, and continuing to work in that niche. But for me, the community was a huge level-up.

I worked in New York for a year, and then I came back to London. I'd already worked in London. I had friends and a network there, but this was in 2008. (This was after the next recession. This is a common theme for me, it seems: as the recessions hit things, I decide to make major changes in my career!)

I came back to London in 2008, which was an important decision for me. At that point, I had about 10 years of experience as a Java developer, but I wouldn't call myself senior: more like mid-to-senior level. I was looking for my next role. I was looking for something. I had worked in the city, in London, beforehand. I'd been working in finance in New York as a consultant, and I found that interesting and challenging. At this point in my career, I was able to know the sorts of things I didn't like, the sorts of places I didn't want to work, and what was going to interest me.

Now, if you speak to recruitment agents to try and get yourself a new job, you can keep having those calls and interviews and going on-site to meet all these people, but what I found when I lived in New York was that there's a great website called `meetup.com` where you can meet people who have similar interests. So, when I moved back to London, I used it to join the London Java Community. I was going to Java meetup events and I was learning about technologies that I was not familiar with, such as AWS. Spring had moved on a bunch, so I was learning about new things in Spring. I was speaking to a lot of people who worked for gambling technology companies; London has a bunch of gambling technology, finance, gaming, and mobile app companies. I was talking to lots of people who worked in these different types of companies, getting a feel for the technologies they use, how they work, what they like about their job, and what they do not like about their job.

Firstly, I used the community in a very selfish way, if you like, to figure out what my next job was going to be and to try and get that next job. It didn't directly help me get that next job, but it did open my eyes to what was around and what people were doing. It got me interested in speaking events and the fact that apparently, normal human beings can speak at these types of events! It's not just experts and book authors; any old developer can do it.

After I got my next job, which happened to be at LMAX, working with Dave Farley and a bunch of other people who ended up becoming quite famous afterward, I was still going to the London Java Community. I got more involved in helping to organize community events and trying to create slightly different types of events, because what I was really looking for was something more networky and more people-talky than just presentations.

Then, I started giving my first couple of presentations and stuff. My first presentation was on the JCP: what the JCP is, what the JSR is, and what the executive committee is. It was a 15-minute introductory presentation, because the LJC had just joined the JCP at the time. Gradually, over a couple of years or so, that really helped me. It gave me a lot of visibility into the technical community, what people were doing, what was relevant, and what wasn't relevant.

Then, at LMAX, we open sourced a technology called the Disruptor. We wrote a white paper on it. We were doing developer-advocacy-type stuff early on: this was about 2010. As a result of that, the Disruptor won the Duke's Choice Award and we got a ticket for someone in the company to attend JavaOne. My boss was already going because he was presenting, so they gave the ticket to me because I'd done a bunch of work around getting the Disruptor known out there.

I went to JavaOne 2011, and that was where the whole community thing just exploded for me in a very positive way. I went with Martin Thompson, who knew a bunch of people in the performance field: people like Kirk Pepperdine and the folks at Azul, and a bunch of other folks who are really well known in the Java performance space. But I was also there with Martijn Verburg, and he knew a bunch of people from the community, from the JCP, and from user groups. I got introduced to a huge range of people. I wasn't just parachuted into a conference and stuck on my own, going, "Oh, I don't really know anyone." I didn't know many people when I got there, but by the end of it, I had made all these amazing connections in a few different areas: user groups, the JCP, performance, and open source. My career was just never the same after that.

I actually co-presented with Martin there, but it wasn't so much the presenting – it was just about the community that was physically there at JavaOne, making those connections, and being included in those groups automatically without having to fight my way in.

From there on, everything snowballed. I had new job opportunities. I had more speaking opportunities. After doing that one thing at JavaOne, I got four or five speaking opportunities off the back of it. I made a bunch of new friends. I ended up doing more blog posts, and I got a following on my blogs. That's what steered me into the developer advocacy thing: JavaOne and meeting the community.

Q: Yes. I remember meeting you there. It's amazing how that pivoted your career, or amplified all the things you'd already been doing to gain skills.

You've started to talk about blogs. Can you share a story about how you have used social media to advance your career?

A: I ended up going to work for Thoughtworks around 2011. Whenever I wasn't placed with a client, I had time to start writing blog posts, which I'd wanted to do for a long time. I had been on Twitter for probably about four years, and a friend of mine, Simon Brown, spoke at conferences and was on Twitter sharing the things he was writing. I thought of him as being way better than me, but he was ultimately at a peer level of me, and he was doing these sorts of things. So, I thought, "Oh, I could write blog posts and tweet about them, and I could get involved in building this kind of audience and community."

It happened very organically. I would write a bunch of blog posts about stuff that I hadn't really understood very well; once I figured it out, I'd write it down. I wrote a bunch of stuff about being a woman in tech because people always want to know what it's like being a woman in tech. I wrote a bunch of stuff about why I got really annoyed about being asked about being a woman in tech because it's very frustrating.

I just wrote about stuff that I wanted to know about, stuff that was based on personal experience. Is it frightening to do that? It's a bit difficult to get started because you're worried that people are going to say, "Oh, I can't believe you didn't know that," or you worry about people piling on about the women in tech thing, which they do sometimes. But ultimately, if you write about these things and people say, "Oh, that's really interesting. I didn't know that," you get a nice positive feedback loop. If you start putting it on Twitter, then you get more people following you because they see that you tweet about your content.

Later on, before I started working at JetBrains, I would read (especially when I had a commute) a lot of interesting blog posts, because I was a big reader. Every time I read stuff, if it was really interesting, I would put a really short summary on Twitter with a link to the blog post. People started following me because I would tweet interesting and relevant stuff with a TL;DR so they don't even need to read the blog post.

So, I started to develop a social media following because I'm a developer who's interested in stuff and wants to share that stuff, not because I have any particular high-level expertise in one area. I'm just interested in stuff; let me share what I'm interested in with you. That's how I organically grew a lot of my social network.

The other thing was when I started going to conferences more. At conferences, we would use Twitter a lot: you use the conference hashtag and you start talking about the sessions that you're seeing or the observations that you've made. I made quite a few friends that way because you'd end up chatting to people who were using the same hashtag.

I remember I was at JAX London. I didn't really know anyone at that conference, but because I was tweeting quite a lot, a few people came up to me – and obviously, there are not many women either. So, people would say, "You must be Trisha. You've been tweeting a bunch about this conference." They come up to you and talk to you, and you make friends and expand your community and your network. That's how I met a whole bunch of people that I now consider to be friends and peers in the industry.

Twitter was really important to me in terms of building a following but also finding a voice. What is it that you're good at? What works for you, what resonates with you, and what do people like about the things that you do? That can help you steer your career as well. That's how I ended up in advocacy. One of the things I'm good at is taking stuff that's complicated, condensing it down, and sharing it with people. Then, because that's the sort of thing that you do, people approach you and say, "Do you want to work for us?" or, "Do you want to write an article in our magazine on these sorts of topics?" or, "Do you want to present at our conference? These are the sorts of things that we want you to present on." It's a positive feedback loop where the more that you do stuff, the more followers you get, the more opportunities come your way, and the more you say yes to those things. Then, you can end up in videos from conferences on YouTube, and you're answering questions on YouTube and you've got a completely different social media platform to follow.

Again, a bit like the Pokémon thing, it's all about trying to gather things for yourself, doing what works for you, using the things that you're good at, and amplifying those things.

Q: It's really interesting how it's advanced your career: meeting people.

I'm wondering if you have any tips to share about consuming technology – Twitter, LinkedIn, YouTube. How do you make strategies for learning or finding content so that you can also have time to do your actual development and the work that you need to produce?

A: That is really tricky.

I actually have a couple of talks on this topic. I used to curate the newsletter when I worked at JetBrains. I used to do the Java Annotated Monthly, and that was quite challenging because it was a case of really staying up to date with the news, consuming it, and figuring out what was relevant and what wasn't. When I was in London, it was a little bit easier because I had commute time, and you just use that time to skim through the things that seem either the noisiest or the most interesting. I got used to that kind of thing – particularly skimming stuff rather than reading things in depth, to get a feel for what's happening in trends and technologies.

That's something that I tend to do on the go. If I'm commuting or waiting for the kids outside school, or if I happen to have half an hour to myself in a bar or while I'm waiting for something, then I will try and skim-read stuff. I'm not great at skim-reading because I get really engrossed and I read things properly, but I will try and just skim through stuff quickly on the go, and because you're doing it on the go, it forces you not to go too deep. It just gives you an idea of, "Oh, this is vaguely what this technology is for. I see what some of these viewpoints are."

My whole thing about staying up to date as a technologist is that it is impossible to know everything that's going on. For juniors in particular, my main advice for them is this: don't get overwhelmed by the fact that there's so much stuff out there because it's impossible to stay up to date, and therefore it's absolutely fine to focus only on the things that you find interesting.

For example, I decided I'm only really interested in core Java – Java the language. I have used Groovy. Obviously, I've used Kotlin. I've done the tiniest amount of Scala. With those sorts of things, I vaguely stay abreast. If there's a major release, I want to see vaguely what's in it. I'm not going to read the release notes but I might read someone else's summary of what's interesting about it, but I'm not going to go away and learn that language. I'm going to do that for Java.

When Java 9 came out, I spent quite a lot of time investigating: what are the things that are potentially going to break? What are the new features? Why is it challenging to migrate? Because that was interesting to me and to people who follow me on social media. What they expect from me is to do that hard work so that I can tell them, "Don't worry about this. Do worry about that."

So, you want to focus on the things that are interesting to you, and it's fine to ignore the stuff that's not interesting. It's fine to just read the headlines and think, "Oh, OK. There's a new version of Angular. Great. OK. That's all I need to worry about right now." It's fine to then dive in later. Let's say you move to a new job that uses Angular: then you can do the tutorials and read more about it. But you don't have to stay an expert on absolutely everything because you won't use 99.9 percent of it. You're only going to use a small amount of it.

But it is worth surfing that tsunami of news. I tend to pick through headlines and things to take the pulse of what's going on. Twitter's useful for that, in that you can take the pulse of what people are talking about. It's not super structured, though, and the algorithms obviously have changed a bit lately. I use Twitter to try and hear from more diverse voices. In the past, when I started, I had a lot of technology news on my Twitter. Now, I hear a lot more about people's experiences, from people who are not necessarily middle-aged white men who work for Twitter. Some of the stuff I get is really eye-opening, but it's not necessarily, "Here's what's new in Angular." It depends a lot on what you want to learn and how you want to learn it.

Q: That is a good point to make – it depends. What you're going to learn about is based on who you're following, so try to make sure that the people that you choose to follow are people whose viewpoints you're interested in, and make sure that it's diverse.

A: Exactly. Especially because the algorithms tend to feed you stuff, I got quite particular about the types of people I was following and the types of tweets I was liking or re-sharing, because I'm aware that I'm feeding the algorithm. If I like something, I know that I'm going to get more of that back. I always make a push to follow as many women techies on Twitter as possible. I don't have to do it but I think that it's important for us to amplify each other's voices because otherwise, we tend to get drowned among everyone else. I generally follow women techies and people from underrepresented groups more than others. Well, I follow plenty of the other folks as well, but I make a deliberate effort to go out and find women techies and people who are not necessarily from the UK or the US – people from different backgrounds.

Q: I think that's good, but you just have to be deliberate about it because the algorithm typically will feed you more of the same, which is just more typical mainstream content, so you have to make an effort to go out there and find diverse perspectives, either from different parts of the world, different parts of the industry, a different gender, or other different underrepresented groups out there.

A: I know that there is a fair argument for how we shouldn't have to do this, but the way the world is right now means that if you want to combat institutionalized bias, which is not always intentional, you have to be intentional about the changes you want to make, particularly as algorithms, machine learning, and AI start to become even more prevalent. We have to be aware of the fact that the way the world currently is is being fed as a model into these computers, so we will continually get the way the world currently is fed back to us as the way the world is or should be. We need to be very deliberate about the fact that our experiences as white middle-class people in Western Europe – for example – are not the same as the experiences of developers in Africa, India, or any other place. It's important to hear from others in any context, but particularly when it comes to AI. The kind of information we're feeding into our models is not complete. It doesn't cover everyone's experiences.

Q: That's always been an interesting aspect for me: the training of AI models and what's going into them and trying to educate about that, so thanks for sharing that.

Summary

In this chapter, we covered the basics of social media for technical career development, personal versus professional social media usage, how to build your online presence, and how to reach out to people and have meaningful and career-advancing conversations on social media.

In the next chapter, we will discuss how in-person conferences, or even sometimes virtual conferences, can be used to advance your career.

10
Build Lasting Relationships

In-person conferences, or even sometimes virtual conferences, can be used to advance your career. Although online relationships can help advance your career, nothing beats in-person contact. In-person events and conferences can connect you to important people and companies, and create a deeper engagement with your network. This chapter will show you the steps to add conferences to your career-building toolkit.

Here's what we'll specifically cover in this chapter:

- How conferences can boost your career
- Finding the best conferences to attend
- Time and money – making your attendance worthwhile
- Making conference attendance an asset for your boss and your company
- Goal stacking – how to guarantee results while attending a conference

Let's begin!

How conferences can boost your career

Conferences can boost your career through deep and long-lasting relationships. So, how do you form these relationships? You network with recruiters and engineers from companies you want to work for in the future while you attend conferences. You may be surprised to find that job offers can result from your efforts to engage with people at conferences. These interactions can form the basis for relationships that may result in opportunities for career opportunities – maybe not now but, more likely, in the future. Most job offers are a result of an introduction via a connection in your network. You may be able to apply for jobs in the future based on some of these interactions. Conferences are a great opportunity to improve your networking skills. Take the time to practice your skills by considering some alternative responses to common and expected questions. You can do this via conversation framing by asking questions, instead of being the one always answering the questions. Guide and frame the conversation in the way you want to steer it, instead of just answering questions.

One ideal response to a routine question is "The better question is…" Be prepared with specific and unique questions that are of interest to you rather than generic or basic small talk questions. As you attend more conferences, your network will expand, and you will be able to connect with even more people. Conferences are an ideal place to connect with other like-minded people in your field. They give you the opportunity to introduce yourself to other people. If you continue to build on your experiences and attendance and be persistent, you will begin to see concrete rewards as a result of these efforts. When you add the intense and intimate setting of a conference and repeat meetings with common interests and continued online interactions, you will find a deeper relationship that can be longer lasting than relationships that are formed through solely online interactions.

You will not only build deep and long-lasting relationships that will boost your career through attending conferences, but you will also learn new things that can help you to advance your career. You can enhance your learning about technologies you already know and use in your work. You can also learn about new technologies, trends, or innovations and new uses for those technologies. The conference is also a place to learn about projects you can join or start as you network with people and hear about their experiences with them. In this smaller and more intimate environment, you will forge bonds and initiate project engagement that can happen through shared experiences.

While you will experience these benefits most profoundly via in-person events, you can also enjoy learning, networking, and forming relationships via online conferences. There are some events where discussions and interactive experiences can help to boost your career. In most cases, these events are better suited to learning, as opposed to interaction, but having a mix of events – some for learning, and some with more in-person interaction – is a strategy that can offer complementary engagement in conferences, allowing you to participate in a greater number of conferences over time.

Finding the best conferences to attend

How do you find the right conferences to attend? Most likely, you have discovered conferences in your area of expertise from co-workers, colleagues, and the internet. Research those conferences by looking at their websites and social media presence. Look at their agendas and review some of the sessions from preview editions. Evaluate the quality of the speakers, the content, and the recordings. You should also review the social media posts from previous editions of the event. Ask members of your team at work and members of any meetups or user groups you attend to share their conference experiences as well. One trend in event organization is that events are becoming smaller and much more focused locally and regionally. There may be one flagship event and then several regional or local events in various regions, based on the main flagship event. You don't need to wait to attend the biggest, most international event in your field. You can find an event reasonably close to you to start your experience and then build from there. Once you start attending conferences, you will find that you discover more and more opportunities, exponentially. You may even decide to travel to conferences outside of your local area, country, or continent.

Since software developers need to know a variety of tools and techniques to complete their work, they need to learn about various programming languages, data structure/algorithms, object-oriented design, database and system design, operating systems, cryptology, source control, cloud platforms, frameworks, and so on. As we discussed earlier in this book, the amount of learning required, both in advance of getting hired and during your career, can be overwhelming. All of these types of tools and techniques have conferences to support the developers and their communities. Use the criteria we discussed to determine which areas you most enjoy and also the conferences that have something to learn from and/or something you want to share with others. Where do your passions lie? Research the conferences in those areas. Once you have attended some conferences, evaluate your experiences at the conference to decide whether it is something you would like to repeat in the future. There are a variety of aspects to consider, including what you learn, social interactions, ancillary events at the event, and other factors that may be crucial to your experience.

If you can't go to all of the best conferences, ask people you trust, respect, and admire about their conference experiences. If they describe an event that sounds interesting and appealing to you, make a plan to attend one of the conferences with them. You might have a desire to attend one of the biggest and most popular events. You will want to consider the bigger events – nearly every platform will have one. In the Java community, the flagship international event is the JavaOne conference. This is the event that draws Java developers from all over the world and has been held since the early days of the technology. This event provides a unique conference experience that doesn't compare to any other. If you are a Java developer, this is an event that you will want to experience at least once. There are also many smaller events and regional events that you can attend. You may decide that you prefer to attend one type of event or another, or you may want to attend a mix of events. This could mean that you attend multiple events a year, or you may alternate events on an annual basis. There are plenty of events to choose from, but overall, deciding on the best events for you will be a largely personal decision, based on your preferences as well as your goals for attending events.

What are your goals for attending events? Remember to go back to your SMART goal framework:

- **S: Smart**
- **M: Measurable**
- **A: Achievable**
- **R: Relevant**
- **T: Time-bound**

Do you want to learn new skills or enhance your current skills? Do you want to network and meet people? Do you want to participate in hands-on activities and get involved in more projects? Depending on your goals, you may choose different events. There are events that will help you to meet your goals. Do your research, and share your experiences while you read the experiences of others to determine which conferences are best for you.

Time and money – making your attendance worthwhile

There is a cost to attend conferences. How do you make the costs of both your time and money worth the investment? The word *investment* is intentionally selected here because it is an investment in yourself. It costs you both your time and money – travel costs, food and beverage costs, and potentially, time you could be billing for compensation at an hourly rate. There are some best practices for attending conferences that will help you to make your attendance worthwhile.

When you are attending conferences, introduce yourself to others – this is the best way to get something out of the experience. When you introduce yourself, remember to be authentic. Be yourself in personality and appearance. Ask for their contact information and social media details. Make sure to follow up with a message, and be specific with your follow-up.

Review the conference schedule in advance – sketch out a flexible schedule and select the sessions you would like to attend in advance. One option is to attend the session with someone you just met at the conference.

Make an effort to attend the sessions. You may be tempted to complete work projects, attend meetings for work, or catch up on emails. However, in order to make your attendance at conferences worthwhile, you need to resist this urge and attend as many sessions as possible. You might be thinking that most of the sessions at conferences these days are recorded, so you will watch them online later. Will you really watch them later? Or, if you do watch them later, will you pay attention, or will you be distracted and multi-tasking? While you are attending sessions, you can think of topics or methods you can present yourself next year at the conference, or other conferences. Share what you have learned on social media, blogs, and so on. Ask questions and introduce yourself to the speakers at the sessions you attend. Voice your opinions confidently and engage in conversations with them. Take the time to express your appreciation to them. Speakers put hours into planning, preparing, and delivering their presentations to audiences.

Go to informal social events. These are some of the most critical moments to network with other attendees, speakers, or conference organizers. You may be tired after a full day of sessions, but if you make the effort to attend, and consider making an effort a vital part of your conference attendance, you will reap more of the rewards of your conference experience. Do not be tempted to catch up on sleep. This is not the time to rest and recover or sit alone in your room. Immediately becoming accustomed to the local time zone is a best practice for global travel and beating jet lag.

Attend the keynotes and closing sessions. The welcome keynotes and closing keynotes are especially valuable because they frame the conference experience. You will not be able to attend all of the sessions during the conference, but the opening keynote will highlight not only the themes for the events but also the top experiences during the week that you will not want to miss. The closing keynote, similarly, will summarize the experiences that happened, giving you a sense of some of the things you may have missed or want to go back to experience. These opening and closing keynotes are also some of the most entertaining and illuminating sessions of the conference. Often, they will include thought-provoking, big-picture concepts relevant in the industry that will not be covered in the smaller conference sessions. Take the opportunity to experience them in person and also to capture some of your favorite moments on social media. This will help to give you visibility at the conference with other conference attendees (make sure to include the hashtags of the conference).

In addition to the social events and keynotes, you should also attend any of the evening sessions. Oftentimes, conferences will hold evening sessions such as birds-of-a-feather sessions, which are typically informal question-and-answer type sessions, or unconference sessions, which are user-directed sessions organized spontaneously without a set agenda or topic announced in advance. Both of these types of sessions are prime opportunities to engage and interact with other attendees and enhance what you learn at the conference.

One of the most underrated aspects of attending conferences is what is often called the "hallway track." This is the time you can use to socialize and hang out in any of the informal spaces in between, before, or after sessions. This is a key time to meet other people, have informal conversations, walk the exposition floor and engage with any exhibitors of interest, and check out any special activities happening on the featured area or stage, hacker areas, or contests happening. These are not only fun but also sometimes result in some of the most valuable interactions during conferences.

Remember to relax and have fun. Be inclusive and make an effort to meet people different from yourself. If you run into any issues or have special requests, you can talk to conference organizers. The organizers want you to have an awesome experience, so don't be afraid to speak up and ask for any accommodations you may need.

Some thoughts about virtual events

There are also an increasing number of virtual (online-only) or hybrid events. In 2020, it became more common for software development conferences to be held in an online format, and also in a hybrid format. A hybrid format is when some people might attend and/or speak in person, while some might attend online. Online conferences provide educational benefits, but it can be challenging to connect, network, and form strong relationships in this format. While you can connect with other people at virtual or hybrid events, it is more difficult and challenging. You can maintain connections with people you have met in the past, and you can make new connections, but the level of engagement will not be as strong. It is difficult to deepen relationships via online or remote/hybrid conferences. That being said, it is not impossible. You should strive for a mix of in-person and online/hybrid events. If you only have the opportunity to attend online events, then, by all means, attend the events that you can online. Take the initiative to initiate connections at these online events. Most of them offer some form of online networking options. When the opportunities to attend in-person events arise, take the steps to attend them. You will be rewarded with richer and more meaningful connections. It is great to attend in person.

Making conference attendance an asset for your boss and your company

In many cases, you are not the only one who is investing time and money for you to attend conferences. If you are employed (unless you are self-employed or an independent contractor), you are also asking your boss and your employer to make an investment in you via time and money. How do you make your conference attendance an asset for your boss and your company? In addition to the steps we outlined in the previous section, you will want to plan your conference selections and attendance based on how your employer will benefit from the experience, not just how you, personally, will benefit.

You can view the conference keeping in mind how the content you learn will benefit any projects you work on for your employer. This can be a project you work on with your team, a project by another team, or a cross-organizational project. Bringing back the knowledge you learn and applying it to either your team or another team will make the experience an asset to your boss and your company.

You may even be able to bring back lessons learned to help inform your employer about a potential project you plan to work on in the near future. Search for these opportunities in advance of your conference attendance. Think about projects and technologies that your employer may benefit from, and have conversations with members of the leadership team about their priorities and trends. This showcases you as an asset to your employer and positions you as a proactive strategic thinker and solver of the problems facing your business. This also reinforces your plan to attend conferences for your own professional development, as well as for the benefit of the company and future projects. This will put you in a position that few software developers will be in – poised for opportunities to advance.

In addition to bringing back knowledge for your employer, you can share the work your employer and your team undertake at the conference. This could be either informally via networking and conversations, or it could be via a more formal presentation (just be sure to obtain the necessary review and clearance before disclosing information about your employer in public). This positions your employer as a top choice and your boss as an asset to that employer. Attracting and retaining top talent is a valuable asset to your employer. You can also search for potential talent and refer people who you meet at conferences to your network, filling specific needs and roles your team or employer may have.

Goal stacking – how to guarantee results while attending a conference

If you want to guarantee success and results while attending a conference, get specific about your goals. Even better, be **SMARTER** about your goals. Make these kinds of goals for each conference you attend (and use this model in general as well). Review your goals before, during, and after your conference experience. If you can dream it and draft goals around it, you can achieve it. Make at least three goals for each conference you attend. They can be in various categories – learning, networking, project-based, for personal professional development, or for the benefit of your employer. They can be aspirational to achieve a new position or become a speaker or mentor. Articulate what it is that you intend to achieve. What are your intentions with this experience? You can guarantee your results if you put your mind to achieving the goals set.

For example, here are three goals when attending your next conference:

- Learn four new features in the upcoming Java release

- Gather experience in two different corporate migrations to the latest Java release to inform your migration project at work

- Talk with five contacts who are participating in open source projects that you use and whose experiences and recommendations you are interested in, enabling you to become a contributor to an open source project

Once you set your goals, share them in advance and review them before, during, and after the conference to ensure you are on track to meet your goals. Hold yourself accountable to your goals by sharing them with someone you trust – a friend, mentor, or colleague. Watch as you achieve your results.

Interview

Ixchel Ruiz

Q: Ixchel Ruiz is a developer advocate at JFrog. She's highly active in the Java developer community and has some excellent stories to share with us about her conference experiences and her career path from developer and consultant to developer advocate. Welcome, Ixchel.

A: Hi, Heather. Thank you very much for having me. I'm super excited about being here with you.

Q: Your stories and your career journey fit so nicely into this particular season. It's serendipitously happened that your story is a perfect fit to talk about this book, how you've managed to shape it the way that you wanted it to be, and how the experiences that you've had participating in the community have helped to bring you to where you are today.

Let's just start with you sharing the story of how that happened, and then I can ask you a few questions about it.

A: Sure. But before we start, I wanted to show you how interesting is this. I'm right now in a hotel room because I was participating in Devoxx UK. Conferences and being in the limelight are part of my life today.

As you mentioned, Heather, I'm a software developer. Java is my tool of choice. I have been doing this for more than 20 years. Before I became a developer advocate (although I still say "become" because it's a work in progress, as our careers always are), I had more than 20 years of experience as a consultant. That means I had a public face because I had to see my clients and move from team to team, but I also had an extra public face. My passion for community work, for sharing knowledge, made me jump into speaking at conferences, and that is exactly what pivoted my career as a developer and took it to the next level. It opened doors for other skills and other opportunities for growth.

Q: Could you share a little bit about how you started doing that? As a consultant, how did you begin to participate in conferences? Sometimes, it's all about that first step. That's what I found because I've also participated in conferences. Once you start to participate, you find the next opportunity arises and you step through that door. Maybe it'd be helpful if you shared how you first started to have those community experiences – attending and speaking at conferences.

A: Attending conferences was interesting. I'm going to be completely frank – the reason why I started to attend conferences was the opportunity to learn and improve my skills. I really wanted to know about new technologies, what to be learning, and so on.

I started speaking at conferences because it was one of the only ways to actually get a conference ticket. At that time, they were too expensive for me to afford. When I started, my company was into the continuous development of their developers. I was still back in Mexico, so my only opportunity to get to different conferences was as a speaker. It was such a challenge, but I'm happy that I took it. There is never a better way to learn a topic inside out than having it to explain to other developers.

Q: Exactly. That's one of the tips that I typically give to first-time speakers if they're not sure what topic to present – pick something you want to learn, and then share your experience learning it.

Maybe you can share what your first topic was, how you selected it, and what it was like when you spoke for the first time.

A: The topic that I felt would be pressure-free to talk about was testing. This was maybe 17 years ago. At the time, even though we knew that testing was super important, it was still the ugly duckling in the family. Everybody knew that we had it, but we knew we didn't want to interact that much with it.

That was my opportunity. I knew that it was my opportunity. I went into testing. I love the concept, and I love making it easy because I know all the drawbacks. At the time, people were saying, "We cannot spend a lot of time on it. We cannot spend a lot of resources on it." I knew that if I talked about it from a perspective that assumed that it was not expensive or difficult but easy, enjoyable, and expressive, that would be a good way to approach it. I talked about my favorite libraries to test.

Q: That's great. I love that example. Sometimes, you feel like everyone else can speak about a certain topic better than you can when you haven't spoken before, and so finding a topic that you don't see other people talking about, having an interest in it, and finding your own niche is perfect.

You had 20 years of working as a consultant, participating in the community, getting your face well known, and expanding your network. What propelled you or motivated you when you decided you wanted to shift from being a consultant to taking a job as a developer advocate?

A: That was interesting too.

When I started traveling and conferences started appreciating my contributions more, I start expanding my network with fellow speakers and conference organizers. We're very involved in the tech community and, in this case, the Java community – it's super supportive, welcoming, and very vibrant. I've met with a lot of passionate people, and suddenly, years later, I might meet them at different conferences in different parts of the world. They know me and they know what I do. When you are a speaker, you share part of your personality, your passion, and what drives you. When you work on different projects, people already know you. You don't have to have those conversations anymore.

One of my friends and colleagues of some years – we're from totally different companies, but we're friends because we have met so many times at different conferences and other events – came to me and said, "Ixchel, there is a spot for you in my developer relationships team. Do you want to come and join?" I said yes, because I wanted to try this new path and it was totally different from the world of a consultant. Sometimes, it's easy to jump between the two; sometimes, it's not so easy. But in this case, it was a good fit because people already knew my work.

Q: And how do you do that – share your passion? Especially for women that I've talked to in their careers, their focus is more on the work. But what struck me in your story of promotion from consultant to developer advocate was that it was fueled by your excitement.

What tips do you have for being confident enough to share a passion and take a break from just getting work done? Because that is really what promoted you from being in your current role as a consultant to being a developer advocate. You shared, and people could see your passion and your excitement for topics.

A: Well, the answer there is a little bit easy and a little bit complicated.

The easy part is to find a dream, an inspiration. When things go wrong, you will still have a bad day – your demo is going to crash. Your computer is not going to work. People are going to leave your session, and you are going to feel miserable. So, you need that inspiration, that dream, that driving force, to make those bad days good days at the end of the day.

In my case (and I think this is something that a lot of women out there can sympathize with), the dream is that I want more women in our industry. I want a woman on the conference stage, and I want other people to say that it is normal to see a woman that is good at technical things, a woman that is good at communication, a woman that is willing to share, a woman that brings a new perspective to current topics or old topics, a woman that actually shows something at the bleeding edge. I want that. I want normalization and inspiration.

That's why I do it, even though public speaking is not my first choice. It's still terrifying for me. I still criticize myself a lot – did I deliver it correctly? Did I bring something interesting to the audience? Is the audience happy? What would the audience really warm to? Did I bore them to death? I still struggle with all of that, but my dream is bigger than that.

Q: Exactly. I think it is important to normalize and share our stories of success because it isn't something that you see all the time. I love what you said about normalizing having women on the stage – I agree. You're providing that example for people.

Can you share with us a little bit about how your day-to-day life is different as a developer advocate versus when you worked as a consultant and attended conferences in your free time?

A: Attending conferences is very demanding on our free time because we usually have events and technical sessions in the mornings, and later on, there are plenty of opportunities to do networking and talk to attendees, speakers, and organizers. So, they are full-day events.

When I'm on the road, I have to focus on all that, but I still have a job. I still need to generate content and coordinate with different teams. For example, as a developer advocate, you do sessions, and most often, you do them with your partners. These are technical partners, which means other companies, so it's a balancing act.

This profession and this particular job role are not for the faint of heart because sometimes, you're on another continent – you're battling time zones, and you're battling people all around the world with different time constraints and different goals. Your team and the teams that you interact with are not like your own developer teams, where everybody has a set schedule and you share a project and a sprint. You have a long relationship with your home team. But as a developer advocate on the road, you face other teams with different time constraints and different domains of expertise. I deal a lot with marketing but also with sales and product managers.

In that regard, it has been an interesting challenge. I still do my developer work (coding) as well as the other public part – attending conferences, networking, and talking to developers. It's a full life.

Q: But a fun one.

A: An amazing one! I mean, look at me. I'm still really passionate about this.

Q: I can tell. I know that you have a great time doing it, and I'm really pleased that you were able to successfully have that career transition.

If there's anyone out there who is interested in becoming a developer advocate, what advice would you give them?

A: Find the technology that you like to talk about because you need to have a lot of passion. If you're not passionate about it, it's going to be a little bit more difficult.

Secondly, there is a lot of learning that you have to do very fast, but that's beautiful in itself. Find a technology, a library, a language – whatever you feel that you can understand and can communicate to others about – and then go deep.

The community is also important. Find an awesome community and you will feel welcomed. You will learn from the developers and other people involved in whatever technology you pick.

Q: Great tips – be passionate, be good at learning and learning fast, and engage with the community. So often you can engage with the community online, but being able to engage in person, face to face, is when you really deepen the connections and engagement that you're able to have. Even if you can't travel but engage locally, you can find those in-person opportunities to forge those deep connections.

A: Yes. Go to meetups, and go to hackathons. Even contribute to open source because when you contribute to open source, you generate a channel of communication with contributors or maintainers of projects. Those are the first steps to engaging fellow developers in a totally different conversation. Believe me, that will open a lot of doors for you.

Q: There's the hands-on aspect too – hackathons, meetups, conferences. They are hands-on activities where you gain experience, learn new skills, and forge relationships. It's almost like everything is all in one place when you are able to find those opportunities.

Well, thank you, Ixchel, for sharing your career story, and congratulations on your transition as a developer advocate. I look forward to seeing you in person again at another conference very soon, and I hope that you enjoy the rest of your time in London.

A: Thank you very much, Heather, and I am so looking forward to seeing you soon face to face because I love hugging you!

Q: Me too, and thanks for sharing.

Summary

In this chapter, we learned how to add conferences to your career-building plans, how to select conferences for the best results, how to make a plan for this effort, how to engage with your employer to bring their support to this activity, and how to achieve the maximum benefits from engaging in-person conferences.

In the next part of the book, we will show you how to create an impact by sharing and leading. We will start with how to build trust with top developers to solve important problems by joining open source projects.

Part 3
Create Impact: Share and Lead

Now that you know how to establish long-term relationships that will drive your career forward, it is time to take the last step: position yourself as a leader, to break all limits in your career growth. *Part 3* will discuss advanced actions that you can take that will differentiate you in the market and will transform the lives of people around you.

This part has the following chapters:

- *Chapter 11, Build Trust and Solve Problems with Open Source Projects*
- *Chapter 12, Scaling Trust through Public Engagement: Speaking and Blogs*
- *Chapter 13, Be a Leader: Manage Up, Down, and Across Your Organization*
- *Chapter 14, Step Up Your Technology Game: Define Technology instead of Merely Using It*
- *Chapter 15, Build Your Personal Brand and Become a Trusted Advisor*

11
Build Trust and Solve Problems with Open Source Projects

The deepest level of trust you can have with other developers is by working together on a project. Open source projects allow you to meet and work with amazing developers and build deep, meaningful relationships that take trust to a new level. This chapter will show you how to do that.

In this chapter, we will cover the following main topics:

- The value of contributing to open source
- Selecting an open source project
- Building trust and getting accepted
- Making open source a core part of your evolution
- Bringing value to your company and customers

The value of contributing to open source

The primary value of contributing to open source projects is that it gives you access to awesome software that you can modify for your needs! You also gain the following:

- Knowledge
- Skills
- Opportunities to work on impactful projects
- Purpose
- Friendship
- Opportunities for networking

- Access to amazing developers

- A portfolio

- The ability to build your reputation

When developers talk about open source, they usually mean participating in open source projects or contributing code to libraries or software they use and like.

The definition of open source itself comes from the **Open Source Initiative (OSI)**. It is a set of rules on how to license software in a way that allows people to learn from it by having access to the source code. You can modify the source code for your own purposes and publish the modifications for others. The open source definition creates the basic ground rules that allow all of us to benefit from and contribute to open source projects. In this book, we're *not* going to discuss open source licensing. But you should be aware of licenses, especially if you start to use open source inside your company.

Many people refer to open source projects and developers as a community. But in reality, because open source is organized around projects, it is more like many communities, each built around a project. This is important because although there is a definition of what constitutes open source software, there is no specific standard of what it is and how a community should organize itself. So, there are as many types of different communities as there are open source projects. After all, there are open source projects about absolutely everything you can imagine. That is why it is easier to think about open source in relation to a specific project.

Think about each open source project as a community by itself. Each is a community of people working together to improve a project or solve a particular problem. Each project has its own community of users, big or small, that it serves.

If contributing to open source is only valuable for other people, that is, for the community and users of the project, it is reasonable to question why you should do it. It is common to hear questions such as why should I work for free? Or, why do so many developers work for free on open source projects? Those are valid questions. Although some developers are paid to work on open source projects, that is not the norm. Most developers participate in open source for other reasons. This is a good place to start our exploration of the open source world. Let us explore some of the reasons why you might be interested in using and contributing to open source software.

A word about meritocracy

A lot has been said about open source and how it is a meritocracy. When you hear that, it is easy to assume that it is because the best and top developers are the ones building open source software. That is their merit. But in reality, the meritocracy that is mentioned is basically who is putting in more effort. In open source projects, people that put more work and more focus into the project tend to be the most respected and end up setting the direction of the work.

You may find that this is very positive because it is not about how good you are today that will allow you to join an open source project, but how much effort and focus you are willing to put into it.

The more effort you put in, and the more help you provide, the better you become as a professional and a developer.

Every open source project needs lots of help! Many developers only think about helping by writing code and becoming a committer of the project. But open source projects need help with everything: from creating documentation to translating the project into multiple languages to supporting users and other developers. There are a lot of opportunities to help promote the project, understand user needs, maintain old versions, prepare for the future, and much more. What we'll be discussing in this chapter is exactly what the value is and how you can start contributing to open source projects today.

Access to amazing software

First and foremost, open source software gives you access to amazing software. The value of having source code access to a piece of software that solves a problem that you have and that can also be adapted to your specific situation cannot be overstated. Being able to incorporate code that is ready, tested, and working in the real world into your own projects, personal or commercial, is a huge value. It is so valuable that most companies will charge you a premium to have access to similar code. And you get it for free. That's the reason why it's very rare to find any projects today that build all they need from scratch and do not use some pre-existing open source software.

Even if you're just using the libraries of your preferred language, you've probably used a lot of pre-built open source components, since most programming languages today are open source.

Access to knowledge

Having the source code available allows you to study the workings of the software. This is extremely valuable. You can learn a specific piece of code or how a project works. But even more interesting, you can learn the best practices. Let's say, for example, that you have a specific problem to solve, such as how to generate good logging, create scalable software, or maybe how to develop a secure login process. By looking at open source software that already implements any of that, you can learn how other developers solve this particular problem that you have.

To build on one of those examples, we are sure you have used the logs from an application server or a web server to debug and identify problems. So, you have confidence in how useful the logging of, let's say, Tomcat, is. If you can access the source code of Tomcat and learn how that team created it, you can implement the same thing in your software.

Learning

You will learn by looking at the source code, following the work of more experienced developers, learning their processes, automation scripts, and even runtime configurations, and understanding how the team interacts, how they handle conflicts, and what happens when someone quits or doesn't deliver their part. There is so much you can learn from open source projects. There is no better way to improve your development skills.

Improve your skills as a software developer

For you to improve your software developer skills, you need to practice. But it is more than that. Force yourself to practice slightly beyond your current skill level. Participating in and contributing to open source projects will give you development skills in all areas that you can imagine.

Not only are there all kinds of open source projects in different technologies and programming languages, using a myriad of architectures, and solving wildly different problems, but also, in any open source project, you have the whole of the development life cycle implemented – from understanding users' needs, to developing software collaboratively in a team, debugging and testing, packaging the software, all the way to delivery and maintenance. Participating in open source projects will give you all the skills needed as a software developer, which brings us to impact.

Impact

A counter-argument is that you could learn and build all those skills by participating in a project in your company. That is true, to a certain point. Open source projects have the added opportunity of working on impactful projects. Not every developer has access inside their company to implement software that will be used by a large number of people, software that provides value to society, or any other impact that you might want to have.

Because there are many open source projects out there, you can always find a project that matches and connects with your objectives and the impact that you want to have, which brings us to purpose.

Open source projects can give you a greater sense of purpose

Psychologists indicate that our sense of purpose is normally associated with helping others. By working on open source projects that other people are benefiting from, you participate in this giving ecosystem. Friends are not only people that we have fun with but also people that we work with on purposeful things.

When you participate in an open source project, you are building something significant together with many other developers. The longer you do this, the more you know who they are and how they work, and understand their code. You meet them at events and have meetings and discussions over email and online. All of these build close bonds between the team. After all, although you work at different companies and may even live in different countries, you're all working on the same project.

Quite frequently, the friendship acquired from an open source project spills into the lives of the developers. Members meet each other at events, go out for dinner, and may even visit each other's houses. Open source participation can expand your contacts and networking to a much larger array of people – and not only developers, by the way. In any open source project, there are also designers, testers, writers, and managers, from different companies and backgrounds. You have access to all those people, which will give you much better access to knowledge, a different set of skills, and even to companies and job opportunities.

Networking

Networking inside an open source project is of high quality, exactly because it is around a common goal. A special type of networking that also happens is having access to developers that are more experienced. There is a widely known principle in management called Joy's law, attributed to Sun Microsystems' co-founder and co-author of the Java specification, Bill Joy. Joy's law states that no matter who you are, most of the smartest people work for someone else.

The principle is based on the idea that the outside of your company is much larger than the inside. What is a good way to meet, interact, and work with people outside of your company? Open source project participation is a darn good one!

For you to have access to the top, smartest developers in the world, participate in open source projects that they are already involved in. Because software development has a big component of arts and craftsmanship, working with developers that are better than you is the best way for you to improve your skills.

Portfolio

One of the best ways to showcase your skills is by mentioning a project that you participate in and the company and people that you work with. Open source projects can facilitate you having a strong portfolio of interesting problems, projects, people, and companies that you have worked with.

One of the best features of open source software is that it is visible and public. This is great for you to learn from it, but it is also perfect to showcase your work. Your contributions are visible on the project site, but also in open source repositories such as GitHub and Bitbucket. Developers even use those visible contributions as part of, and sometimes as, their main curriculum. Most companies looking for developers will consider your visible contributions as proof of work that you've done and as a way to evaluate your experience.

With all of that, participating in open source projects helps you build a strong reputation as a professional developer. You are showing your experience. You are working alongside great developers. Your code is publicly visible, showcasing your experience and skills. It helps you build those skills to begin with. There is a lot of value in participating in the open source community and open source projects. Now, the biggest question developers usually ask is, how do I find a project to be part of?

Selecting an open source project

Although there are millions of open source projects, not all of them will be suited for you and your goals, so here are a few things to consider in selecting open source projects you may want to participate in:

- Work on projects that are related to what you know

- Work on projects your company uses and depends on

- Work on projects you are interested in

- Participate in a foundation (Apache, Eclipse, Linux, etc.)
- Work on projects your friends are part of
- Start your own project

Projects you are already using

A good place to start your open source participation is on projects that you are already using. You're probably using programming languages, libraries, and tools that are open source already. Do any of those interest you? Do you see things that you would like to change or improvements you'd like to make? Starting with a tool or library that you are using will make it much easier for you to look at the source code, understand how it works, and even propose improvements or changes.

Since you are already using those libraries, you may even have the source code in your artifact repository and ready to load into your IDE or debugger. Depending on your stack and build process, you may already be building the source code along with your own source. This makes it very easy for you to inspect the source, debug a problem, and get started with the open source part.

Projects your company uses and depends on

It can be even more rewarding if there are open source projects, libraries, or tools that your company uses today, and maybe even depends on, to go deep into those projects. Being knowledgeable about and even participating in open source projects that your company depends on may allow you to work on open source projects during your work hours. Eventually, you could put yourself in the very interesting position of being paid to work on open source projects.

Using this strategy, many of the top open source developers in the world are paid to work on their own projects. Because they work on them full time, they are much more effective and able to contribute a lot more. Remember that the "meritocracy" has to do with who puts in more effort. Being paid to work on their own project makes a developer a stronger member of the community.

Projects that are related to what you know

Another way of choosing an open source project is by looking for projects that are related to something that you know and are good at. It's much easier to participate in projects where you are already familiar with the technology.

If you are a Java developer, it is easier to participate in projects related to Java. If you're particularly interested in data or databases, you might know the details of how a database is implemented and may be interested in participating in open source database projects.

Using whatever existing knowledge you have is a great way to get involved. Your knowledge might be exactly what the open source project needs to implement a new feature or improve an existing piece of code.

Projects you are interested in

Expanding on this idea a little, you can look for projects on things that you are very interested in and would love to get more involved in, beyond the technology realm.

Let's say you like a sport, such as surfing, biking, or soccer, for instance. You could participate in the myriad of open source projects related to sports. This works for any interesting activity that you love. You may be a lover of franchises such as *Lord of the Rings*, games such as *Dungeons & Dragons*, or toys such as LEGO. Look for open source projects around those areas. You will be surprised by what exists out there!

It also works beautifully for religious and spiritual interests. There are open source projects focused on helping people from all faiths and beliefs to deepen their spiritual lives. This can also apply to software that solves more mundane, day-to-day problems, such as databases of members or streaming meetings.

Being able to contribute to things you enjoy and are part of, using your soft development skills, will give you a sense of purpose, connect you more with the community, and get you to meet and interact with people that share your interests.

Projects your friends are part of

Exactly because interest plays a big role in your willingness to participate and contribute, if there are open source projects that your friends are involved in or are using, they might be very interesting for you to participate in.

Working with friends is more enjoyable and motivating. Even more, it is easier! They already trust you and know how interested and committed you will be. It is also easier for you to ask questions and have conversations. This can even deepen your friendship.

Participate in an open source foundation

Extending that idea of working with friends, another good place to look for projects is by getting involved with an open source foundation, a user group, or even a company that you would like to be connected with.

Many companies have their own open source projects, and if you are a fan of their work or would like to work for one of those companies, you would do very well by looking at what open source projects they are involved with, the ones they sponsor, or even the projects they run themselves.

If you would prefer to contribute to the projects of a specific company, there are many open source foundations that you could get close to, the Apache Software Foundation, the Eclipse Foundation, the Cloud Native Computing Foundation, and the Linux Foundation, among many others. Not to forget OSI! These are non-profit organizations behind some of the top, most used open source projects in the world. If you align with their goals and beliefs and how they work, you would do very well in choosing a project that they sponsor.

One interesting result of working with a company or a foundation is that they usually have the whole contribution process very clear, documented, and explained. They also try to adopt the best practices of project organization. You do not have to guess how things work. It is not uncommon that developers that already understand the process end up participating in multiple projects of an organization, because they are familiar with the process.

Start an open source project

Besides all that, anyone can start an open source project, so you can always start by creating your own. However, while it gives you some visibility and builds your portfolio, it is not the most recommended strategy.

This isn't because it doesn't work, or is a bad idea in itself. After all, most open source projects, if not every software project, started because someone at some point, in some place, decided to solve a problem and started writing code. But starting your own open source projects will not give you great visibility or immediate access to other developers, best practices, or learning from others. To gain all of that, you will have to build other skills, such as promoting your ideas and attracting developers to your project. These are great skills, but are hard on themselves.

So, before you start, or maybe during, your own project, it may be a good idea to practice by participating in a few other projects, so you gain the skills and experience necessary.

These tips will help you find an open source project that you're interested in participating in. You might even find several that are interesting to you.

Finding projects is a good start, but it's just the beginning. Now that you have a few projects in mind, the fun begins. Let's discuss how you can get accepted to an open source project!

Building trust and getting accepted

One of the biggest mistakes developers make in trying to participate in open source projects is thinking that an open source project is just there for the taking. Developers may think that just because the source code is available, anyone can just come in and do whatever they want with it. That could not be further from the truth.

An active open source project is developed by a community of people that are very passionate about their code. You could imagine that their project is their little baby. They take care of and protect it. Although open source developers are particularly open and accepting, they need to trust you before you can actually contribute anything.

Imagine if it was one of your projects and a random person that you have never seen before just comes in, makes decisions, changes your project direction, or tells you what you should be doing next. You would probably not be very happy. You would need them to start slowly, make a few suggestions that you would be glad to accept, and in general follow your lead on where the project should go – at least until you know who they are and you form a connection. That is what building trust looks like, and that's why when you approach an open source project, you have to start small. Building trust is a process that can take some time.

Developers on open source projects want contributions, but we all know that code maintenance is a lot harder and something we spend more time on than creating code to begin with. You will not be surprised to hear that people come into a project, suggest something, and disappear. That just leaves behind lots of unruly code that will need to be maintained for a long time, and this type of behavior is not very welcome.

The first principle you should adhere to when you try to participate in any open source projects is to be helpful. That might seem easy. You know your stuff, of course, so anything you do will be helpful, right?

That is not how it works. Being helpful does not mean being the smartest person or contributing the most amount of code. Being helpful means thinking about the current users and maintainers of the project. Help them to do what they are trying to do. Help them solve problems instead of creating problems for them.

To illustrate that, let's consider a concrete example. We already mentioned that maintaining code is where most of the work on software happens. If you plan to join an open source project and contribute a lot of code to implement something that you think is important, but you don't plan to stick around to maintain that code, you may be tempted to believe that you are being very helpful. But in fact, as you are creating code that needs to be maintained, this ends up just leaving more work for the maintainers.

It is for that reason that when you browse any open source project that has a bit of traction, you will find lots of pull requests, which are basically proposals of changes, many times with dozens of lines of code, which instead of being incorporated into the project sit there untouched by the maintainers. I'm sure the developers that contributed those pull requests thought they were being helpful. But in reality, they were just leaving extra work for the maintainers. They now have to analyze the submissions, validate whether they really work as intended, consider whether the changes are necessary or valid for the project, test whether they break compatibility, incorporate the changes, build tests around them, and maintain the functionality for all future versions.

If you are really serious about participating in and contributing to open source, you should approach projects in a more helpful manner and consider them as a longer-term strategy. You will be much better received. Let us now discuss in more detail some tips on being accepted to contribute to an open source project. .

Build trust

Participating in open source projects is all about trust. This is similar to any project where you work with others, but open source projects need a higher level of trust. In your company, for example, there is a hierarchy, and your manager organizes things and directs the developers on what to do. Your manager can tell you what to do because they have a level of power over you and your work.

In an open source project, things are more self-managed. The developers work for different companies, and most of the time there is no hierarchical relationship. Even the leader of the project doesn't have the power to tell you what to do. The relationship is one of influence and trust. Trust is not something that you can just take. Trust has to be earned.

Start small

To build trust, you should start small. Small contributions are a great way for you to know more about the project, and the maintainers to know more about you. Small contributions are easier to get accepted because they don't bring a lot of overhead.

Try to start with the smallest thing possible. That will give you a better idea of how the project works, how things are organized, and who is doing what.

Start by building the project, running tests, and making small changes for you to know where things are and how they work, and where help may be needed. Look for small things to contribute to. Look for little fixes or improvements in the documentation or non-critical areas, such as tests and example code. Some projects even list easy-to-fix issues that you could take a look at.

Test the waters. Experiment with the process. Get people to start knowing who you are and seeing that you are serious about it.

Join the mailing list

Among the small, important things that you should do is to join the mailing list and communication channel. Open source is a very distributed process, so communication is paramount among the team. Every open source project has either an email list, a Discord server, a Slack channel, or some other form of communication. That's where developers and users communicate, and you should be part of that from the beginning. Observe for a few days and understand who is who in the project. Try to figure out what is going on and how things work before trying to contribute or change things.

Don't try to impose your own ideas

Listening and patience are probably the most important skills when working in open source. Although you may have amazing ideas, and an amazing vision of where the project could go, listen first to understand where the project is actually going. Committers and maintainers may have their own reasons why the roadmap is the way it is or why the priorities are what they are right now. It's rude to try to change things before you have an understanding of what that is and are accepted into the group.

Instead of coming up with amazing new ideas, try to be helpful. Find out the ideas that already need to be implemented and fixes that need to be done that you could start helping with immediately.

Think about the project users first

Think about the project users first; after all, the reason for an open source project is to help solve a problem that someone has. Even in very small projects that have just a handful of users, or where the users are the developers themselves, the focus is still on the users. Since the owners of projects are probably thinking about the users, you would do very well if you did the same.

A good way to put users first is to keep an eye on the main list or other user channels to see what problems people are having. Is it hard to get started? Are there installation problems? Is the tutorial not very helpful? These could be good places for you to volunteer to help.

The more you understand the needs of the users, the more helpful you are going to be to the project and the maintainers.

Start with things where you do not need permission

Open source code can be analyzed, copied, modified, and distributed without having to ask anyone's permission, but to become one of the committers and be able to modify the project itself, you do need permission. Until the day you become a committer, you are probably going to need approval, reviews, and some hand-holding. Some projects even require a sponsor to vouch for you and work with you in every contribution you make. Before you get that kind of access to the project, you can help with things that do not require any permission.

Examples of things that do not require permission are answering questions in the mailing list or helping beginners to get started using the project. You can help both users and developers of the project to do things they are trying to accomplish by researching and clarifying how things work. You can write articles or even present about the project. These are some of the many helpful things that you can do that do not require permission from anyone.

Let us take a look at two particular things that do not require permission and that are extremely helpful: promoting the project and answering questions.

Promoting the project

One of the most important things that you can do that does not require any permission is to promote the project. Every open source project needs to be seen – it needs to be visible and used by many people. Any promotion that you can do of the project is helpful for the project and for you.

While you are studying and understanding the project, write articles and create social media posts. Discuss the project on Facebook, write articles on LinkedIn, create tutorials, put step-by-step instructions together, including screen captures, and teach classes on YouTube. Whatever you would like to see as a resource to help you use the project, create that for others. You can do that even if those resources already exist and you believe you can bring a new angle or approach to help someone else.

You can start by promoting the project inside your own company or at your school. The more people that know and use the project, the more valuable the project is, and since you are associating yourself with it, the more valuable you will become too.

Answering questions

Another place where you do not need permission is to answer questions. You might think that as a beginner in the project, you do not know as much as others. But you are here for the long run. The more you look into the source code and understand the project, the more you'll be able to install, use, and configure the project. It will be easy for you to find beginner questions that you can answer.

Answering questions on the mailing list, forums, and blogs will help the project be easier to use and attract more people. It is a feedback loop because you will know more about the project. When answering a question, you might need to look at the source code, understand a piece of the project, or learn a command-line option. That research will help you understand the project better and will make you a more useful contributor when the time comes.

Moving on to help more closely

It will then become time to start moving on to help more closely. For any contribution to be accepted, you will initially need to get some kind of approval. Here is where you will need to understand how your chosen project works.

How are contributions accepted? What are the specific policies? How do you submit your contributions? Are there any legal documents or agreements that you have to sign? What other process should you be aware of? Different projects have different policies, and larger communities will have more processes than small ones. Also, companies and foundations will have specific requirements.

That is one more advantage of starting small. Even larger, more bureaucratic projects have simpler processes to accept small contributions. Things such as documentation changes, misspelled words, corrections, and even small code fixes are usually allowed without complicated agreements.

Larger contributions, even if it is just adding a test to the project, may trigger a more formal relationship, such as signing a contributor agreement or other legal documents for the particular project. Companies and non-profit foundations are usually more aware of those processes and have clear documentation for getting them done. In smaller or less formal projects, those things may be non-existent, or just not very clear.

Improve the documentation

Documentation is usually the point of entry for newbies in most projects. Having good documentation that is consistent with the latest version of the project is very important for the success of the project.

You can start by closely following introductory documentation, such as a tutorial or a README file, and see whether it works, follows the latest version, and is clear to someone that has never used the project before. If you find problems, non-clear parts, or commands that don't work, you can submit a pull request to have the documentation fixed.

Even a single misspelled word, which may not seem like much to worry about, is a good place to start. Maintainers will gladly accept corrections like this, and it will be easier for them to approve your contribution than to reject it. That is a great step toward building trust and starting to participate in the project.

Improve testing and project delivery

Another thing that you can do is to improve testing. There is no such thing as too many tests in any project. You could start by looking at the existing tests and try to see whether you can improve or add new tests to the project.

See whether you can help with project delivery. Help automate things such as packaging, running tests, or automating the development environment. You can also work on creating Docker images, setting up CI/CD pipelines, handling backups, site infrastructure, or a myriad of other automation and configuration work that is not the main goal of the project and that in many projects, no one is really responsible for or willing to take care of.

Help with upgrades

Every project needs help with upgrading things – be it the libraries the project depends on, the version of the language that is being used, or the tools that the project uses. You can run the project on a new version of the runtime, switch the version of the library being used, and identify the problems. Sometimes, this is easily accomplished just by running the build and tests.

You can also see where the project may be using outdated or deprecated libraries or methods, and work to upgrade those to more recommended versions. Also, if security issues have been found in libraries, it may require the usage of a new version or applying a fix to the project. Sometimes, if you can just make the assessment, this is enough to rally people to fix things.

Some languages and runtimes come up with major improvements from time to time. For example, there is a new version of the Java runtime every six months, sometimes with significant language or library improvements. It is similar to when a new version of Perl or Python comes up. In those cases, there may be a need to change the code, call better versions of the API, or use a faster, more secure version of the API.

In large projects, those might represent hundreds of places where those things should be fixed. In many cases, some of those fixes are simple and can be automated by your IDE. You may think that this is easy because of that, but fixing them and testing and creating the pull requests are all time-consuming steps that could totally be done by a newcomer in the project that doesn't have a lot of other responsibilities. That's where you can suddenly become very useful to the project.

One condition for large things such as this is to make sure that the team is considering such a move, or at least is open to it. You can then volunteer to be the person to do it.

Fix small issues

Every project has small things to be fixed that no one has the time to do. Some projects even create beginners' issues to help people see what they are capable of helping with and get started.

If the projects that you are looking into have something like this, take a look at the issues that exist and see whether you can fix one of them. You can learn the whole contribution process by doing this. Look at previous small fixes that have been done by other people to see whether you could have come up with the solution yourself, and how others have submitted solutions in the past.

Do things no one wants to do

Many people that want to be part of an open source project do so because there is something in particular they want to work on. Hopefully, by now, you can see that there's much more that goes into open source projects. Open source is valuable and can push your career forward really fast. So, it could help to approach it from a different angle than initially expected.

When you start thinking about what the users, especially the maintainers of the project, want, you will quickly find out as many things that they do not want to do. These are things that have to be done, where it would be good if someone did them, but the committers are too busy to do them.

That is why we suggest things such as documentation and testing because, usually, those are parts of the projects that developers are least interested in working on. Once you volunteer to do things that no one else wants to do, you build for yourself an open space for you to work inside the project. No matter how small that space is, it is enough to build trust with people in the project. You will more clearly see the value that you're bringing to the project and they will want you to do more.

Do not be afraid of doing those things, thinking that you are going to get stuck doing them forever, because that is not how it works. As we discussed before, open source projects are based on meritocracy, which does not mean that the best person has merit, but all of the people that do things do. The more things you do, the more responsibilities you will have in the project.

To summarize the preceding, there are five steps to successful participation in open source:

1.   Select a project – pick a project that is of interest to you.

2.   Communicate with the leaders – it is a two-way street. Share ideas before coding solutions.

3.   Research the project – read the discussions and issue trackers and download the drafts.

4.   Decide on action items together with the project leaders. Remember to discuss ideas before submitting a pull request!

5.   Contribute and share your actions on the mailing list, issue tracker, or repository for the project.

Making open source a core part of your evolution

Once you understand the value of open source, have selected open source projects to participate in, and have built trust to be accepted into those projects, you are ready to incorporate open source as a part of your career evolution.

When the team accepts you, take your responsibility seriously

It's not uncommon for developers to do some initial work on a project just to have something to put on their resume or to secure a new job. Once they get the results they were looking for, they stop helping and go do something else (maybe enjoy their new job!).

On one hand, there is nothing wrong with this. Really. There is no obligation or commitment in open source. You are a volunteer and you work as much and for as long as you would like to. You are not forced to continue helping indefinitely; however, it takes effort from you and the project maintainers to get someone (you!) up to speed and set up to contribute. You end up building a relationship with the people and the users. Your code is there, being maintained. When you decide to contribute to and dive deep into a project, take it seriously. Work on projects in which you see value for your career in the long term. That way, you can really put in the effort and keep working on it for enough time to make a mark on the world.

By making small contributions to open source projects, you can gain valuable experience and make a positive impact without requiring a significant investment of time and effort from either yourself or the project maintainers. As you become more involved in a project and take on greater responsibility, you will also have the opportunity to build relationships and expand your professional network.

Taking this responsibility seriously can lead to significant benefits for your career. Not only will you be able to showcase your skills and contributions to potential employers but you will also be able to demonstrate your commitment to open source and the value it can bring to your work. Start small and gradually work your way deeper into projects that align with your goals and interests. The friendships and connections you make along the way, as well as the impact you have on the projects themselves, can be truly invaluable. As we mentioned in other parts of the book, there are five main skills needed to improve yourself and your developer career. The cool thing about open source projects is that they can help you with all of your development abilities.

This is huge! In the past, if you wanted to have an opportunity to work on sophisticated projects, built by a team of experienced developers and serving large numbers of users, you needed to be hired by a company doing all of that. Open source turns this on its head. You can now do all those things, no matter where you live or where you work. Let us see how participating in open source can help you with all five umbrella skills.

Reading code

Reading code is a fundamental ability for software developers. It is the basic skill that you need for everything in your developer career. Knowing how to read code in different languages and versions, with increasing levels of difficulty, and implement multiple patterns and architecture are critical to your success as a developer and also your ability to contribute effectively to open source projects. This skill – being able to read code – is the basis to help you achieve all the other skills!

As the name implies, the basic freedom that open source gives you is the freedom of reading the source code. Imagine what that means. No matter what you are going through right now in your development, regardless of the language, library, or development problem, there is some piece of source code, somewhere, that you can read.

This skill will give you access to insights, experience, and art and craftsmanship. It is going to help you understand the problem better and get clarity on the solutions. There are open source projects that apply every possible design pattern and use any architecture you can think of. Reading open source code will help you get a real-world, deep understanding of software design.

The following are some practical suggestions and a few things you can do to improve your code-reading abilities.

Read code from libraries

The easiest thing you can do related to open source is to read code from the libraries that you use and that you call. Any software development project that you are working on will use some open source library, whether it is the language that you use, which has basic open source libraries, some of the libraries that your project is utilizing, the framework you are basing your project on, or the open source infrastructure you are using, such as application servers or databases. From all of these, you can read and understand how the libraries work or how the frameworks you're using manage requests. Spend some time every day reading the source code from the libraries that you use. A simple thing to start is to choose one library that you're currently using and open the source code just to take a look.

Read code you do not understand

Also, try to read code you do not understand. It is how you improve every skill – by pushing it a little above your current level. The best way for you to improve your code-reading abilities is to try to understand code that is not clear to you, and that can be code in different programming languages that you are less familiar with or code from more difficult parts of the frameworks that you are using. Read code that's badly written or very confusing to understand. Read code that solves a problem you are trying to solve. All those exercises will make your code-reading abilities a lot better.

Change and step through the code

Another interesting activity that you can do is to make small modifications to the source code of an open source project and see what results you get. That may require a bit more than simply reading the code. You may have to compile and build the project, but it is going to help you have a much better understanding of how the code works. While you're doing this, you can spend some time stepping through the code on your debugger, to see what the code is doing. This is also going to not only help you with reading the code but also improve your debugging skills.

Writing code

Writing code is the skill most associated with software development. It is no doubt the most visible result of your work and the thing that most people associate with contributing to open source. This makes many developers imagine that to practice this skill, you need to write code from scratch. That can work, but it is not the best way. You also need to write code that you can compare with other code.

Refactor code

To really use open source to improve your code-writing skills, you can refactor code. You first use refactoring to understand code better. By breaking down its parts and understanding what each part is doing, you will have a clear vision. You can then try to refactor the code to make it more readable, more efficient, or cleaner. When doing these exercises, you probably will not even contribute the changes back to the projects and just use them to improve your skills. This will help you contribute to the project in the future, since you will better understand how the code works, and with that, you will also be able to solve problems. Refactoring code, even if temporarily just on your IDE, is a great way for you to understand where the code is breaking before you can fix a problem or a bug.

Update and upgrade code

We already mentioned updating and upgrading code and libraries. This is a great code-writing exercise. It is something that every open source project needs at some point, and many projects have even done full rewrites to use new versions of the language or runtime. Experiment on a project to find out what it would take for the code to be updated, and especially, what new versions of the libraries could bring to the project, in terms of performance, security, and maintainability. This can be a great contribution to the project and an amazing boost to your code-writing skills.

Delivering code

Another important skill that you should have is delivering code. Understanding the full life cycle of software development will give you superpowers in our industry. This is a very broad set of skills that touches everything from understanding the problem to writing the code to testing and packaging. It will give you skills from delivering and deploying to running and monitoring, not to mention things such as infrastructure as code, zero downtime, cloud deployments, scaling, containers, and CI/CD. You can practice most, if not all, of those skills by participating in open source projects. Here are a few suggestions that would be very helpful to any open source project, and can give you practice and proven real-world experience in delivering code skills.

Code analysis – help with the project quality

We do understand that quality is an overloaded concept and can mean a lot of things to different people. But in terms of improving your skills, any work you do to improve the quality of a project can aid in your understanding of the development process.

A good place to start is with code analyzers. This is because you can run them in the existing public source code, so you do not need any permission. You can just go and run them for your preferred open source project. Also, those tools will analyze previous versions of the project that are available in the code repository. You get an immediate view of how the code is evolving, who is doing what, where changes are concentrated, and what the hotspots of potential problems are. A good tool to give you all this information is SonarQube, which is itself an open source project. As an added benefit, those tools can flag many potential security issues. That can be another area of focus if you are interested in security. Tools such as SonarQube are very helpful, especially for projects that aim to be used in large software projects. If you are interested in a project that does not run code analysis, maybe you could volunteer to start an initiative like that.

Testing, testing, testing

OK, you may be tired of seeing testing being mentioned here. "I want to be a coder, not a tester," we can almost hear you thinking. The thing is that testing is a differentiation skill. Developers that are test-conscious and understand the implications, the trade-off, and the value of quality have a higher value in the market. Once, a Java virtual machine engineer talking about the skills needed for a position said, "We can teach Java to people that join the team, but getting them to think about testing is much harder."

If you do not have these differentiated skills right now, it can easily be changed by helping some open source projects solve their testing issues. That is another helpful thing about testing: every project has a testing issue! This could be running, automating, or writing tests to fix issues that show up. This can be an open door for you to enter and start helping.

Going a little deeper, and cranking up your skills to high gear, some projects and technologies will even have strong testing requirements. For example, in the Java ecosystem, any open source project implementing a Java specification has to run the **Test Compatibility Kit** (**TCK**), to provide a compliant implementation. Helping with these efforts could be extremely fruitful for the project and you.

Package and deliver the project

There are way more people using an open source project than developing it. There are projects such as OpenSSH, a project that is used basically on every computer system in the world, and at one point was being developed by a handful of developers. Because of that, the process of delivering a new version and getting it easily into the hands of users is a crucial part of the project. This includes things such as packaging it as a Docker container, making it ready to use in a repository such as Maven Central, or making sure it is easy to install.

If the project already has those processes, you can participate and help with the initiative. If not, implementing and automating these efforts can make the project a lot more professional and easily usable by many more people. A couple of other suggestions are packaging and distributing the project. This is something that can be done without requiring a lot of permission from the maintainers and can be easily promoted to users and maybe later incorporated into the project.

Solving problems

This brings us to the next big skill, and probably the most important skill as a software developer: solving problems. No doubt that open source projects focus on solving problems, so being part of an open source project will help you improve that skill, but here are a few things you can do to make it even more effective.

Use the project in your current position

The first thing you can do is to use the open source project! Find ways you can use the project in your daily job. Use it as a way to solve problems in your company and your current projects. This is just the obvious. Of course, you can fix problems in the open source project itself. To be amazing at solving problems, you need to be an expert in identifying the correct problem and understanding what is going on. Every open source project has complaints from users where the details are unclear or the user was not able to articulate the issue. When it is not clear to anyone in the development team what the problem actually is, it cannot be fixed. You could be the person that identifies issues on the project's mailing list or forum and then digs deep to identify exactly what is going on and what the real problem is. Doing that will make you amazing at getting clarity and solving problems. Even if you cannot go and fix it, because you do not have permission or maybe you do not know how to fix it, just understanding the problem is half of the battle.

You should also go deep into problems in the open source software that you are using. If something is not working, open the source code and try to find out what is wrong. Maybe it is just that you misunderstood what the library was doing, it is a problem with the documentation, or it is a bad implementation or a corner case. Who knows? You can find out! Solving problems is about creativity, so be creative. Apply solutions found in open source projects to your current project. You may not even be contributing to a project, but you can get inspiration from it and apply the same solutions to fix problems in your project or company.

Sharing – bringing value to your company and customers

The last umbrella skill that we are going to discuss here is sharing. Sharing what you learn is an amazing way to deepen your understanding and improve your learning process. It is also a fantastic way to build your professional reputation. We even have several chapters about different ways of sharing in this book. Using open source is a great way to improve your sharing skills, so here are some ideas that you can implement.

Share what you learn by working in open source

Start by sharing what you've learned from everything else that we've talked about in this chapter. When you read the source code of a project or you write something, fix a bug, or solve a problem, you will learn things. You should then share what you have learned, even if it is something small. The knowledge you acquired is very important, but just as important is that people see that you learned that from the project! It promotes you and the project. Sharing what you learned helps you get a deeper clarity and understanding of the project. It will also attract people to use and even participate in the project. Another advantage of sharing what you learn is that you inspire people to participate in this or other projects, and you spread the idea that being part of an open source project is a good way for them to also improve their careers. Everyone wins!

Share the project

Another easy and important thing you can do is to share the project itself. After all, you probably became interested in the project in the first place because it solves some interesting problems that you have or had. Maybe the project helped your company achieve better results or solve a customer issue. Sharing all the things that the project has done for you or your company will really help the project to be more visible. It will also help you have clarity on how to explain things to people and how to share the pros and cons of something. Last but not least, sharing the project with someone will help them solve their problems.

The big advantage of sharing the project is that you will have a lot of information about it available, from README instructions to tutorials, examples, and even the source code. It is a lot easier to share something when the materials are already available for you to draw from. That is a win for everyone – for the project, you, and the people that are having problems.

Share the principles

Your chosen project does something well, does it not? I can imagine that you were attracted to it because it has some technically interesting challenges or solutions. Maybe it has a strong architecture, uses a new programming language, applies some technology in an interesting, innovative way, or uses some new idea or tech. How about sharing those principles, so people can use them in their own projects? You can focus on large principles, or even some small implementation trick or pattern, the way the project uses its data, or even some secrets about the language that the project is being developed in.

This is the secret: you can do all of that even if you're not part of the project! You can learn principles by reading the source code and running the project, and then share what you learned with other people. Sharing about the project is something that you do not need to ask permission from anyone for. It is once more a win for everyone involved. It is a win for you because you get more visibility and improve your reputation. It is a win for the project because more people see the value that they are creating, the results of the project, and the novel methods that they are using. It is also very important for the people that will be reading or watching your content because they can understand and apply the same principles to their projects.

Share how to participate

The last suggestion for you is to share how to participate in open source. After all, you are doing the work of getting involved, of being accepted and contributing. You can then help other people to do the same. You already know your project, and know where and how to get started. You can help or even mentor new people in your project. Or you can apply the strategies we've mentioned here in this book and share how they worked for you, so other developers can work their way into their project of choice.

Sharing is a win-win proposition for everyone involved, so anything that you can share about your current project and what you're doing, or about participating in open source in general, is extremely helpful for you and everyone involved.

The following are examples of bringing value to your company and customers:

- Solve problems faster by adopting open source solutions
- Bring improved solutions to open source communities
- Build a knowledge base of solutions for your company
- Combine open source software for a more complete solution
- Build on top of existing open source projects
- Learn from solutions and patterns implemented in existing projects
- Apply proven open source processes inside your company or for your customers

Bringing value to your company and customers is key. Working on open source projects can be extremely interesting and unbelievably valuable because it builds your reputation, your knowledge, and your skills. Sometimes we forget that open source also brings amazing results for your company and customers. Once you realize that this happens, then you can start working on open source in your current job. That is interesting because, as we said at the beginning of this chapter, many open source developers get paid to work on open source projects, and the way they do that is by bringing clear value to their company and customers.

There are a few things that you can look for and do to make sure that the open source product you participate in is bringing value to your company and customers. You can solve problems faster by adopting open source solutions. Often, companies spend substantial amounts to build frameworks and libraries and solve problems. If you can find an open source project or even a small part of an open source project that can solve the problem that you are trying to solve, or that you can use as a basis for something that you are trying to solve, then it accelerates your projects and accelerates the results of your company.

You can do the same thing by expanding that and combining multiple open source software projects to build a more complex solution for your company. Instead of just looking at one project or a small part of a project, what if you could combine a few open source projects that would solve 50-80% of the problems that you are trying to solve? That could be an amazing result for your company. You can bring a product to life much faster. You can get results and even your first customers by building on top of something that already exists.

Sometimes there are open source projects that are either infrastructure projects or base-level initiatives that you can build on top of. Even complete projects can be improved upon, or they can be used as a basis and then modified. You can create a completely different new product, or you can repurpose a project. An open source project can be used in different industries in diverse ways. Building your software solution on top of an open source project can help you achieve results faster.

Every time you do that, invariably, you will end up improving the open source project itself. Every time you make a point of bringing back the improvements that you created to open source communities, that is one of the major ways that open source grows and becomes more prevalent and more important for everyone. People that are using open source software and building on top of it bring those improvements back into the wider community. Many people confuse that with giving away your product to the open source community. Most of the time, you are going to be using an open source product as a base, and that is something that is completely different from what the open source project does. Your improvements on the open source base can be brought back to the community even if you do not want to share the exact product that you are creating.

You can also use your knowledge of multiple open source projects that exist or your visibility of what the projects are doing and how they work to build a knowledge base of solutions for your company. One of the most advanced things that you can do to really bring lots of impact for a company is to contribute standard architectures. They can be reused throughout all your company projects. So, if you make the effort to map and define the open source projects that your company is going to be based on and how the company can benefit these communities in return, and you help the company forge a relationship with the open source project that you will be dependent upon, that is going to be extremely helpful. Another thing that can be helpful for your company is when your company has problems, such as performance problems, compatibility problems, or difficulties with their software solution, to learn from open source projects and how they solved similar problems. Their solutions can be re-implemented in your company's project. That allows you to build on top of and learn from the many hours top developers spent solving those problems and utilize their solutions in your current projects. By doing this, you also build the knowledge that you need to bring improvements to those projects themselves. You and your company win and the open source project wins.

The last thing that we'll mention here in terms of how you can bring value to your company and customers is when you apply proven open source processes inside your company to help your customers. Open source projects, especially the larger ones, are built with many developers that work for multiple companies, sometimes spread out in large geographical areas, using quite different communication styles. What happens inside of a company with requirements, in terms of maintainability in evolving the projects in a way that does not cause disruption to the large number of users who are using this project? Most companies do not have the level of requirements in terms of usage and widespread adoption that some open source projects have. To learn how those projects evolved, how they build their systems, and how they actually work, you must incorporate software development best practices into the project. You can help your company implement best practices. That is valuable because that is a skillset that is difficult to teach people, and it is much easier to learn it by participating in a project like this. So, once you understand something by participating in an open source project, then you can repeat the same thing inside your company. Thus, you are helping your company to become more sophisticated and professional. These soft development skills will really benefit your company's projects and every single customer that you have. If you are a consultant or you do development work for customers, you can also apply the same strategies with your customers, benefitting everyone around you.

Delivering value to your company and customers

Participating in open source projects can be extremely interesting and valuable for your career because it helps so much with building your reputation, knowledge, and skills. You should not forget that open source also brings amazing results for your company and customers. Once you are able to start doing this, you can start working on open source in your current job. As we said at the beginning of this chapter, many open source developers get paid to work on open source projects. The secret to doing that is bringing clear value to companies and customers. Next, we will explore a few things that you can do to make sure that the open source project you participate in brings value to your company and customers.

Solve problems faster by adopting open source solutions

A lot of times, companies spend huge effort building frameworks and libraries and solving particular problems. You can try to find an open source project or even a small part of an open source project that can solve the problem that you are trying to solve. You can also use one as the basis to do something that you are trying to solve. This usually accelerates projects and the results of the company.

Combine open source software for a more complete solution

Expand that idea and combine multiple open source pieces of software to build a more complex solution for your company. Instead of just looking at one project or a small part of a project, what if you could combine 3 or 4 open source projects? What if by doing that, it would solve 60% (or maybe 80%!) of the problem that you're trying to solve?

That can provide amazing acceleration for your company, and you can bring a product or feature to life much faster.

Build on top of existing open source projects

You can use open source projects and frameworks to build almost anything you want. There are a lot of projects that are either infrastructure projects or base-level initiatives or platforms that you can build on top of. There are even complete projects that are maybe focused on something else but can be used as a whole or in part, and modified to suit your needs. You can create a completely different new product, repurpose it for another industry, or use it in different ways. You get a base that has been developed, tested, and is ready to be reused, making your work much easier.

Bring back improved solutions to open source communities

Every time you do any of the previous things, invariably you will end up improving the open source project itself. Make a point of bringing back the improvements that you created to the open source community. That is one of the major ways that open source grows and becomes more prevalent and more important for everyone.

You should not confuse that with giving away all your products to the open source community, because that is not a necessity. Most of the time you're going to be using an open source project to create a product that is different from what the project does. Your improvements to the core of the project can be brought back to the community, even if you don't make public the exact product that you're creating.

Build a knowledge base of solutions for your company

You should also use your knowledge of multiple open source projects that exist and your visibility of what the projects are doing and how they're working to build a knowledge base of solutions for your company.

After all, one of the most advanced things that you can do to really have a big impact on a company is to contribute to company standards and architecture decisions. Once you help build those, they're going to be reused throughout all your company projects.

If you make the effort to map and define what the open source projects that your company is going to be basing its projects on are, and how the company can return value to the open source community, you are not only helping the company to forge a relationship with the open source project that you use and depend on, but you are also defining the architecture and frameworks that all the developers of the company will work with and how to use all that software together.

Learn from solutions and patterns implemented in existing projects

Another thing that can be very helpful for your company is to use open source to help deal with large, complex problems. Examples could be performance, compatibility, integration, and scalability problems. Whatever difficult problem exists in their solution, you can find and learn from open source projects and how they solve it.

You can then re-implement similar ideas in your company's project. That builds on top of many hours of top developers solving those problems. Not only can you learn from and utilize those solutions in your current projects, but you also build the knowledge that you need to bring improvements to those projects. Again, you and your company win. The open source projects win too.

Apply proven open source processes inside your company or for your customers

The last thing that we will mention here in terms of how you can bring value to your company and customers is when you apply the processes that open source uses to get highly distributed teams to build software together.

After all, open source projects, especially the larger ones, are worked on by many developers that work for multiple different companies, sometimes spread out in large geographical areas, and usually with very different communication styles. Many open source projects have requirements that only the largest companies will ever have, such as high maintainability and evolvability. Not to mention the project's need to grow without affecting the large number of users who are using it. Most companies also don't have the level of requirements in terms of usage and widespread adoption that some open source projects have.

Learning and applying how those projects evolve, how they build their systems, and how those projects actually build software are best practices that can revolutionize the way your company builds software too. Those processes are not easy to learn, but you can learn how to do them by participating in open source projects. Once you understand how to do something, you can repeat it inside your company.

Making your company a more sophisticated and professional software development house will benefit your company's projects and every single customer that you have.

You can apply the exact same best practices with your customers. If you are a consultant or you develop for customers, applying the same strategies in working with your customers will promote even more professionalism to everyone around you.

In short, participating in open source communities and open source projects will help you hone your technical skills and improve your career in many ways. It is an effort that can bring benefits to you, your company, your customers, and the wider development community.

Interview

Josh Juneau

Q: Welcome, Josh Juneau, Java Champion. We are sharing career stories and talking about how developers have advanced in their careers.

Josh, you are someone who's well known in the community and has had great success in your career and the Java developer community. Bruno and I want to hear from you about your career. Tell us just a little bit about you and your career and what you're doing now.

A: Well, first, I really appreciate you having me, Heather and Bruno. I'm very honored to be here.

I am an application developer by day. I also am a database administrator; that's my full-time job. But in my off time, I work a lot in open source, and I also do a lot of authoring: articles, books, and so forth. That's where I spend most of my time. I also do lots of podcasting – I have a couple of podcasts that I'm a regular on, so I enjoy doing that as well.

Q: Podcasting is fun, and it's a good platform to be heard and make an impact.

What is a story you can share that really made your career start to move in the direction that led you to this point?

A: I did lots of work with Java and learned it on my own through tutorials, which were great. I was interested in learning other languages on the JVM, so I got into Jython because I was familiar with Python at the time. I started to get involved in the mailing list and to speak with some of the developers, and I asked what I could do to help contribute.

I started by contributing to the website – I totally redesigned the website for Jython. Then, I started to work on the Django on Jython project – I was one of the leads on that. I made a pretty good impact in that community, starting off with Django.

From there, they asked me to be the lead author of the Jython book. I went ahead, worked with Apress, and got into authoring there. That kick-started my authoring career.

It happened quickly, and I enjoyed every minute of it because I enjoyed working with Jython and the community. Making those connections with others in the community was a big deal; it's very important.

Q: Sometimes, I hear developers say, "I want to get started. I want to participate in open source." I think that's a very common topic that people bring to us when we talk about careers, and there is often a desire, but people don't know how to take that first step. I think you touched on it a little bit when you said you joined the mailing list. What was it that motivated you to take that first step? Can you explain how you got initiated into the community and how it built organically from there?

A: I started off by asking a few questions on the mailing lists because I had questions about the technology, and then I began to interact with the members of the group. They started to say, "You've got some good ideas. Why don't you help?" And so, that's exactly what I did. I started to contribute back, and just went on from there.

If you've followed me at all out there, you know I've got a few books, and that's something that I was interested in continuing. I worked with a couple of people in the publishing industry and had some ideas, and they liked my ideas, so I continued to pitch new ideas and they continued to like them. I would write books about those ideas, and getting that foot in the door really helped with that part of it.

Then, to build upon that, I knew lots of people from the conference space because I started to attend meetups, Java User Group sessions, and conferences. You start to make connections with networking, not only meeting people online through the mailing list and through the different projects but also meeting face to face, which makes a big impact and is very important.

I was then asked to start writing articles, so I began to do some book articles. Then, I got interested in other open source projects as well, so I started to be introduced to even more projects. I think just being a part of the community has got me into so many different areas. It's really helped my career.

Q: And it sounds like along the way, you're expressing or verbalizing your thoughts and ideas and sharing your intentions, saying, "I want to write a book, I have these ideas," and getting feedback from people.

A: Indeed. You have to not be afraid to provide your feedback and input. If you sit back and listen and don't ever speak up or provide any feedback, nobody will hear. I think it's important that you get involved and communicate – don't be afraid to share your opinions.

Q: I think some people think that their opinion isn't significant enough or they don't have enough experience, and they end up being reluctant. Or, on the other side, they might just assume people know they want to be an author or contribute to an open source project, and so they just wait to be asked.

A: It's really important to take those steps and go out to your JUG, or to a conference if you can. You'll probably see people walking around that you have met online or that you've seen elsewhere before; don't be afraid to go out and introduce yourself, because that's how these connections get started.

Q: Don't you think that progressing in your career after a certain point is more of an art than science? Not every recipe works for everyone. For example, some people may have last or equivalent experience both to careers while you're stuck. Have you ever had the feeling that people were growing and you were stuck?

A: It can be like that sometimes. You can feel intimidated by others moving ahead and advancing and feel like you're stuck. But at that point, you have to reach out and do some work to learn more technology, or learn in more depth about the technology you're already working with. Engage yourself and learn more so that you can produce more.

Q: Josh, there's one question I want to ask because I am asked this question a lot: many developers, when you're talking about participating in open source and contributing to podcasts, will say, "But that's not development. Those are extra things." Do you think that doing those things makes you a better developer? People say, "All I want to do is be a better developer. I want to do it for a certain goal, and so doing all of those other things would detract from the goal. It seems to be a waste of time, doing podcasts and writing books instead of becoming better at developing." How do you feel about that?

A: I don't think it's a waste of time at all. I enjoy writing books and articles because it keeps me well informed about what's coming up or what's new. In order to write a book or an article, you have to be very knowledgeable about the subject. I've never written a book or an article where I didn't learn at least one or two things, because you're always going out, learning more, reaching out to the community, and finding out more information, and that's one way to help further your development; it's very important.

Another thing is that with podcasts, one of my favorite times of the month is when I get together with my friends and discuss Java and other things that I'd like to talk about, because I learn what they've been up to, what's new in their world, and things I've never even heard about. Every time I record a podcast and every time I write an article or book, I'm furthering my development.

Q: Can you share a little bit about the impact that you think you've made in your career as a result of being involved in these open source projects and as a result of the articles, books, and podcasts?

A: The first big impact I had was with the redesign of the Jython website, because that impacted the whole community. It rejuvenated the Jython language.

With respect to the books and the articles, I hope that people are enjoying the content and learning from what I have to offer. I know one thing that has had a big impact is the mailing list. That's one of the easiest things you can do: get involved by providing feedback to the different communities out there and giving insight using your perspective. That definitely has a good impact because you can further those technologies.

Q: And it's impacted your career as well, and benefited it?

A: It has. It helped me learn more. Every time I do things, I learn more, and so it does have a big impact on the future of my career.

Q: How much time do you spend a week on open source projects versus work for your employer?

A: That's a good question.

It changes every week. It's never constant. If I have more free time one week, I may spend a few hours on open source. If I don't have any time, there are some weeks that go by where I don't spend any time on it. It just depends.

That's one of the things about open source that I think is similar for everyone; it's one of those things where people will make a big impact when they have the time, and it's just natural that sometimes you are busy with other activities or your full-time job, and you don't have as much time to commit to the open source project. But you should still continue to stay engaged, and then, as time allows, make your contributions.

Q: What was the impact of the open source community on your career?

A: It's had a significant impact. Even being here today (at the event) and talking with all of my fellow developers and people in the community I've learned new things about what people are doing. I'll go out and research those different things and learn more, and maybe I'll get more into those avenues – and maybe not. But it's always good to engage with the community and work with others that are doing similar things and dissimilar things. Even if they're doing something that's not similar to what I do – if somebody's working on a different tech that I'm not familiar with – I still like to try and understand what they're doing and why; it might be something I'm interested in looking further into. The community is very important, as is paying back to other individuals and always communicating with your peers.

Summary

In this chapter, you learned about the value of open source contributions, how to identify open source projects that are relevant to your career, the steps to get involved and start participating, how to find the time and resources to keep participating, and how you can make open source contributions valuable for your company and your career growth. In the next chapter, we will discuss how to incorporate public speaking to have an impact on your career journey.

12
Scaling Trust through Public Engagement: Speaking and Blogs

In the last chapter, we talked about contributing to open source projects to increase your skills and advance your career. Trust is one of the most important currencies for your career growth. You need it for both contributing to open source projects and for public speaking. When people trust you, you have access to better positions and more interesting projects. So far, you have been building trust by working closely with people in communities and open source. Now, it is time to build trust at scale. Public speaking and sharing allow you to do that, and that's what this chapter is all about. In this chapter, we will cover what public speaking really is, how to overcome fear and anxiety, how to generate and present your content, and how to find where to start sharing.

Trust is one of the most important things in our careers. When we have trust, we can get amazing jobs, get offered better positions, and gain more responsibility. We can then work on more interesting things. When we have more responsibility, we become more of a leader and get a better salary.

Trust and responsibility go hand in hand. The more trust you have, the more responsibility you can acquire. Trust is hard to build. It requires people to know you and see who you are, and understand what ideas you have and how much knowledge you have about a particular topic. It is extremely hard to trust someone that you do not believe has the requisite knowledge.

Trust has a lot to do with what people believe about you. Reputation is precisely what people believe about you. So, trust and reputation, although not the same thing, go hand in hand.

One powerful method to establish trust at a large scale and build a strong reputation is through sharing. This can be achieved through various means, such as expressing ideas through written content in blogs or delivering impactful presentations.

Although both writing and presentations involve sharing, they differ significantly. Writing generally consists of a more solitary process, allowing ample time to refine ideas and incorporate input from others.

However, since the act of writing occurs behind the scenes, the final product is the only visible aspect that others witness.

Public speaking, be it in a presentation or on an online seminar or video, tends to be done face to face with others. They are different formats, but in terms of creating and defining the content and understanding what the audience needs, they are similar. This chapter deals with sharing ideas in general: speaking, blogging, and writing.

In this chapter, we will discuss the following topics:

- What public speaking really is
- Listening: public speaking for introverts
- Generating unlimited content ideas
- Building and presenting your content
- Finding the right places to share

Before we begin, it's important to acknowledge that sharing can be intimidating. When you put your content and ideas out there, you become visible to others. People see and hear you, read your writing, and become aware of your presence. This vulnerability can potentially invite criticism and judgment.

When you share your knowledge and ideas, others have the opportunity to assess your expertise and evaluate your authenticity. They can gauge your true understanding of a subject and scrutinize the validity of your statements. It is natural to feel uneasy about being vulnerable and exposed in this way. Sharing can indeed be a daunting prospect, evoking fear and apprehension. It is exactly because it is scary that it is so powerful. Most people realize that it is hard, that it is scary, and so believe that they would never be able to do it. They think, *"I would need to be a master to do it. If you are doing it, it must mean that you are an expert."*

This is especially true for public speaking. People have such a deep fear of public speaking, that it makes public speaking an extremely effective way of building trust, especially when done in person and even more so at big events where lots of people are watching. This combination is also immensely powerful, and it is something that we can use to grow our careers, our visibility, and our reputation.

Let us see how we can use this tool as a career and reputation booster because it is not as hard as it sounds. It is scary, for sure, but not hard.

What is public speaking?

Public speaking can be thought of as a form of sharing via a conversation. No matter whether you are talking to someone one to one, in person, or even over the phone, be it in a meeting at your company, with a few people in a room, or at a big event with hundreds of people in a room – it is still a conversation.

Even when you are recording a video or authoring an article, sharing is always a conversation with a person. Even at an event where speakers are talking on a stage, the best speakers look at each person in the audience. The speaker talks, and the other person responds by nodding their heads or smiling. They reply to you visibly, or in their heads.

Sharing is always a conversation. That is true also for writing: when you write, you're talking to someone. When you read a book, there is always a conversation. The author is talking to you and telling you what is going on, answering the questions that are in your head.

When you see speaking and sharing as a conversation, it makes a lot more sense and it is easier for you to understand what to do and how to do it. When you think of sharing as a conversation that has the potential to help more people, it is also easier to decide to start sharing yourself.

Heather has experience of learning to share when working with a professional coach on her leadership and communication skills. The coach, John Bates, had worked with her many times on sharing her stories. At one point he became frustrated and asked her, *"Why are you being so stingy with yourself in your presentations? You are sharing stories here with me now, and you have the potential to help so many more people by publicly sharing more of your stories."* This encouraged a shift of mind toward thinking of helping others by sharing.

There are many formats that you can use for sharing, but they fall into three main categories: text, audio, and video.

Text is the most prominent format and the most popular. You can share text content through blogs, articles, and books. You can write posts for your blogs, articles for magazines or websites, and even on social media. You can also share text through both traditional books and e-books, and over email.

Audio is another popular way of sharing. Podcasts and audio-only conversations on Twitter Spaces are a couple of examples of this. Audio is a great format for sharing knowledge because lots of people like to listen to content on the go. You can listen to content in the car or while you're walking or cycling to work or on the subway. It's easy to download and have on your device to listen to any time you want, and as a result, audiobooks, for example, are very popular. Audio allows you to have a conversation with your audience, interview other people, or even host a multi-party conversation.

And the last way is sharing through video or visuals, such as a presentation on YouTube or on a stage for example, where people can see you. This could be in person, at an event, or at a meetup. It can also be transmitted to people watching it remotely. It can also be recorded and then watched later as a fully online video. This combination of audio, video, and slides with text is a really strong combination that many speakers use to present their content in all those formats.

In all of these formats, you have one person sharing their content with many people listening, reading, or watching. You can also have a few people interacting with each other to create content, such as interviews or panels where different people share their views and then others can watch and listen.

The idea behind sharing is to transfer knowledge and experience so more people have access to it. That's why we consider sharing a way for you to build trust at scale, because once you have a piece of content that has been recorded or written, then it can be accessed by many people.

Even in an event where there's no recording but tens, hundreds, maybe thousands of people participating, you're doing the same thing. You're building trust at scale because everyone that's watching your content will see you as an expert on that content, not because you necessarily know more than they do, but because you're willing to put the work into clarifying, formatting, and curating the content, and presenting it in a way that helps people solve their problems, get inspired, and take action. And this is probably the most important thing about sharing: you want people to take action.

Sharing is not only about you speaking and creating content, but also about that content helping people to solve a problem, to take a step forward in their careers, in their projects, and in tackling their problems. And so once you share your knowledge, other people can take action on what you're sharing and use your content to solve their problems. That's when the cycle becomes complete and that's the highest level of trust: when people trust you enough to take action on your proposals based on what you're teaching them.

This action could take many forms: going back to their companies and applying that technology or experimenting with that new project that you've talked about, or maybe integrating a specific technology or technique into their project. All of these involve people taking action on what you're sharing.

So in general, public speaking and blogging are parts of this ecosystem where you learn and experiment with something, and so you become good at something. You are then able to clarify, curate, and explain that knowledge to other people. Then you can use text, audio, and video to share that knowledge.

Other people will then understand what you're doing and be inspired to apply the same techniques and ideas in their own lives. Once they do, what happens? They start trusting you more because you are now a trusted advisor that helps them solve that particular problem.

That is how we build trust at scale. Those ideas distributed in text, audio, and video can really help you reach large numbers of people. There are technical presentations with millions of viewers on YouTube, for example. We don't have to aim for massive scale or widespread recognition to see success in our careers. It's not necessary to *go big or go home* to achieve meaningful results and make progress in our professional lives.

We need first to affect people that are close to us. Even if all you are doing is writing or presenting your knowledge to others inside your company, such as writing a document explaining how to apply a given technology to your project and then a few developers read that document and take action on your proposals, then you're also influencing and becoming trustworthy inside your company. Never mind hundreds of millions of views; working inside your own company is enough to deliver you plenty of results in terms of your career.

Public speaking for introverts

When it comes to sharing, particularly for introverts, it's understandable that there can be hurdles to overcome. For introverts and those who fear being in front of people, engaging in conversations and sharing ideas can be challenging, limiting their ability to share effectively.

While extroverted individuals often naturally feel more energized and comfortable being in front of others, it's important to note that being an extrovert is not a prerequisite for sharing. Both introverts and extroverts can benefit from a powerful technique: listening. Listening plays a crucial role in sharing because the essence of sharing is not solely about talking; it's about understanding and helping others take action to overcome their challenges.

Would you believe that Heather is an introvert? By employing her natural strengths of listening and her genuine desire to help others, she was able to utilize public speaking to listen and help others. She shifted the way she thought of public speaking and then built the skills to excel at public speaking. In the process, it became one of her greatest skills.

As an introvert, you likely excel in listening since it comes more naturally to you. By actively listening, you gain insights into your audience's problems, difficulties, and experiences. This knowledge becomes a valuable resource for creating relevant content that resonates with your audience. Extroverts can also employ this technique by actively listening to people's concerns and challenges shared during social interactions or events.

How does it work? It can be applied in various situations, such as one-on-one conversations. For instance, when a friend confides in you about their struggle with implementing the latest Java version, actively listening and understanding their problem enables you to create content that addresses and solves that specific issue. By consistently creating valuable content that helps people overcome their obstacles, you establish your reputation and gain visibility in your field.

Contrary to common misconceptions, you don't need to search for universal problems or cater to a wide audience to create valuable content. Even if you address the challenges of just one person and provide a solution, chances are you are also helping others facing similar problems who may not have voiced their concerns or sought assistance elsewhere.

By solving real problems for individuals, you exponentially increase your reputation and visibility, regardless of whether you identify as an introvert or an extrovert. The key to generating valuable content lies in listening. Start small by listening to your own challenges and difficulties. Look around you and listen to the problems faced by friends, colleagues, or individuals in your network. By asking questions and actively listening, you can identify their challenges and gain a deep understanding of how you can help.

Listening not only boosts your confidence but also allows you to explore solutions implemented by others. By understanding the actions they took to overcome their obstacles, you expand your expertise and learn from their experiences, enabling you to provide even better problem-solving strategies.

Once you have listened to people's difficulties, problems, and solutions, you can create content that genuinely helps others implement effective solutions and navigate their challenges more effectively.

Generate content ideas

One of the hardest parts of sharing is to decide what kind of content on what topic you're going to share. It's easy to look around and see that for anything that you can imagine, someone already shared something and so there's nothing that you can add. This couldn't be further from the truth; just because someone else has already discussed a topic you want to talk about doesn't mean you have nothing valuable to add. You have your own experiences, your own problems, your own particular situation. This is one of the most powerful presentation topics, especially (but not exclusively) for beginners – adding your personal experience to the presentation or content. When you're applying a technology, for example, you have a specific context inside your company that can lead to different problems down the road, and you have different environments, different existing problems, and different resources. The same solution that may prove incredibly valuable and useful for a large company with a sizable team can be an ill-suited and problematic choice for a start-up with only a few developers.

Depending on the context, the environment, and the resource you have available to you, there are different solutions, and different experiences will come from these. So, if you're looking for a topic to write on, you can share your own experiences. This also builds trust. People will want to know how that solution actually worked for you. Did it make a difference? Did it rock your results? Did it shake up your project? They want to see if they can relate to your experience and find a parallel with their own situation. If they do, then they're like, *"Hey, this could be the answer to my problem too! I can totally handle those challenges just like you did."* That's why sharing your experience is a game-changer. You bring a unique perspective that can be a goldmine for others.

But that said, we understand that choosing the right content to share is hard. So, here are some ideas for you to select and decide what content to share. You can use it to help create unique content – above all, consider sharing your personal experiences. Every time you share something that is personal to you, something that happened to you, to your project, or your company, you're always adding a different perspective and creating content that is unique to you.

You can share your experience with a problem that you faced in the past, or that you still face today. You can discuss how that problem affects you, how it affects your project, how you're trying to solve it, the experience that you had while solving it, and what other problems your solution caused. All of these could be important ways to add your own experience to your content. You can also share a solution that you implemented or would like to implement. Talk about how you would (or did) apply the solution to your project, the pros and cons, and how you use that solution in your company now.

You can also share things that you learn. If you're studying something, share it with others so they have an easier way of learning what you're learning right now. Share your personal experience of learning it, too.

Another way is to share your thoughts on a popular topic. Popular topics pop up all over the internet. It could be a new technology that comes along or a new version of an existing technology everyone's talking about. It could be a particular situation that happened, a company that had a problem or had a good result, or launched a new idea that everyone is commenting on. It could be something from outside the technology world, such as a sports event like the soccer World Cup or a prominent movie that's coming out that your audience is interested in. Maybe a new Star Wars series or a new version of The Lord of the Rings.

All of these things are popular. You're going to see many people talking about them. Your immediate thought might be that everyone's already talking about it, and there is nothing for you to add, but it's actually the other way around. When lots of people are talking about it, many people are interested, so you have more people to be interested in your content.

When you have a trending topic like this, there is the opportunity to share your perspective on it. You can dive into why the World Cup matters to the tech world or explore the software development happening around the latest blockbuster movie. You can discuss how you've implemented a trending technology in your own project.

While everyone is buzzing about the new Java version, you can chime in with your experience using it in your current project. Share the challenges, benefits, and problems you encountered. Talk about how it impacts your work. For instance, if everyone is talking about ChatGPT, you can discuss how it will impact your specific tasks and daily life, illustrating its broader impact. In all of these cases, the key is to make connections to the technology you want to discuss. For example, if you are a frontend developer creating content for mobile devices, you can talk about how ChatGPT will change the design of mobile applications – this is a different take than most people have. Another example is if you're implementing an API, you could talk about how ChatGPT can help you task the APIs. All of these are ways for you to connect the popular topic that everyone's talking about to something that you are doing right now and that will make your content unique.

Another great way to make your content unique is to share some situation you have in your life. Even normal day-to-day things can become content. You had a discussion with your friends, how might that connect to technology? How does that connect to a discussion that people might be having inside a team? You had a special interaction with your pets. How does that connect with something that you're doing at work or with the technology your audience is working on?

That may sound strange, but it's completely possible. Maybe you saw the video of two dogs fighting through a gate, and then the gate opens and they just stop fighting and start becoming friends. Maybe you can make a comparison with how developers discuss technology on social media and yell at each other, but when they sit down to work on the same project, they quickly see that they have the same problem and collaborate to implement a solution.

You can always see situations in your daily life and try to apply those situations to things that are happening in your projects. You can also create comparisons or metaphors for things that you said or experienced in your life. Maybe you watched a movie that contained a metaphor that can be applied to the Technology Award, for example. That is a great way to create and generate unique content.

Another thing you can do is remix content that's already out there. What would that entail? It could mean comparing different content. So, you could say, here are two different developers talking about different technologies. You can compare those two different technologies based on what they wrote.

You can curate content from others. You can provide the best content to solve a particular problem; for example, curate an archive of the best articles on solving the refactoring of legacy code. That's great curated content.

You could also respond to or expand on existing content. If someone suggests a solution, you could respond with what problems that suggestion might create, or expand on how that solution could be applied to other situations.

In all those cases, you give your perspective on some piece of content that already exists. You can amplify, criticize, agree, or disagree with any kind of content that already exists and that helps you create unique content also.

You can also join forces with other content creators. You can run interviews, panels, and discussions to bring together the opinions of different people and what they think, what challenges they're going through, and how they can solve those challenges. You can do this live with people or you can send questions to other speakers and bloggers. In the latter case, you could watch someone's presentation and send them a set of questions that they can respond to. And with that, you're both creating content together.

That's not an exhaustive list, but should give you some ideas of how you can always create unique content. No matter how much content on particular topic already exists on the internet, you can always create something that's new, different, and adds to and improves on what already exists.

Find the right place to share

Now that you know how to find the right types and topics of content, you need to find the right place to share it.

There are many places where you can share your content, but the most important thing is to know where your audience is. Every time you share content, you're sharing to help someone take action, solve a problem, and improve their lives. Your content is geared toward a special person. We call this an "avatar," a representative of the type of person that needs to hear, listen, or consume your content. Wherever you publish your content, the right audience, your avatar, needs to be present because that's where they're going to find your content and benefit from it.

If you're writing text, one of the most common places to share it is social media. If you have an audience on social media, sharing content there can help you promote content that's published somewhere else, or you can use social media to write content directly. Places like LinkedIn and Facebook allow you to write and publish long-form content. Some other social media, such as Twitter, will only allow short-form content, but you can create multiple posts in a thread, which allows somewhat longer content.

Another avenue for sharing is through blogging platforms specifically designed for content creation and publication. Platforms such as Dev.to, which caters to developers, or Medium.com, which has a broader audience, offer excellent opportunities for posting your content and reaching a wider readership. These platforms act as distribution channels, ensuring that your content reaches a larger audience. These are particularly useful if you want to write one-off pieces or standalone articles. Those platforms will promote and distribute your content to lots of people even if you don't have your own special audience.

You can also use that technique to write articles for places such as Dzone or Foojay, or even magazines like Java Magazine. These are great places where you can write longer formats, and multiple pages of content. Also, many companies have their own places for articles – consider checking with yours.

And of course, you can have your own site. We talk about this one last because when you have your own site, you have to build the audience yourself, you have to attract people to read your content. With the other destinations for content that we mentioned so far in this chapter, the platform or company will promote your content for you so it's easier for you to reach more people. Despite that, having your own site is great because it's a place where you can keep all your content together and can attract the right audience that you want. There are different tools you can use to run your site, including WordPress or GitHub Pages and Jekyll. You can use different tools of your choice to publish content on your own site.

If you're doing audio, of course, you can publish your audio on your own site. And if you have a site with your own blog and audience, you can publish your audio content there. But there are also several platforms for podcasting. You can publish your content on places such as Spotify, Apple, and Google, all of which offer strong podcast platforms that allow people to easily download and listen to your content. There are many other platforms like that. You can choose what works for you.

A more recent trend that's very important and very useful for audio is audio discussion places. Places such as Twitter Spaces, Clubhouse, and even Discord servers will allow you to do host these audio-only discussions with other people. Discord is an interesting place because you already have an audience on public Discord servers that you can join, including servers for user groups or communities, and you can run audio discussions there.

And last but not least, we have video presentations. That's the top level of sharing. There are many places you can do these. You can start inside your own company, presenting to your colleagues. You can expand to more people inside your company. Maybe your company has an auditorium or an online place where you can present something if you want to do more public things.

Another good place to get started is at universities or sometimes technical schools, where you have people that might be interested in your content. Often, students may not have lots of access to industry players, so they're going to be an easier audience that you can talk to. You can be more informal and create and present your content there. For career-minded people, there are places such as meetups and user group meetings. We discussed user groups more extensively in an earlier chapter.

If your audience is, for example, Java developers, then looking for Java User Groups could be a great place to start. If it's Python developers, Python also has a strong community that does meetups and so you also go find them there. You can also participate in online events run on Zoom or other online events platforms such as Hopin or Airmeet.

These platforms allow you to run events yourself if you want, but often there's someone else running the event itself and you are invited to submit talks as a speaker so the event attracts an audience. You have online events like this, but you can also have physical events. Places such as DevOps, the Developers Conference, and many other events exist worldwide. There is certainly an event near your city in your country where you can submit talks and present.

We have a whole chapter here in the book that talks about conferences, events, and calls for papers. Conferences are a great place for you to meet people and present your content. As a reminder, look for conferences in your technical community of interest. You can ask people in your network for recommendations of conferences to attend and share your content. You can also observe on your social media channels the conferences people in your network are attending.

Since we're talking about presentations, a great place to do these is video platforms such as YouTube or Rumble. These are video platforms where you can create your content and distribute that content for people to see. Those platforms allow ads on your content to sponsor it, but usually you do not have to pay. If you want a little bit more control over advertising or sponsorship of your content, there are other platforms, such as Vmail, where you pay to publish your content. Whether you host your own podcast or audio-only content or appear as a guest on someone else's platform, these are all good places to share your content as well.

Organizing, building, and presenting your content

Creating content can be challenging, especially when it comes to the process itself. Now that you've listened to people's problems, difficulties, and challenges, and you want to offer a solution, the best approach is to envision a journey for your audience. Consider where they currently stand and where they aspire to be. Then, identify the specific steps they need to take to progress from their current situation to their desired destination. With these steps in mind, you can create content that assists your audience in navigating each stage of their journey.

This approach of envisioning their journey helps you create valuable content by addressing the gap between your audience's current position and their desired outcome. Your content can fill that gap by providing a clear path and outlining the necessary steps they need to take to progress. This can be highly specific, such as addressing a particular challenge like *"How to build a Docker image."* By offering precise solutions to specific problems, your content becomes even more relevant and useful to your audience.

Then, you can provide specific steps accompanied by code, examples, and detailed instructions. This includes tasks such as installing a particular tool, executing specific commands, or adding code snippets. On the other hand, you can also create content with broader topics, such as *"How to start an international career."* While these topics may not have exact step-by-step instructions, you can still outline more general steps such as preparing a resume in English and researching companies of interest. In both cases, you are guiding your audience through a journey, explaining each step, and outlining the necessary actions. This approach works well for various content formats, including articles, blogs, presentations, and even podcasts. It helps you effectively organize and structure your content while inspiring and motivating your audience to take the required steps towards their goals. Another way that you can do this is via a less structured process.

If you invite someone to have a discussion with you, and plan some items to discuss in advance, these topics can be a little less structured because different people can add information. You can make it very interactive and involve your audience. You can let the audience ask questions and make comments so it becomes more interesting for them, as now they can participate, ask questions, and get their specific problem solved when they interact. The best presentations are interactive, where you listen to what people need and adjust your content to help them with the specifics of their situations.

When you present your content, you should present using an appropriate level and register of language for your audience. If you're talking to a more formal audience, such as your team or your boss, you might decide to use more mental representations, numbers, and details. Match your language and content to the needs of the audience. If the setting is a technical event, for example, where people are more informal, you can also present in a more informal way. If you go to a university, maybe you want it to be more informal to allow you to connect with the students.

It is always important to align your tone, attire, slides, and voice with the specific audience you're presenting to. However, the most crucial aspect is the audience itself. When you share your knowledge, the main objective is to benefit your audience. By sharing your expertise, you enhance your visibility, reputation, and gain trust from others. But remember, the focus should never be solely on you—it should always be on the audience and their needs. People are attracted to your content because they want to achieve or acquire something. Your content should provide a solution to their problems or help them attain their desired career, job, or project goals. Whether they aspire to be a junior developer or a team leader, your content should guide and inspire them to take action. Therefore, every time you create content or decide where to share it, keep in mind the impact it will have on your audience and how it aligns with their desires and aspirations.

Finding the right places to get started and share

You should always be thinking about the audience that you are targeting your content at. That way, your content will always match your audience. Once you have that in mind, you can then apply all the things we talked about so far in this chapter – listening to your audience's problems, understanding their situation, and helping them tackle their challenges; organizing your content the right way and generating content that will help them; finding the places where they are so you can present your content to them; helping your audience to achieve what they want; and tailoring your tone and formality to inspire people to take action. Once you do all of that, what happens?

When your audience gets results, they trust you. When they trust you, your reputation grows and your visibility in the market increases. That takes your career to a new level.

Now, let's consider some myths about sharing that we can dispel right now.

You need to be a master to share. No, you do not. To share great content, you only need to be a step ahead of the people that will consume your content. If you just learned something new, you can share it with people who don't know it yet. Even if you are not a step ahead, you can still share good content. You can share the problems you are facing, or difficulties you are going through. You can ask good questions to people that know more than you. There are all kinds of ways to share that do not require you to be a master. But the reality is, the moment you start sharing, people will see you as someone that knows their topic. That is both a responsibility and a benefit. It helps your career because people are going to see you as someone that knows the topic. But it's also a responsibility as you need to be one step ahead of your audience.

The other myth is that you have to be an extrovert to share. We discussed this earlier in this chapter – how introverts, because they are good at listening, can use that ability to share content that's valuable for people. You don't need to be an extrovert to share. There are many ways that you can share that don't require you to show up in person, such as audio-only conversations, so you don't have to show up on video; or a podcast, for example, or by text. You don't actually have to talk to anyone if you don't want to; you can still share good content.

Another myth is that *it takes too much time.* In a way, that is true. Sharing does take time, but it does not necessarily take too much time. What takes the longest is diving deep into a topic, so now you're able to share it. There are many ways that you can share that don't require a lot of preparation; for example, being interviewed by someone, where you generate content based on your experience without having any preparation or spending a lot of time writing things. Answering questions from people is another way that you can create content without a lot of prior preparation. The biggest time commitment involves deeply researching a topic so that you can actually create content about it. That is most likely what you're already doing in your career anyway. You are diving deep into things to do with your projects to learn about technology. The sharing part does not necessarily need to take very long.

Another myth is that *sharing is a waste of time because it does not improve your expertise.* If you're going deep into a topic to apply it in a project, for example, you're building expertise. When you then go to share your knowledge with someone, you'll notice any gaps you might've missed, and things that you don't actually understand very well. That will allow you to become much better at something that you're already interested in, allowing you to solidify your knowledge by applying it and reflecting on it. The sharing part essentially involves you reflecting on what you did, on what you learned, and then organizing this to share with other people. And that will really deepen your understanding and make you a powerhouse. So yes, sharing does improve your expertise, but more than that, when you share, you build trust.

When you build trust, you grow your reputation, and people will invite you to work on more challenging projects and give you more responsibility. This in turn increases your expertise and skills. So actually, sharing is the *best* way for you to increase your expertise.

The last myth we'll talk about here is that sharing is only done in events or public spaces. That's not true. You can share with your friends, your colleagues at work, and your team. All of those ways to share are valid, important, and will build your reputation. You don't need to have a public worldwide reputation to make a difference in your career. If people in your team, people in your company see you as the expert in a certain area, you will get more responsibilities and access to more interesting projects, and will grow in your career and in your company – even if you don't share that information publicly. But doing this publicly will actually increase your reputation in other areas for other companies. This can lead to you meeting amazing people and getting access to other experts. This will be beneficial for you, for your company, for your project, and especially for your career. So although you don't *have* to share publicly, it will be really beneficial for you.

Techniques for engaging audiences with your content

As we close this chapter, let's talk about engaging your audience. We talk in other parts of the book about techniques for effective storytelling. Humans remember and engage with content through stories. This is how you connect with other people and gain understanding. There are a few key points to remember when you use these storytelling techniques. One that is especially important is to focus on your opening, or your hook, that you will use to engage your audience as you share your story. Equally important is your closing, which should retrace your opening points as a way of closing the story you are sharing.

You will also want to incorporate visual aids when you are sharing your content. Consider adding visual aids to all of your content. If you are sharing in person, utilize props to convey your points or get into character. Something like a hat, glasses, shoes, or any other signature item can set the tone and be incorporated as an element of sharing your content. For example, Bruno will typically wear the Brazilian flag as a cape when he is sharing his content. Also, consider your use of slides when you are sharing content in a presentation. The slides should help to communicate your content as an aid or a prompt. You should not be reading your slides – this is commonly known to disengage an audience. The bullets on slides should guide you as a speaker and the audience to follow your story, but they should not be competing with you for attention. Your audience will either focus on reading the slides, or listening to you. You want them to listen to you. In general, think about ways of engaging your audience. This could be asking questions, or asking them to participate or share suggestions in response to your content. Ask them to share feedback with you. Effective sharing and communication is a two-way street.

Interview

Jim Weaver

Jim Weaver now works for IBM. He's been a Java Champion, developer, and evangelist for many companies over many years. He has travelled around the world and gone to many places. But right now, Jim is the quantum computing man.

Q: Can you tell us where your career started?

A: In the early days, I went to school for computer technology but then dropped out due to the pressures of life: wanting to get married and start a family, and I thought I could make more money in the restaurant industry. I put the dream of being a computer scientist on hold and went eight years in the restaurant industry, but became increasingly unhappy. This was in the 1970s, a long time ago.

But as I was in that industry then and I had a TRS-80 level 1, so I decided to go ahead and create the first ever restaurant drive-through ordering point-of-sale system, because I wanted to sell that and buy a model 3.

I created an assembly language in Z80 – dialogue 80. If you had a basic program, that was no problem. You'd just load it, and then you could save it to the cassette tape. If you bought the game Space Invaders, a game that was written in machine language, it wasn't a basic program. If your tape messed up, you were out of luck. You had to buy the game again.

So, I created an application in a dialogue machine language to copy tapes from one to another to bring the tape into memory, and then I could save it to another tape. In that era, I was managing a restaurant and decided to use a point-of-sale system. The TRS-80 had three components to it: the keyboard, the monitor, and the tape deck. So, I mounted things into the drive-through. Then, people could take the order with the funky TRS-80 keyboard, see the order, see the lanes, and see the maps of the cars. Some of the routines were in assembly language so that it would be very quick when somebody's order was fulfilled. I didn't even own a TRS-80, so I would hang out at Radio Shack and learn how to do it (that's where I was when John Lennon died).

I had a lot of my life experiences back then while I was working at, managing, and building things for the restaurant, such as inventory systems. I was also moonlighting for other companies to create applications, such as building applications for a golf course.

Then, at one point, I decided that I'd just quit my job, go into this full-time, and start a business. Then, I lost my shirt. Things were lean, and I was married. I really had a couple of lean years before I got into more consulting – that's about when the IBM PCs came out. I learned dBASE and some other technologies, including a technology called Framework. I built a consulting practice, learning new skills along the way. I was hired by EDS and worked there for 15 years, mostly supporting engineering computing, scientific computing, and then factory floor automation. In 2000, I started an educational technology business, sold it in 2008, and struck out on my own again as an individual contributor, creating JavaFX applications for companies. I also worked for Oracle, and then Pivotal, and now IBM.

Q: When I hear the story of how you started your career and how it evolved, I realize you've had a lot of transitions in your career. Often people are, for whatever reason, either forced to make a transition or want to make a transition based on having realized certain things. Do you have any learnings from all those transitions that you had, or tips and advice that you can draw from your career?

A: There is no one size fits all, but generally, you should always get into a situation where you can be passionate about what you're doing because if you don't, you'll be unhappy. If you can help it, don't be unhappy. Don't consciously go into a situation or role where you know you're going to be unhappy. Don't try to force yourself to fit into something you've talked yourself into, saying, "*I can tolerate this for a while.*" It's almost never, in my experience, a good thing. It's better to really think it through and not be unhappy for big periods of time: find things that you're passionate about and do those things.

For example, there is a trap that I've run into where I thought to advance my career, I was going to have to take a management track, and through experience, I've found that I'm not really happy being a manager. I've found out over the last 20 years that I'm much happier in an individual contributor role. If I knew back then what I know now, I would have tried to stay in an individual contributor role, even if the advancement wasn't so quick and the pay wasn't as great, because I could be passionate and was more suited for that role, rather than being unhappy in management. Think it through: what are you really passionate about?

Q: That's good advice: follow your passions. We talk about this in the book too: having a plan, a vision, and a map, keeping in mind your passions, and staying true to what your interests are.

Can you give an example of your transitions? You worked at Oracle. You worked at Pivotal. Now, you're at IBM, and you're a quantum computing developer advocate – how did that come about?

A: About seven years ago, at a JavaOne panel, there were some prominent people. There was James Gosling, there was the guy that invented CCPIP, there was Vint Cerf, and there were some others. They were talking about the direction of computing. In an offhand way, Cerf said, "You know, I've been looking at Shor's algorithm, thinking that quantum computing could offer some exponential increases in the speed of some algorithms." I had never heard of Shor. I hadn't really looked into quantum computing at all, but based on the fact that Cerf said it, I wiki'd it, followed the rabbit, fell into the rabbit hole, and became passionate about it.

That was when I was working at Oracle and Pivotal. I started steering my career toward quantum computing and putting it into my talks. At Pivotal, I was educating my developer community not only in Spring and Java, but also in quantum computing. That led to IBM reaching out to me and saying, "We hear you are doing the work of an IBM developer evangelist, or an advocate. Why don't you come do it for us?"

Q: How do you get success in life?

A: It's a textbook question.

First of all, success is the progressive realization of a worthy goal: I set goals, and then progressively realize those goals by breaking them down.

Q: We can talk about balance – you mentioned that when you were more junior in your career journey, your marriage was important to you. You have a good story of balance. Oftentimes you have your wife with you when you travel, and you make sure you include your wife. Do you have any stories about balancing your home life and work life in your career?

A: For sure. I'm fortunate that I will have been married to Julie for 47 years this November, and she's put up with a lot because my career is very important to me and translates to supporting the family. That's very important to me, of course, but so is the content of what I do in my career: I love it. I probably won't ever retire because it's my hobby.

As a parent, you need to work to make sure that the family is supported. But then, if you add to that the fact that you love what you do anyway, it's easy to get out of balance, and you could justify that loss of balance sometimes: "It's my work and I have to do it." But in reality, I don't think it's ever necessary to do that. You can rationalize it, but your process of rationalization is often a cop-out to either satisfy your desire to do the fun thing that you're doing or to overemphasize your need to provide. How much do you need to provide? How much do you need in a 401k? How much do you need to spend doing what you're passionate about?

As I've gone through my career, I've found that I don't need as much as I thought. It's like eating, or any other thing that brings pleasure. When you're talking about the joy that you get out of your career, the first bite is the best. After a while, it's just a chore to eat, but you're doing it because you're still getting a little bit of a dopamine hit.

It's the same with working. I don't need to sit at a computer for eight hours working on a problem. Why not try to do it efficiently, prioritizing work and using whatever tools you need to? Have you heard of Pomodoro? Sometimes, you work too much, but I've found that that's almost never necessary, because through planning, prioritization, and being realistic about how much money you need and how much you really need to satisfy your desire to code, you can actually attain that.

This is a success-in-life thing. One component of being successful in life is deciding what you're going to sacrifice: what you're going to give for success. Whatever it is that you say, that's what it will cost you. So, if you say, "I'm going to work 40 hours a week," or, "I'm going to devote this much time and this much energy and this much cost to something," then it just seems like the way that it's worked out is that that's what life requires of you. You gain those benefits that you have agreed to in life.

You could say, *"I'm going to spend 120 hours a week working and traveling."* Somebody else could say, *"You know something? I'm going to give 35 hours a week of concentrated effort, and I'm going to give my family time and balance it.*" Either will be successful. Either will give you monetary and pleasure rewards. It's just what the contract says. Why not agree with life itself and say, *"This is the way it works"*? Why not say, *"OK. I'm going to give this much to this, this much to this"*? You then end up with a more balanced life while still getting the things that you and your family need.

I wrote a very short book to help people going through exactly this process. You need to think about your whole life. What are your goals – personal, professional, and financial? Most people get stumped because they only think about career. That's why people don't have a life-work balance because they only think about work. How can you have life-work balance if you only think about working?

Q: Exactly.

Do you have a story of where you feel like you made an impact by participating in the community? That would be motivating to people who aren't yet engaged in a community.

A: This story ties into career progression as well as impact on the community.

I gave a presentation at JavaOne 2022 on QiskitBlocks. It's a program that I wrote about three years ago: it's a Minecraft-like program in which high-school students, college students, adults – whoever – can learn quantum computing concepts. I wrote it and put it out on GitHub, and it's been very successful. It's been downloaded, starred, and forked, and it's been very helpful for thousands of people in learning quantum computing.

Oftentimes, people ask me, *"How can I get into X field? What's the best way?"* What I've always told them is to first make sure that you like X. If you like X, you're naturally going to be coding some technology and you're naturally going to want to write things in whatever that technology is. You're going to want to build things if that's your passion. When you build things, give them to the public. Put them on GitHub. Make them accessible to other people, and then blog about it. Teach people how to use the thing that you built because the best way to learn something about X is to teach it and build in it.

QiskitBlocks is a prime example of it. I did that while I was working at IBM, but let's say that I was working somewhere else and I was trying to get into quantum computing. Let's say I was working for another company, getting passionate about quantum computing, and I built a similar thing, only it was a musical application. It was a quantum toy piano, and it helped me learn quantum computing. It helped me get exposure to the point that someone reached out to me and offered me a job in it.

My advice, then, would be that if you're passionate about some technology, don't feel discouraged that you're new in it or you're new in the industry. You have way more power and influence than you think you do. If you create an application that people can use to have fun with and learn about it and you put it out there for people, then you learn, they learn, and you become perceived as an expert in it (or at least someone that people can call to help them).

As for the job market, if you're on the outside, the perception is, *"I can't get in."* But if you're in a company and you're looking for people to fill a position that requires an expert in something, you find that a lot of times, you can't find those people. So, if you as a recruiter then connect with some open source project that you see that's really cool that somebody has built, aren't you going to reach out? You're going to at least check them out.

The other answer I was going to give was to say that success is where preparation meets opportunity. An opportunity presents itself because someone needs what you can offer. They see your project, and then all of a sudden, you're working for that company.

Q: That's great. You mentioned the perception that people have of you. The perception that people have of you is reputation. That's exactly the definition of reputation. Reputation is what people think about you and believe about you, and if you don't show up – if you don't help others, if you don't present, if you're not visible – then people don't know about you.

A: That's the whole thing with servant leadership: Heather and Bruno, you're our poster children for servant leadership. You both are, and that is, in my opinion, what you want to be for career success.

Q: So, we have Bazlur and Mimar. Bazlur was on the Java education initiative. So is Mimar.

What did you think of the Java education initiative and the JCP, Mimar?

Mimar: Firstly, I want to say it's a great honor to speak with you. I am so excited.

Q: Let me help you out a little bit here. Mimar sent me all his stories written down.

Heather: I know Mimar. He's from Turkey. I met him there in person. He sent me all his stories. He says that he prepared the first Java video in Turkish in 2008. It was 150 hours across five DVDs. .

Mimar: Thanks.

Heather: Thanks for this training. Many people in Turkey got to know, loved, and learned Java. Thanks. He loves Java and he has produced content, and he's very excited. It's a great honor to speak with you, Mimar. That's awesome.

Mimar: Thank you.

Heather: I've been learning Java since 2001. I have been invited to 10 countries. I have given more than 100 seminars. I have talked to universities and companies about Java. I have written 5 books and published more than 500 hours of video cards and Java technology. Thanks, Mimar. That's awesome.

Mimar: This is my first book, *Java Server Pages*, and this is *Android and Java*, my third book. This is my fourth book: *40s Hibernate and Java*. This is my fifth book: *Spring Framework*.

I want to continue. At the moment, I create with Java microservices and the Java blockchain. I will write about these subjects. At the moment, I'm writing two new books for the Java community.

Heather: That's good.

Mimar, you seem to have had a lot of success in Java in your career. What is the message that you want to give to other developers?

Mimar: In my experience, I've come across many fellow developers who've faced similar challenges. I initially started out as a frontend technologist, navigating the complexities of various technologies throughout my career journey. These transitions were consistently tough, and I truly understand the hurdles that new developers often encounter.

My primary focus has been on teaching Java, a language that's known to be quite intricate. Despite its reputation for being challenging, I've been able to create effective guides that streamline the learning process. By employing methods such as simplifying explanations, using visual aids, and conducting interactive seminars, I've been able to demonstrate that Java can indeed be comprehensible and approachable.

As of now, there are roughly 2,000-3,000 developers in Turkey. However, I believe this number has the potential to skyrocket, especially if I continue my current efforts. I consistently provide valuable insights and share a plethora of new information, playing my part in shaping the ongoing evolution of development practices and contributing to the future of this dynamic field.

Heather: Bazlur is a recent Java Champion – tell us a little bit about it. How do you become a Java Champion? What do you have to do?

Bazlur: First of all, it starts with passion. I'm a very passionate Java developer. I've been doing Java for over a decade.

I did a couple of things. First of all, I started a Java JUG group back at home in Bangladesh, and I continued to be a leader of the Java JUG group, doing a lot of sessions. I've been doing the Java JUG group thing for a while. I've been doing a lot of in-person sessions and online sessions. I also invite a lot of Java JUG group leaders and Java Champions to my Java JUG groups. That way, I build a network.

I have also done a lot of writing. I write on various blogs – InfoQ and others – and I also have my own blogging platform. That's also contributed to me becoming a Java Champion.

Apart from that, I have also written a couple of books in my native language, which is Bengali. I have written four in total. All of it contributed to me becoming a Java Champion.

It means more recognition from your peers. You have to be outspoken, so that when you meet people and other Java Champions, they can see your work and your contribution. You can be an expert individually. You can work for a company for a long time – that's definitely amazing. It will give you a steady income as well. But if you want to achieve other things – such as the honor that I have been given – you have to be outspoken. You have to network with people, do community work, and write stuff.

I don't speak a lot, but I have started to grow my speaking career recently. I love to write. That's the one thing that I keep doing and have been doing for a while. It helps your inner life. You could be writing on any interesting technology that you work with, but when you articulate it in the written form, that's where the challenge comes. When you develop, you'll find a lot of things that you probably didn't know, so that's really important. You know you know things, but when you have something to teach to others in some medium or other – whether speaking or writing – it's always challenging. It forces you to learn a lot of new things. That's what happens for me.

Along the way, doing all of those things, I made a lot of friends. I met all of you, in fact. That's essentially how I became a Java Champion.

Heather: All right. That's awesome. You've shared books, you've presented, and you've written a lot; you like to write. For developers, writing is such an important skill, because that's what we do. We write code. If you write well – if you're able to write an article, for example – you're going to be a better developer. You're going to write code better. Those two things are very much linked in the brain, writing code and writing articles.

You've done all this writing and become a Java Champion. But my question to you, Bazlur, is this: has any of that impacted your career? Are you better off because of it? Was it worthwhile? Is there anything that happened to you in your career that made you say, *"Man, this is awesome. It really helped me"*? Or is all of this just a distraction?

Bazlur: It's definitely not just a distraction. I have received many opportunities because of all of this. A lot of interesting opportunities have come to me because of all the things I do. You mentioned a couple of things: writing is definitely one thing that has led to opportunities.

For example, I worked in InfoQ, on a renowned tech content platform. If you write content, they pay you. They reached out to me because of all the things I used to do. So I can write and get paid. That's an amazing thing.

I also get to know about opportunities. For example, I found out about the current job that I have because I know someone who used to work with that company, and we have been friends for a while. He told me that there was an opportunity there. So, you get to know about opportunities; sometimes, opportunities come to you because you do a lot of these things. If you are visible to the community, people see you and people start to trust you. When you're working, you want to be someone who people are happy to trust and give responsibility to – but they need to trust you first. They cannot give you any responsibility if they don't know you.

That's why I would say these things are really important. I've been a Java Champion for a few months, and it has helped me in expanding my network. People I used to follow and look up to I was not able to reach directly – now, I can do that. Hopefully, that will help me in future to get more opportunities, as this is definitely helping me to expand my network.

All of the things that I've been doing are awesome. I don't think they are a distraction. These are very beneficial.

Heather: OK. That's awesome.

I just want to quickly mention Hussein saying, *"Please give me the motivation to study."* Hussain, I cannot give you motivation. For motivation, you have to look around. Look at your family. Look at your life. Look at the things you want to do. You will have to build motivation by looking at your situation.

There are two main ways, Hussein, to have motivation.

One is looking forward to somewhere you want to get to: a happy place where you want to be. Look at those things that you want, that you want to become, that you want to have. Look at the things that you want to be in the future – that's one way to get motivation.

Another way to get motivation is to think: where do you want to run from? What are the pains in your life right now? What are the things that are hurting you? What are the things that are hurting your family? What are the things that are bad for you right now? Our brains love to run towards something good, but our brains want much more to run away from bad things. Run towards good things, run away from bad things: that's a great way for you to build motivation.

All right. Bazlur, thanks a lot for being here with us. Thanks a lot for giving your time.

Bazlur: Thank you.

Summary

In this chapter, you gained valuable skills and insights to enhance your public engagement and establish trust on a larger scale. Firstly, you learned how to leverage public speaking as a powerful tool for career growth, understanding its significance and the potential it holds. Additionally, you discovered strategies to overcome the fear and anxiety often associated with public speaking, enabling you to confidently share your ideas and expertise.

Furthermore, the chapter provided guidance on generating impactful content ideas, allowing you to create compelling and valuable material for your audience. You also explored techniques for effectively organizing and presenting your content, ensuring a coherent and engaging delivery that resonates with your listeners or readers.

Lastly, you discovered the importance of finding the right platforms to initiate your sharing efforts. By identifying suitable channels to reach your target audience, you can maximize the impact of your message and expand your reach.

In the next chapter, we will delve into the subject of becoming a technical leader by mastering the art of managing relationships across the organizational hierarchy, including managing upwards, downwards, and across departments.

13

Be a Leader: Manage Up, Down, and Across Your Organization

To be a leader and a top-level developer, you need to understand leadership and be able to deal with your team and your managers. Having the skills to manage up – talking and negotiating with your boss, other managers, and executive directors; to manage down – inspiring your team and peers; and to manage across – reaching out to people inside and outside of your organization, will allow you to lead and have a larger impact inside your team and company, and also outside, in your communities.

In this chapter, you will learn how to be a leader. Even if you don't have a leadership role, you will learn how to lead by serving and helping, listening and asking questions, inspiring people to take action, and using your leadership to build trust in the market.

In this chapter, we will cover the following:

- How to be a leader, even if you don't have a leadership role
- Lead by serving and helping
- Lead by listening and asking questions
- Inspire people to take action
- Use your leadership to build trust in the market
- Tips for job opportunities and interviews

Being a leader even if you don't have a leadership role – take a leadership attitude

Do you need to have a leadership role to be a leader?

"A boss has the title, the leader has the people."—Simon Sinek

One criterion for technical professionals to be considered for advancement is leadership. You may that leadership does not relate to technical careers, but you would be wrong. You are a leader. Even if you don't have the official title of manager or team lead, you are a leader. You are the leader of your own career journey. In his bestselling leadership book *The First 90 Days*, Michael D. Watkins talks about the importance of your responsibility to manage yourself. Part of this responsibility is your relationship with your manager. If you want to progress toward senior levels of your technical career, you will need to be perceived as a leader. Senior developers may not have a team lead designation, but they are often expected to be a leader in their roles and to demonstrate leadership abilities. One common question then is how do you demonstrate leadership without anyone to lead? You need to expand your understanding of leadership. As Grace Hopper said, "You manage things; you lead people." The ability to lead others starts with the ability to manage yourself. One of the most important tips for this is "plan to plan" – devoting time to planning your day, your week, your month, and your year; and also focusing on the important work.

This is somewhat similar to the *Big Rocks* approach we talked about earlier in this book. It is easy to get caught up in meetings and with emails, Slack, and social media. All of those things are necessary, but you must dedicate time to do the important work. *What is the important work?* you may ask. The important work is the work that will help you to achieve your goals and how you ensure that if you achieve your goals you will be promoted. This is where your relationship with your manager comes into play. Many developers and employees in general take the approach that they do what their manager tells them, and will even avoid meetings with their manager because they don't want to be given new tasks or hear complaints about their work. This is where you can establish yourself as a leader by taking the attitude of a leader and being responsible for that relationship, taking the initiative to schedule meetings, determining your goals and priorities, and establishing the criteria for success and promotion. This attitude will showcase your leadership even though you do not (yet) have a leadership role. By establishing your goals and criteria for success together, you will gain an understanding of the priorities of your organization, your group, and your executive management and find out how you and your contributions fit into the overall success of the organization.

When Heather was working early in her career, she made the mistake of thinking that if she kept her head down and worked hard, she would be rewarded. She did not understand the importance of being perceived as a leader, and doing the work that was perceived by her management to be important. Once she understood how to demonstrate her leadership to her management, there were subtle shifts in her career toward advancement.

While you do need to work hard, you should not work long hours just for the sake of "putting in the time." A community member shared a story with us of a former colleague who was a hard worker (as was he). They would often be the only ones in the office until the late hours. During one of those late nights, the colleague confided that they would often "accidentally" leave papers in the printer so that their manager would see how late they work, thinking this would make a good impression. The community member shared that he really was not impressed with that approach.

Instead, look for ways to amplify your results and the work of yourself and your team members. While you should do your best, when you are working on the correct things and taking responsibility for your manager, you will be recognized for your contribution. Artificial theatrics such as the technique used in this example are transparent and will be recognized as such. Look for authentic ways to promote your work, such as achieving your performance goals and success metrics.

If you want to advance in your career, you need to be the master of yourself. There are some core components here in addition to the leadership skills we mentioned. They are humility, persistence, and a positive mental attitude. Heather learned these three skills early in her life from her grandfather, who served in the United States Marines and went on to be a successful businessman, public speaker, and philanthropist.

Here's an excerpt from his obituary: *As the first to attend college in his family, he graduated from USC in June 1941 and traded his civilian clothes for a Marine Corps uniform and a commission as 2nd Lieutenant. Earning his wings, he flew missions over the Islands before and during the battle. For this, he was awarded the Bronze Star with a combat "V." He retired from the Corps as a Lt. Colonel.*

Heather learned many of these details about his service only after his death in 2014. He was humble and only spoke of the future and what he planned to achieve. He spoke of the things he wanted to do. Anytime someone asked him about working on a project, he would say, "That sounds wonderful, when can we get together to talk more about it?" These are lessons we can internalize and carry into our work in our technical careers.

He also shared a quote about the value of persistence by Calvin Coolidge, former President of the United States, and lived by those words from his early career days working at the *Los Angeles Times*.

Persistence – press on

Nothing in the world can take the place of persistence.

Talent will not;

Nothing is more common than unsuccessful men or women with talent.

Genius will not;

Unrewarded genius is almost a proverb

Education alone will not;

The world is full of educated derelicts.

Persistence and determination are omnipotent!

He instilled in her the power of a positive mental attitude and believing in yourself. One of the life lessons he used to teach this was the power of a first impression – always have a positive attitude when meeting people for the first time since you never get a second chance to make a good first impression. That lesson seems so obvious but the power of a positive attitude was ingrained into Heather from a young age and she is known in the developer community for her positive outlook on life and the people in her life. One of the quotes she often draws on for hiring or advising others on hiring is by American businessman Herb Kelleher: "You don't hire for skills, you hire for attitude. You can always teach skills."

This is so true. As we talked about in a previous chapter, there is always something to learn, but if you embrace learning and become a lifelong learner, you can always learn new skills. It is much more difficult to change your attitudes and beliefs. To become a master and be the creator of your destiny, take this approach in your career and with your management. It will serve you and your team well.

Leading by serving and helping – act as a leader in the team

As we talked about in previous chapters, building trust is essential to your career advancement. This is true, but once you build trust, you will need to further build upon that trust to take your career to the next level. You will need social capital or an emotional bank account with the people on your team.

Simon Sinek tells a story about the United States Navy SEALs – they are one of the highest performing organizations in the world. A former Navy SEAL was asked who made it through their selection process, called BUD/S. He said, "*I can't tell you who makes it but I can tell you the kind of people who don't make it. The star college athletes and the tough guys with ripped muscles don't make it through; the preening leaders who delegate everything don't make it through. Some of the guys are skinny, scrawny, and shivering out of fear. When they are emotionally and physically exhausted, somehow they are able to dig down deep inside themselves to find the energy to help the person next to them.*" Service and the willingness to help make the highest performing teams in the world – not their strength and not their intelligence. It's their willingness to be there for each other.

To be a leader in your team, whether you have a designated team lead or manager title or not, you need to serve and be willing to help your team members. There are many ways to lead your team. You can offer to mentor new team members and teach them about the workflow or offer to pair program with them or provide peer coaching. There are skills you can master that will establish you as a leader in your team, such as running meetings, having crucial conversations, giving and receiving feedback, and attracting key talent.

Let's start with running meetings. As chairperson of the JCP program, Heather has become an expert at running meetings successfully. Being able to lead meetings is a skill that will establish your authority and leadership in a team. Learn from some of her tips:

- Decide on the best way to hold the meeting, whether this is virtual, in person, or hybrid. Usually, a combination will work best.

- Spend at least twice as long planning the meeting as you expect it to last. Prior preparation is key to a successful meeting. You should prep all topic speakers and leaders with not only the agenda and details but also the expectations of the content, how you think the content will be received, and a review of the content in advance of the meeting.

- Stick to an agenda with a timeline. While it is tempting to let certain topics go on for longer than the allotted time, it is important to set the expectation that the meeting agenda and everything on the agenda will be covered. If you need more time to discuss a particular topic, suggest another, future time to discuss the topic in more detail. You can also guide the conversation back to the agenda topic as necessary to keep the conversation on track.

- Ensure that you are hearing a balanced view of the participants. You want to solicit the opinions of a majority and have a diversity of thought in meetings.

- Plan breaks in the meeting every 70-100 minutes. Ensure that the breaks are long enough to allow for some informal discussion or quick phone calls/emails in between topics.

- Arrange the meeting room and schedule the timing to suit the majority of your participants. If you are meeting in person, ensure the position of the seating is appropriate and there is seating for all. If the meeting is remote or partially remote, ensure the sound and audio-visual equipment is adequate for all participants. Scheduling can sometimes be difficult in distributed and global teams. Make an effort to vary the times between early morning and later in the day for the needs of all attendees.

- Invite only the required attendees. If there are too many unnecessary attendees or bystanders/observers in the meeting, it will decrease the impact and participation level overall.

- Prepare opening and closing remarks. When running a meeting, you should have customary introductory and closing remarks or action items planned in advance to ensure efficiency and that nothing falls through the cracks or is not followed up on after the meeting.

- Ensure all attendees are heard. If one person is sharing all comments and feedback, suggest that you appreciate their perspective, but you would like to hear from other people before coming back to hear more about their perspective. If you think someone may have an interesting perspective but is not speaking up, suggest that they share their thoughts on the topic or encourage their participation. A well-run meeting will include varying viewpoints and feedback.

- Take meeting notes/a summary and distribute them to attendees.

Now that we have discussed how to be a leader of your team or within your team, let's focus on attracting new talent to your team.

Attracting top talent to your team

One thing that is tremendously valued and shows leadership in a team is the ability to conduct interviews and review the resumes of candidates.

Resumes should not be too limiting in scope but should be specific and focus on projects that were completed or collaborated on, not just jobs, certifications, and training/degrees. Ask candidates to reference stories and examples from their experiences, summarizing key points, facts, and solutions. If you are applying for a job, you should also have stories and examples for interviews. In an interview, ask candidates to demonstrate critical-thinking or problem-solving skills. One of the best ways to evaluate problem-solving is to check whether candidates can do the following:

- Break down the problem

- Realize it's been done before in all likelihood, so do their research

- Recognize that issues/roadblocks will be normal

- Research services and tools

- Test solutions and debug

The goal is to attract and hire the best talent so that you can make the team successful. Once you have played a critical role in the hiring process, look for ways to onboard and peer mentor team members. Increasingly, peer-to-peer mentoring and pair programming are being implemented in corporate environments. Gone are the proverbial days of coders sitting alone and delivering code without speaking to anyone.

Let us not forget about retaining top talent. Even in a tough economic period, it is a valuable attribute to be able to retain talented team members. It is disruptive not only to you and your productivity but also to your team, management, and company overall to have a high level of attrition or turnover of team members. Do what you can to welcome and provide support to new team members. Help them to assimilate and onboard into their new role. This will be appreciated and noticed by your supervisors and team leaders. That leads us to our next area of focus. Let's talk a bit about feedback.

Leading by learning how to solicit and receive feedback

Leaders know they should give feedback but it is often avoided because it makes them feel uncomfortable. It brings up anxiety, fear, or criticism in many people. Think of feedback as sharing observations on work performance and behaviors. It can be positive or negative feedback, but if you view it as an opportunity to reward and praise good work or suggest improvements in a constructive way for the future, it can be an overall rewarding experience.

A key to soliciting and receiving feedback is learning how to listen and ask questions.

We talked about listening earlier in the book when we discussed public speaking. Listening is also key to leadership and feedback. And again, as we have said before in this book, you are responsible for your relationship with your management and, specifically, with your manager. You can lead this relationship with your management by asking questions and listening to the answers. This will provide you with so many insights. One of the best questions to ask is how to communicate. Which method is best for them and at what frequency, and at what level of detail. Communication, as we have stressed throughout this book, is a vital skill to advance your career, and even more so with your management. You want to communicate in the style they want, so adapt to their preferences and ask whether your communications are meeting their needs: am I doing this right? You also want to ask how you are contributing to your organization or your group's success. Time and again, when asked about opportunities for advancement and promotion, this is a required element to advance – how you contribute to the overall success. How does your contribution justify a promotion or raise?

You should be asking for and giving feedback on a regular basis. That means that it is a process that continues throughout your employment and career journey – not just at the times you are requesting a promotion or raise but as part of an ongoing dialogue with your manager. Another thing you should be asking about is what you should be focusing on this year or this quarter. You want to ensure that you are aligned with the priorities of your management chain and that you are working on the items that are of critical importance to your organization. One thing that you can be sure will make you one of the favored team members is to think about how you can make your manager's life easier.

Even better, ask them: how can I help to reduce your workload? Not only will this help to direct and guide the projects you work on, but it will also be a signal that you care about helping your management with the workload they carry. You also can check in for feedback on your performance periodically. Do not wait for the requisite performance evaluation period. Have an ongoing conversation where you are asking for feedback.

Managers are often reluctant to provide feedback because they are not sure of how well it will be received. If you are willing to ask for specific feedback, it will create the space and the opportunity for your management to provide it. You can then incorporate the feedback into your performance on an ongoing basis, and by doing so, you increase your opportunities to be rewarded for your performance and strengthen the relationship with your management. Ask how you are doing in any given circumstance, and ask whether there is anything that you may have missed or that you could have done better. Often, it is automatic to answer the question "How am I doing?" with "Great," "You're doing fine," or "Keep up the good work." This is not necessarily helpful or specific. On the other hand, when you ask "Is there anything that I can do to improve?" or "Did I miss anything?", there is more actionable information in the answer that you will receive that will help you to adjust your performance and work habits. These are all fundamental questions that can help you in your career. Asking them is essential, but listening and incorporating the answers into your daily work will be required in order to achieve the benefits.

Sometimes we ask questions but we do not really want to hear the answers. We like to think that we know the answers or that we are doing amazing work, and that may very well be true! However, you need to be vigilant to actively listen to the information that is provided in the answers. Active listening is an important communication skill that helps you to understand problems better and also helps you to effectively collaborate with your peers and manager(s). Active listening will not only make your conversations more successful but it will also help other people feel more valued and heard. When you are actively listening, you are engaging with the speaker, and you indicate your understanding by using eye contact, being present in the moment, using gestures such as nodding, asking open-ended questions to receive more feedback, summarizing what the other person has said, and asking for agreement (have you understood correctly?). When you practice active listening, you are listening for understanding, not waiting for your moment to respond or provide a rebuttal, and not judging; you are coming from a place of mutual understanding to really listen, hear, and apply what the other person is saying. When you ask the right questions, that is only the first part. To reap the benefits of asking questions, you need to be willing to listen and hear the answers for understanding. If you can ask the right questions and listen to the answers, you are setting yourself apart for advancement and recognition of your communication skills and organizational abilities in your career. You can also extend these skills to peer feedback and coaching.

It may feel awkward at first to give feedback regularly but it is an integral part of being a leader. Feedback increases self-awareness and enables continuous improvement. A major study showed that employees who receive feedback have a lower turnover and increased productivity and profitability compared with employees who receive no feedback.

You can give feedback in all directions in the organization. You can think of it as a continuous feedback loop to improve your team as individuals and as a whole to increase your overall performance. Remember that feedback is not a one-way street. You can give feedback to people who are less senior, in different groups, peer-to-peer on your team, and also to your management. Think of feedback as part of a partnership with your employees – a mutual commitment to helping each other improve. It's an investment in the organization's long-term success.

Learning how to have difficult conversations

When you are interviewing team members, onboarding team members, giving and receiving feedback, and having peer-to-peer coaching sessions, you will need another skill in your leadership repertoire.

You will need to learn how to have difficult conversations. In the book *Crucial Conversations*, by Kerry Patterson, Joseph Grenny, Ron McMillan, and Al Switzler, they lay out a framework for having these conversations and being successful with them. They call it *How To Spot The Conversations That Are Keeping You From What You Want*:

- **Get unstuck**: This is the law of crucial conversations. If you find yourself stuck, there is probably a conversation that you are either not having or you are having it and it is not going well. The first step is to identify where you are stuck and the second step is to unbundle it with the **content** (the problem), the **pattern** (a pattern of behavior over time), and the **relationship** (define how the problem affects your relationship).

- **Start with the heart**: Change starts with the heart and this begins when you focus on trying to improve yourself. Here, you can focus on asking yourself some questions about what you really want…for yourself, the relationship, and the organization.

- **Master my stories**: Here, the steps are separate facts from the story. Watch for clever stories (victim, villain, helpless) that propel or justify behaviors and then tell the rest of the story in terms of what you should do to bring the story to a successful outcome.

- **State my path**: This is how to speak persuasively to express your views in a way that is candid and respectful to others. Share your facts, tell your story, and ask for other perspectives. Do this with confidence and curiosity.

- **Make it safe**: The book makes the case that people do not become defensive about the content of what you say but about why you say it, or why they think you are saying it. When people are at cross purposes, they can become offended. There are two skills highlighted here for crucial conversations: apologize when appropriate to address misunderstandings between what others think and your real motivations.

Using the tools in this book, you will be able to have these high-stakes conversations, with opposing opinions and strong emotions. This ability will certainly lead to you being perceived as a valuable team member and a sought-after leader within your organization. Being a person who can collaborate and bring varying opinions together for the benefit of the team and organization means that you are a person who can be trusted and it will enable you to build social capital with your team members.

Optimizing your presence – hybrid environments and global teams

Your presence will also impact how your leadership ability is perceived. Today, a lot of teams are remote, hybrid, distributed, or decentralized in some way. When teams are set up this way and accepted as the norm, we can forget about the value of "face time" or seeing each other's faces. In the *Face time still matters* article from the *Harvard Business Review*, they discuss the current dynamic of hybrid and global teams. They offer the following advice and strategies for being intentional and even creative with deciding when and how to show your face:

- If you have the opportunity to go to an office to meet with colleagues, make those days about communication, whether it is individual meetings, group meetings, or just informal conversations. You will be able to make a greater leadership impact this way. Share the dates when you will be in the office to make yourself accessible to team members who may also be able to be present in the office on that day.

- Use video as a backup and embrace it by keeping your camera on – you can show your face virtually. This is especially important during projects that are difficult or complicated. This will also help you to demand focus and attention from your team members.

- Don't forget your nonverbal communication either. You can align your nonverbal cues with your messages and the leadership you are projecting in all of your meetings, whether they are virtual or in person. Keeping your body language open will help with this – your posture should be open, upward, and leaning toward the other parties or your camera. Think about the expression you have on your face when you are speaking or listening – this is also part of communicating with your colleagues.

It may seem insignificant to consider how you are perceived in regard to your physical presence, but this is an important element to consider as you are positioning yourself as a technical leader creating an impact in your team and across your organization, and one that executive management will surely notice.

How to inspire people to take action

As you start to practice demonstrating leadership in your role, you will also need to learn how to develop specific leadership competencies. We have discussed many leadership competencies already earlier in this book. As you develop your skills and practice using them, you will find that some skills come more naturally to you than others. Some of the most useful skills to develop to demonstrate technical leadership are decision-making, conflict resolution, and strategic or critical thinking. These are skills you develop by practicing them in your team. Make a conscious effort to develop these skills and to evaluate your strengths.

In the classic bestselling book *The Leadership Challenge*, written by James M. Kouzes and Barry Z. Posner, they describe the five practices of exemplary leadership. This is a book that Heather has drawn on in her career, and it has been described as the foundation and roadmap of leadership skills. The principles of leadership they cite in the book are the following:

- Model the way – set the example you would like to see followed

- Inspire a shared vision – communicate a vision that compels action

- Challenge the process – question the standard operating procedure of how things have always been done

- Enable others to act – remove the roadblocks that prevent progress toward the shared vision

- Encourage the heart – celebrate and encourage the successes of team members along the way

All of these principles work together to inspire action by other people. You will find that there are practices that align more closely with your skillset and style. Develop this style, but also learn to incorporate other practices or styles as you grow in your career and in your leadership abilities.

When combined, these principles incite action. We believe that at the heart of leadership and inspiration is storytelling. This is the most underrated skill for developers, for leaders, and for all people. It is the world's oldest skill and the way we pass on knowledge, skills, and experiences – sharing stories. How do you learn these skills? You learn these skills through practice and guidance. We will share with you our guidelines for sharing a story:

- Use an example from your life that you are proud of that relates to the topic

- Convey your point in a concise way early in the story and explain why it matters

- Explain your specific role in the story

- Convey the impact

- Express gratitude and be authentic

When you combine these elements, you have the ingredients for stories that will not only teach but also inspire action. We suggest that you have some stories in your portfolio – either on your phone, tablet, or computer; perhaps even in a notebook so that you are ready to share them in moments when they are needed. In the moments when a leader is needed, sharing a story can help the community around you and also put you in a leadership position. What are some stories that every developer should consider preparing? We have listed a few prompts for your consideration:

- A project that had unclear responsibilities and how you resolved this
- A project where you had to lead without direct authority
- A project where you had to rely on yourself to complete a task or project that should have been a group project or task
- A project you worked on with unclear or incomplete information
- A project or a time that changed your outlook or thinking
- A time you had to make a bold decision and the outcome
- A time you had to speak up in a difficult or uncomfortable situation
- A project where you fell short of your own expectations or standards
- A project where you came up with a simple solution to a complex problem
- A project where you used large amounts of data to develop a solution
- A project where you had to correct a problem or mistake

These are examples of stories that you can use to inspire people to take action and highlight your successes. These are useful for job interviews but also for personal leadership and branding. No matter what your role is in the organization, there is always an opportunity to step up and demonstrate your ability to motivate people to act. Find the types of projects that you are passionate about and share that passion to inspire the people around you. This is the type of person who is continually viewed as a leader of high potential.

Using your leadership to build trust in the market – build visibility for you and your cause

The best senior developers have a basic technical foundation – not necessarily the best technical skills, but they have excellent problem-solving and critical-thinking skills. They possess a deep understanding of projects that they work on, they have developed leadership and engineering management skills, and they are organized and efficient communicators.

Technical leaders are mature. They accept the reality of the market. Rather than thinking their solutions are always best, they realize that there are dozens if not hundreds of ways to do the same thing. They know that code will never run on the first try and testing, unit testing, automated testing, and debugging skills are highly valuable – not something to be handed off to another department or sent to another team for **Quality Assurance (QA)**. They realize that 75-80% of software projects are brownfield maintenance projects – nearly everyone in a technical role cites greenfield projects as preferred, but expecting to always work on greenfield projects is simply not realistic and is the sign of an immature software developer. Working on long-term projects with or without technical debt requires skill to ensure the maintainability of the code and strategic thinking to design and write code that will integrate with the existing code and be current with standards at the present time. It also requires strong debugging skills to test the code when new features are added and investigate and solve issues that are introduced and bugs in the code base. Technical leaders value and nurture teamwork – mentoring new members and collaborating via peer programming or other tools to branch, merge, and resolve conflicts with other team members. Software development team members do not work in isolation. It is a highly choreographed yet often imperfect symphony of players. This is where your soft skills and honed attributes in collaboration and communication allow you to shine.

There are specific challenges that software developers may face in managing up, down, and across their organization in a technical context and challenges that community managers may face in building and maintaining relationships with software developers. It would be helpful to explore these specific challenges and provide guidance on how to navigate them effectively.

Interviews

Victor Grazi

Q: Victor Grazi, thanks for meeting with me. I'm eager to hear your career story because I know you've had so much success in your career. Let's start with you sharing a little bit about how you got started in your technical career and some of the things that you were doing when you first entered.

A: I've always been in love with technology.

Many years ago, we had a family factory: a linen business. We were delivering things per order. We'd get a cluster of orders, and somebody would go and pick out an order, and if anything needed to be manufactured, they'd go upstairs and they'd manufacture a few dozen of that order. I looked at this system and said, "Well, what are we doing here? We're manufacturing little bits of this and little bits of that. They have these computers now that mean you can consolidate these things!"

So, we bought a computer, I learned Business Basic, and I programmed a program that took all our orders and told us exactly what to manufacture at once. It actually told you how to allocate the orders, so we created slots on the warehouse floor, and we were able to allocate our manufacturing production accordingly.

That was my start. As for getting into the real world of computing – Java and everything – it's a funny story. Around 1995, my brother and I heard about some new technology called the internet and how you could do some really wild stuff using something called Java and applets: it was just starting around that time. Using some of the programming experience I had from Business Basic and some experience I had with mainframes, I got to work learning HTML, Java, and SQL Server. I had to be my own DBA.

We created a dot-com company called Supermarkets to Go. It was something of a shopping franchise, where we would brand websites for supermarkets, telling them, "Everybody will be looking for you online." That was our tagline.

That worked really well until around 1999, what with the dot-com bubble bursting. So, I had to look for a real job. I got into the financial industry around then, and I've been there ever since and really love it. I think the financial industry is great; I'm an executive director now in a major financial firm.

Luck is a big part of it, hard work is a big part of it, and so is contributing to the community. Right now, with GitHub and so many available resources, such as Stack Overflow, it's very important and very easy to get involved. In the olden days, you just didn't have these opportunities, but now there are so many. If you're a Java developer, you can go and look at the Java Community Process, you can look at all the JSRs, and you can make a difference by contributing to these things. It's important; it's great resume experience.

About 15 years ago, I was doing some investigation into concurrency. Concurrency was really hard to understand, and I think it's still hard. I do dozens of interviews with expert Java developers, and so many of them just don't get concurrency. I started poking around, and I think that's something that's really important for people to do if they don't understand something. Download it, start poking around, and get into the intricacies of it.

As I was looking into concurrency, and I started building little programs to show me what would happen if this thread did that and this thread did that, or if they tried to do this at the same time. Then I said, "It would be very easy to animate these things." So, I started creating animations, and before you know it, I had animations for all of the major concurrency components. So, I said, "Let me open source this thing," and we put it online. Now we get thousands of downloads, and I've been all over the world presenting this thing. I call it Java Concurrent Animated.

That's just an example of something that you have to do – get good at something and find problems that are hard. Don't duck away from the hard problems but immerse yourself in them. Try to really understand them. Be the go-to guy or girl for that particular thing, and that's how you get on the map. I think that's the secret.

Another really big secret is to be nice. Keep a smile on your face. This is our lives – let's enjoy it. Help people enjoy it and give back to the community. I think we're in a super industry. We're poised to soar into the next generation with things such as machine learning and AI. These provide opportunities for technologies far beyond any other industry, so this is something that people should be capitalizing on in this industry.

Q: That's a common thread that I hear in my work and when talking with developers who have progressed in their careers. It typically does come down to the community having some interest. You have that story of how you first got started in the community, and that is almost like a lightbulb moment, where you realized that participating starts by understanding that there's a problem you want to learn more about. You take it further, make progress, and get involved in the community.

But in terms of working inside a corporation, I think you have a lot of insights to offer as well. Maybe you could share a story about influencing across an organization. Tell us about building relationships and how you can use those influencing opportunities to advance your career.

A: It's a hard question. Getting into the company is always the hard part. Once you're in, there's trying to find those hard-to-solve problems. Managing relationships is really difficult, and a lot of times we're thrown in with difficult people. Just learning how to navigate that is really important.

But again, keep that smile on your face when working with people, and try to provide value in whatever you're doing. Don't be shy or embarrassed to move up the ladder. Reach out. Without stepping on toes, reach out into other areas; try to solve problems that are firmwide. In an enterprise, there usually are problems. Sometimes they're difficult to solve, but if you can be the person that solves them, you're going to be well on your way to a successful career.

Also, reaching out publicly is very important. I have a public profile. My speaking engagements and the fact that I'm becoming well known in the community help me when I'm looking for a new job or I'm trying to navigate internally within my enterprise. People look up to me because they know that I have those skills. So, creating a public profile is really important in helping you, even internally in your own career.

Q: As for stating intentions, sometimes people are reluctant to do that because they feel a little bit of imposter syndrome or assume it's known that they want to advance to a certain level.

A: Don't be shy – definitely don't be shy.

Q: So, do you have any suggestions or tips for how to put yourself out there, especially if you're trying to be humble, as is often the case with people that I meet?

A: A big problem in our industry is that people tend to be a little bit geeky or shy sometimes: we tend not to be outgoing. But sometimes, you can look in the mud and find some diamonds, and that's something that I'm finding. Often, some of the shyest people are really the ones with the most talent, but a lot of these people will get laid off or just won't survive because of their shyness.

It's very important to reach out and try to overcome that humility that you were describing. You want to be humble and nice, but you also want people to know who you are, and it's important to extend yourself a little bit to get there.

Q: You obviously are an author and a speaker. Any suggestions for how to get started doing those things? You shared a little bit about the project and how you started it, but there may be some things that seem obvious to you that you did to become an author and start writing about the work that you did, develop a talk, and submit it to a conference to be a speaker.

A: A lot of it is around understanding technologies. Nowadays, that is another thing that's really easy. You can go to Udemy, LinkedIn Learning, or Pluralsight and become really good at any technology. You get good at it. You can master it. But even before you master it, you can take what you've learned and start creating little training pieces and presentations.

I'm not saying to plagiarize anything, but you can go on to Udemy and learn how to do something, and then present what you've learned. Try to immerse yourself in it. Learn a little bit more about it. Try to learn how to answer the questions that you have as a learner. Try to figure out what those answers are.

By immersing yourself in that technology, you can become more of an expert, and then you can put that into a presentation, and that's what you submit. There are lists of conferences online: Java, Python, AI, machine learning, ChatGPT. Learn something. Become good at it. Learn how to figure out the answers. Prepare a talk and submit it. You could submit it in the Java world; there's also Oracle, of course. I don't know if we're still going to have JavaOne this year, but hopefully we will.

There are so many different forums that are looking for good content. Just prepare the content. Prepare a good summary and submit it in the calls for white papers. Eventually, you'll get picked. Nowadays, there are a lot of virtual conferences. A lot of these conferences will pay for you to go. I've even had conferences pay for my wife to go. They generally tend to pay for your airfare and your hotel, so it's really good. Just prepare content and submit it. You won't get hits from everybody, but you will get some hits.

Q: I think it is a numbers game, to some extent. You have to have a lot of nos to get to the yeses. It's not necessarily personal.

A: The sale begins when the customer says no.

Q: You mentioned ChatGPT. How do you think that will play a role with developers? I just got back from meeting with a bunch of students in Singapore, and that was one of the most common questions that I got. A lot of junior professionals are looking at AI and machine learning, ChatGPT in particular, and wondering, "Is that going to make my job obsolete?"

A: Obsolete? I don't know.

There are two sides to ChatGPT. One of them is using it to solve your problems. I recently had somebody in my firm, who is not a developer at all and has no coding experience, come to me and say, "Can you give me an example of an interview question that you would ask a candidate?" I gave him a basic question and I gave him an intermediate one, and within a minute he came back with an answer. I said, "Are you studying this? How did you do that?" He replied, "No, I just asked ChatGPT." I didn't know what it was at the time, but he came up with the perfect solution.

So, on one side, we as developers can use ChatGPT to help us figure out how to code stuff. I'm a Java developer by profession, but I've been getting heavily involved in Python as well, and I always have questions: what is this really arcane construct doing in Python? I can go on ChatGPT, paste it in there, and say, "What does this mean, ChatGPT?" It'll reply, "Here are some examples, and this is what it means." It's really useful to us as technologists for helping us solve these problems.

Another side is figuring out how to index our internal data and use it to create chatbots and things like that internally in our own programs. I have less experience with that, and I'm interested to learn more about it.

Q: It's interesting. I was curious because I do get this question a lot from younger students getting ready to graduate.

A: It's such a great technology. The other day, I started to have ringing in my ears. Normally, I would call up the doctor and say, "What should I do about this ringing in my ears?" I went on ChatGPT, and it said, "Oh, you have tinnitus. It's very common, and this is what could be causing it, and this is what you need to do." It became my doctor!

Q: That's funny. I talked to Frank Greco quite a bit about it when I saw him in Atlanta earlier this month. He brought up some interesting things – cautionary tales. He talked about coding it and then, of course, the legal implications of rights to the code if you were to use it.

A: Well, I have to tell you something. Remember that story that I told you about the guy who wasn't a developer and he asked me for a code challenge? ChatGPT coded the solution perfectly, but it was actually a trick question – there would have been a much simpler, more elegant solution, which it didn't get.

Q: That was what Frank Greco said. He said half the time it'll work, and half the time it won't. It probably won't be as elegant as it could be – there are still skills needed that only people could supply.

Do you have any tips on interviewing? Especially if you're interviewing a larger company and there's going to be a series of interviews, that is something that causes a lot of angst – how do we pass those interviews?

A: I've been doing tons of interviewing lately. One thing is that, sometimes, just having a good personality gets you much further than answering a question about an algorithm. Be upbeat, smile, and crack a joke.

Of course, you have to have the fundamental talent that they're screening for. And of course, never put things on your resume that you don't have. Sometimes people put on their resume that they know how to use AngularJS, and then I ask them how they would do something in Angular and they don't know.

So, don't put it on there just because you have used it once in your life or you took a single training session on it. Don't put it on your resume unless you can answer interview questions on it.

Prepare for your interview. We have CodeWarrior and all these sites now where you can go and take tests and get better. But most of all, just use your charm.

Q: Critical thinking is one thing that I've found that a lot of employers ask about – the candidate's ability to think about a problem.

A: 100 percent. It's not always back-calculating the algorithm and figuring out the right solution. It's about being able to answer, "We're having this problem internally. We need to optimize such and such. How would you go about doing that?" Sometimes we can spend months thinking about that kind of thing, so if a candidate can think about it in 30 seconds and come up with two or three good solutions, or at least start to propose a high-level solution, I'd be impressed.

Q: Just showing that you have the ability to think about a problem is important.

I guess that interviewing, just like a call for papers, comes down to a numbers game. You're not going to be accepted at every call for papers; you're not going to be accepted at every interview. But the more you do it, the better you get.

A: Yes.

There's one thing that's really important, and it was a horror story that happened to a friend of mine. He was looking for a job, and he was having a hard time. There was not a lot of hiring going on. He finally got an offer, and then all of a sudden, they withdrew the offer. The reason was that two recruiters had submitted him to the same company! So, before you allow anybody to submit your resume, make sure that they clear it with you. Make sure that you're not duplicating.

Q: Yes, because that would be a conflict for the company – that's definitely a good tip.

More advice from Victor on job opportunities and interviews

Jobs in the technology industry tend to wax and wane, but at the rate the world is developing new technology, I would put all my money on that horse!

That said, we must consider that post-pandemic, with inflation at an all-time high and the United States Federal Reserve endlessly raising rates, we are seeing a downturn in business and hordes of layoffs in every sector.

This year alone, Amazon laid off 18,000, Meta 15,000, Alphabet 12,000, Microsoft 10,000, and so on. These are skilled people, all competing for your job!

So how do you compete and how do you survive?

I will give you some tips from my perspective:

- First, use a professional to craft your resume – robots screen your resume before a human ever sees it, so you want to make sure it checks all the boxes. You can also search online for resume-building techniques.

- If you are still in school, do your very best to get a summer internship at a recognized enterprise in your target field. This will become your first resume entry, and if you can get that, it will shine!

- You generally do not want to lie on your resume. But if you are going to lie about some skill or some experience, you better be sure you can answer interview questions around that topic or you will be embarrassed, and chances are you won't win that role.

- Prepare! They are going to ask you hard questions during interviews, and it is best to have canned responses. Some questions I've had in interviews are the following:

  - What was the toughest problem you faced and how did you solve it?

  - What are the steps to bring a requirement to production?

  - What was the architecture of a recent project? Be prepared to drill down and discuss very specific details. Talk less about the specific project and more about your contribution to it. Talk about how you made it better.

- Ask questions about the role:

  - What is the hardest problem you are facing today, and what problems do you expect to solve in the near future?

  - What do I need to do to get an "Exceeds Expectations" rating?

- Don't view a rejection as a failure! They say Thomas Edison tested 1,600 materials for the lightbulb filament before he came upon tungsten. When they asked him how it felt to fail 1,600 times, he said he never failed but succeeded in finding 1,600 materials that don't work! If you are rejected after an interview, consider it an opportunity to refine your technique. Prepare answers to the questions you were asked, so that you will be less nervous when you encounter them in your next interview.

- Subscribe for job alerts, but when you see them don't apply through third-party sites – rather, go to the hiring job board directly.

- Keep good notes on the jobs you applied for.

- If you are getting rejections, think about revising your resume.

- Use your free time to study! It is well worth the money invested in a Udemy personal license.

- Nowadays, interviewers expect you to solve very difficult algorithms in live coding HackerRank or CoderPad sessions. If you are great at algorithms, you are all set. For the rest of us, I would suggest spending a lot of time practicing. But at some point, just become familiar with the important data structures: List, Map, Set, Stack, Priority Queue, and so on. When you are asked to solve an algorithm, think about those structures, and think about which would be the best fit.

When I am interviewing candidates, I always ask this as the final question: What makes you great, and why should I hire you?

When you get that question, remember the acronym "ACT", which stands for:

- Achievements – tell them about specific accomplishments you have delivered
- Capabilities – tell them about your specific skills
- Transferable skills – tell them how your skills can be transferred to their business

But the most important advice I can give is to prepare and study. Look at the technological requirements of the role and invest days and weeks in learning these. If you are not employed, you have plenty of free time to study. Do not squander it!

Wellington Rosa

Wellington Rosa shares his experience in building relationships with communities and software developers, including impacts, events, and success cases

Q: Tell us how it all started – your professional trajectory in the field of community and software developer relations.

A: Over the years, I have had the opportunity to work in this fascinating area, building meaningful connections and fostering mutual growth. My professional journey in this industry started with a passion for the social aspects of technology. Caring about people and improving my connections led me down this path early on; I realized the transformative power that communities and software developers could exert. I joined an innovative company, where I had the opportunity to dive head-first into this universe and develop relationship, communication, leadership, and networking skills.

Q: Can you highlight when you have participated in important events and technical meetings and share some success stories that have shaped your career?

A: Over the years, I have had the honor of participating in several events and technical meetings relevant to the industry, and in all of them I had the opportunity to make important connections that have helped me evolve throughout this journey. These experiences were fundamental to expanding my knowledge, establishing valuable connections, and contributing to the dissemination of knowledge. I'll highlight some of these moments in my current company:

- The opportunity to design work in the best format and connect with developers, inside and outside the company. This included the creation of an internal committee, in a multidisciplinary structure, to design the organizational chart. The result of all this was contact and relationships with other professionals from other large companies as well as leaders of software communities.

- The opportunity to develop and strengthen internal actions, with a presentation of the improvements that this type of action would add to the business. This involved the indiscriminate involvement of professionals from all hierarchical levels.

- Launching and being involved in the internal strategy for the entire company, and getting approval of the strategy from the public.

During my career, I have had the opportunity to experience moments of great impact and significant achievements. Some success stories that have shaped my career include the following:

- **Developers advocate internal**: A concise description of a project where the main objective was to show the importance of this group within the company. It was basically a success because we had an approach of notifying the top management of the company of the main alerts and showed improvements in the results. We got approval and support to give sequences in external actions, with greater access to resources and funds.

- **I hit the car of the VP of the company**: Arriving at the company for a meeting at 08:30, and with a very tight deadline, as I maneuvered my vehicle, I hit the side of the car of an employee. The valet arrived and advised that it was the VP's car and they did not know what to do. After identifying whose car it was, I went up to their floor and calmly asked whether he would be driving home. He laughingly said "Yes," and I said, "Today, you will need to go by Uber." I told him that I had already taken the necessary steps to fix it but that I wouldn't have a spare car. At that moment, I told him a little bit about what we were doing in the area with the group of developers and how this would affect the business. It opened the door to a relationship and he became one of the main sponsors of the initiative inside and outside the company.

- **Campus party event**: We were at a moment of growth in our strategy and it was identified that participation in a very large event would be important to consolidate our work. As we already had the door open to contact a VP, we went to the general manager and showed him how important this action would be for the company, as well as his position as a representative of the brand. We explained what we could do, including being offered the main stage at the event. We received approval and the event happened, which became a major milestone for the company particularly among the younger public. We gained strength and visibility, especially through the figure of the person responsible for Brazil.

Q: Is there anything else you can share?

A: My professional trajectory in relationships I have built with communities and software developers has been full of learning, enriching experiences, and impactful moments. Since the beginning, I have been motivated by a passion for technology and the desire to build bridges between people and knowledge. By participating in events and technical meetings, I have had the chance to improve myself and expand my horizons. Moreover, the success stories along the way have shown me the power of engagement and collaboration. I am excited to continue this journey and contribute more and more to the growth and development of communities.

The other important point is that in situations where I have observed that relationships are needed, I have always managed to get closer and establish better contacts and relationships within the company and outside the company, especially treating anyone regardless of their position – treating all hierarchical levels – as equals. I have become more respected and listened to. In all interactions, I try to align my communication with each person. In addition, whenever I participate in conversations, both internal and external to the company, I try to discover, through social networks, connections in things that we have in common. This approach facilitates the creation of empathy and improves relationships for future initiatives.

Summary

In this chapter, you learned how to communicate for impact up, down, and across the organization, including how to take a leadership attitude, act as a leader in a team, act as a leader in the organization, how to cause transformation by helping people to take action, and how to build visibility for you and your cause. We also covered some tips for interviews and finding future job opportunities.

Next, let's continue the discussion on making an impact on your technical career path by discussing how to make a plan to get involved in standards organizations, how to choose a few organizations to participate in to get started, how to join and participate in the process, how to bring the concerns of your company and team into the process, and how to find ways to get involved on a deeper level.

14

Stepping Up Your Technology Game – Defining Technology Instead of Merely Using It

Once you are leading your career and are helping people around you to transform their lives, you can invest in growing your career by impacting the technologies that you use. This has the potential to transform the lives of millions of developers around the globe and will also help you grow inside your company and give you the visibility to grow outside of your company. This chapter will show you how.

We will discuss the following in this chapter:

- How technology is standardized and what it has to do with your career.
- Identifying technologies and organizations. Learning about your programming language – how it is standardized, the basics, the features, the classes, pre-defined libraries and functions, the threading model, the intricacies of the language, and the ecosystem.
- Getting involved with standards organizations – the conventions and best practices and common libraries and frameworks used in the language.
- Aligning your company with standards, identifying technologies and organizations, and getting involved on a deeper level.

Let's get started!

How technology is standardized and what it has to do with your career

Technical skills are required to participate in standards organizations, but there are many other things you need to know and can learn through participating in standardization activities. One of these things is that there are hundreds of ways of doing the same thing. When you start getting involved in standardization activities and participating in the discussions, you will see this through learning about how others use the standards.

Once there is a standard defined, you will see that your first solution proposal will probably not run in production the first time, and you will learn the importance of testing and writing tests and test automation to enable standards to be widely adopted and used. You will learn that even though writing code for new features and working on greenfield projects is exciting, there is so much more involved in the evolution of a standard – you will need to maintain existing builds and projects and evolve and fix bugs – not just for the benefit of your own project, but for the other tens, hundreds, millions or billions of projects.

This will require developing patches, backporting, and debugging – essential skills for a senior technical professional at any level. And to be able to evolve to this point in your career, you will need to learn teamwork (this requires also some of those skills we talked about earlier in this book), and if you are maintaining a project, how to use some specialized tools to evolve projects by branching, merging, and resolving conflicts.

Standards have the unique ability to empower interoperability, enable choice and portability, and provide developers and customers with the flexibility they need to create solutions for their enterprise independent of development, licensing, or delivery method. Standards are relevant to customers of varying sophistication across all levels of the market – from developers to end users. Some of the properties of standards include the following:

- Are developed through a defined collaborative process in which all interested parties may participate
- Use varying mechanisms to license associated intellectual property – across a spectrum of costs and obligations
- Regularize interfaces across varying products to achieve compatibility or interoperability, leaving the specifics of implementation up to developers
- Exist on a spectrum – specification development activities can be more or less open

At times. standards can be confused with open source. We talked about open source participation earlier in this book. While both are complementary tools used in modern technology environments. they are different and not directly comparable, but there is a relation and similarity in participation. The following are some differentiations.

Standards do not require open source – specifications can be implemented under various development and licensing models.

Standards are essential for open source. Without standards, open source software would struggle to provide interoperability when unable to implement proprietary standards that require royalty payments or have other restrictive terms.

Standards implemented in open source code can help developers understand the technology and increase open standards' adoption. One leading example of this practice is the developer adoption of Java, offering an open source implementation of the technology and related development tools.

Technology is standardized by bringing together a set of users (companies, institutions, and individuals) who want to use or currently use technology in different ways. One way, a more traditional way, to develop a standard is to define how a type of technology should be used, for example, cloud computing. A set of companies from various countries and industries agrees to standardize and then raises and forms a group in a standards organization to develop the terminology, specifications, and technology to define it. Traditional standards organizations such as ISO, W3C, OASIS, and so on all have their own sets of policies and procedures to follow in the development process of a standard. They work together to develop the specification or standard and then they adopt the standard using code to develop their solutions.

Another way to develop standards is to start with an existing technology. If there is enough interest in the industry to establish a standard for that technology, which will often start as an open source project, then the competitors come together to evolve the technology and write a standard and documentation such as specifications around that existing technology.

A third example is more of a de facto standard, where a company may donate some technology code or APIs to a standards organization, and then other companies and organizations begin to adopt that technology, leading eventually, to it becoming a "de facto" or "de jure" standard.

Identifying the technologies and organizations

You can identify the standards organizations to get involved with by taking an inventory of the technologies that you are using. Take a look at your development environment and your development stack. Learn about your programming language – how it is standardized, the basics, the features, the classes, pre-defined libraries and functions, the threading model, the intricacies of the language, and the ecosystem.

Learn about the software and hardware you are using. There are inevitably some components that are based on standardized architecture, APIs, and specifications.

Investigate which technologies you might be implementing or using as a solution in the future. There may be technologies you want to use that are based on a standard. Learning about the standard will sometimes take longer than learning about the technology, but once you identify the technology, you can go deeper into learning how that technology is developed and which organizations are involved.

You can be viewed as a leader in this area inside of your company by taking the time to understand the dynamics at play by learning how the technology evolves and who is responsible for that evolution. Investigate the licenses and the **Intellectual Property** (**IP**) flow. Take the time to find out the costs of participating and contributing to the standards and what the process and costs of participating at various levels are. Many standards organizations are fee-based, so this is important information to be able to convey to your management. Assess whether any fees are worth the investment balanced against your ability to influence the standards.

There are many benefits to software and hardware products that conform to standards, including interoperability, portability, longevity, stability, and compatibility. Be prepared to communicate those benefits, along with a comprehensive assessment of your potential involvement in the standard.

Getting involved with standards organizations – the conventions and best practices

The first thing you should do to start participating in standards is to determine your role. Will you plan to lead this effort or are you looking to contribute or just to observe? Are you there to monitor, influence, or drive? Is this effort going to be long-term and strategic or a short-term engagement?

As we discussed, there are many benefits to participating in standards – finding out the latest developments, preventing unfavorable or "bad" things from happening, getting cross-industry perspectives on issues, and encouraging collaboration and innovation. Standards activities can influence standards important to you or your company.

There are also perception-related advantages to participating in standards such as communications, marketing, and mindshare increases in the market. Remember that standards participation is a two-way street: standards influence products, and products influence standards.

In addition to technical standards, there are increasing standards around interoperability, portability, compliance, regulation, and sovereignty issues. Standards bodies are probably an unfamiliar environment for you, different from your technical or community participation activities. They are sometimes described as a technical and political activity. They are not typically operating with a top-down hierarchy and decision-makers. There are new processes, not just related to code or engineering. There are politics, meetings, motions, and Robert's Rules of Order to follow. Many standards organizations follow or loosely follow Robert's Rules of Order.

Robert's Rules of Order is a manual of procedures for governance. It was created in 1876 by Henry Martyn Robert. He wrote it as an application of the rules and motions used in the United States Congress. You can read the rules online (`https://robertsrules.org/robertsrules.pdf`) or purchase a book describing them to become more familiar with them.

Some of the other principles in play that you will need to be able to adapt to include balancing short-term and long-term objectives, establishing influence for continued participation, and long-term influence in an organization. You will need to build good working relationships with people working in other companies and in other geographies. You may disagree with them at times, but it is vital to do so without being disagreeable. This is where your conflict resolution skills will be useful, as well as your emotional intelligence.

For standards development organization meetings, there will be a mix of **face-to-face (F2F)** meetings and virtual meetings, and you should attend in person whenever possible. Much like the usefulness of office chance conversations, in standards organizations, there are also these types of "hallway conversations" that happen at standards organizational meetings.

In addition, there are many social hours, and meals – lunches, dinners, and breakfasts – providing such opportunities during face-to-face or in-person meetings. Strengthening your personal relationships will allow you to create influence and form strong relationships, and in addition to the formally scheduled meetings, this will require a mix of direct phone calls, emails, and both group/private conversations, in person and online. You will need these relationships to give and receive feedback on ideas and proposals. Also, it will give you the ability to understand why everyone, including you, is participating and the objectives and goals of participants.

Bringing together the disparate viewpoints of others and understanding the strategies, tactics, and risks that exist needs to be managed carefully. You should coordinate internally within your company if multiple business units are represented. You will need to negotiate and compromise to resolve conflicts and create collaborations, so the better you understand your holistic strategy, the easier this will be for you to do. Remember that you do not have to satisfy every use case. It may be helpful to keep in mind that with standards development, timeliness is important. If the window of opportunity is lost and no one implements the standard, it is not useful. You will need to differentiate between critical, important, or nice-to-have elements.

There are several possible paths to choose from when you are trying to come to a resolution and reconcile the needs of various participants. Some options include waiting for the next version of the standard, relying on building blocks, or a Lego bricks style of evolution – layering multiple specifications or extensions (standard or proprietary). When you meet with other groups internally, ask them whether it will have a significant impact on services/products: present or future.

There is an advantage to leadership in standards organizations. Advantages of leadership include the ability to influence technical decisions, strategic direction, the timing of standard development, and the pace and direction of the evolution of the standards. Leadership is useful for long-term interest in a standard or an organization. Be advised that leadership can lead to a potential conflict of interest – be mindful of that possibility. It is important to keep trust in the fairness of the process and the presence of a level playing field. This can be a challenge: treating everyone fairly within standard processes while not undercutting your own interests. When there are particularly controversial issues, if possible, having a different employee team member represent a different point of view can help preserve the other positions that you may have taken in the organization.

If you do decide to take a leadership role in a standards organization, ensure that you know how to write a design and specification document – you can learn this by reviewing existing ones. You will need to learn how to incorporate feedback and move to resolution quickly in these documents. You will also need to know how to run meetings efficiently, stay on track with an agenda, and hear viewpoints from different participants in the meeting. You can practice running meetings in your development team to start and practice resolving conflicts in the meeting. You should learn how to influence another team member or team to use your solutions. Practice mentoring and modeling behaviors you would like to see emulated in your team and across your organization. Learn how to lead a project to completion and how to explain your viewpoints to others who may not have a technical background. Often, in standards organizations, there is a mix of technical and non-technical individuals.

There are varying methodologies incorporated into standard-setting organizations or standards-related organizations. They will typically have a development approach that includes transparency, participation regulations, licensing, and **Intellectual Property Rights (IPRs)**.

In addition to languages and frameworks, there are common libraries that are part of language ecosystems, which may also be standardized or developed as open source projects. Often, there is synergy between standards and open source projects. When you decide to participate in standards activities, it is helpful to learn from some of the standards that have a history of successful collaboration and adoption of the standards.

Drawing on our extensive experience in the Java ecosystems, there are some best practices when doing so that we have gleaned. These are summarized in the following list:

- Ensure that there is a wide range of contributors, not only corporations but also individuals and educational or non-profit groups, such as user groups or open source groups, who are interested in contributing to and adopting the standard.

- Involve the broader community early in the standardization process. Include and gather input on the functionality as well as specific features that are required in the standards.

- Create an open and collaborative culture among the participants and ensure that the standards body operates openly and transparently – communications, issue trackers, and development should be out in the open.

- It is essential to have open feedback mechanisms for user feedback as the standards are being developed and after they are finalized to ensure future versions incorporate how the technology is being used, and also to allow for requests for support and new features.

- Allow and encourage multiple implementations of the standards and flexibility in the licensing.

- Allow the standard and the implementation to be developed concurrently and in the open.

- Streamline the processes for standardization to embrace current software development methodologies such as agile and continuous delivery/trunk development.

- Develop test suites to validate the conformity of multiple implementations of the standard.

- You should become familiar with not only the standardization process but also the ecosystem of development for the frameworks and libraries developed to support the language.

When you decide to get involved in a standards organization, remember the reason you are participating and be mindful of whether you are there for your personal interests or whether you are participating on behalf of your company. The purpose and role should guide your participation in the organization. Now let us talk about connecting your company to standards.

Connecting your company to standards, identifying technologies and organizations, and getting involved on a deeper level

Once you have started contributing to a standardization effort, it is often necessary to bring your company into the effort in order to have maximum impact. Assuming you start as an observer versus a participant in a standards activity, the first thing to do is educate yourself and become familiar with the standard and the organization, as well as how you think your company products currently could use the standard. Review the current discussions and issues to become acquainted with some of the current considerations being contemplated in the next release or version of the standard.

The next step in this process is to have a conversation with your management and discuss some of your ideas about how your company can contribute together. You can also find the contacts at your company to discuss this with within other product or development organizations and also whether there are procedural contacts in place. Many companies either have an office in the **Chief Technology Officer (CTO)** or architecture group dedicated to standards and/or open source. Sometimes, you can also find contacts via a legal representative. Ensure that you have the proper agreement on your participation and then you can pursue formalized membership in the organization or perhaps contributions at a level before membership. Typically, organizations have (and should have) a **contributor license agreement (CLA)** in place, which you should also discuss with your legal contract before agreeing to any terms.

After you receive the approval to participate, it is a good practice to find other people in your organization interested in the standard and solicit their feedback and contributions.

Sometimes, people are busy and may not respond to your requests, but try to be patient. Be direct and clear with your requests for feedback and provide a clear date by which you would like to receive any feedback from them.

If you receive feedback that needs clarification or there is any contradicting feedback, it is often helpful to set up a brief meeting to discuss and resolve how to move forward representing your company as a whole.

Start contributing to the standard project(s) based on these positions and look for opportunities to advance your company in the standards organization. This could be through working groups, executive boards, expert groups, contributions, or evangelizing the work to the public.

Provide interim drafts to your colleagues internally and solicit their feedback again.

It will be important to contribute the agreed feedback or input, but also to ensure there is agreement on how it was incorporated and whether there are second, third, and fourth-round comments. Encourage others to experiment with the standard or implementation and provide feedback that you can incorporate. These steps will expedite your company and its ability to develop its own products and implementations of the standards more quickly and easily. This allows the solutions to be out in the marketplace with customers much sooner as well.

When you have successfully contributed to a standards activity, make sure to communicate and share the results with everyone in your team who has provided feedback or comments. This is also a good time to investigate whether there could be mention of the activity in a blog or press release. You can check with your communications or public relations contacts, usually in the marketing department. This will ensure that your company leadership role and your own contributions are impact are highlighted.

In summary, you should learn how the standards organization works, and the processes for moving from different roles such as observer to participant, member, author, editor, reviewer, leader, and so on. Observe and find mentors and sponsors and grow your network of connections inside the organization. Communicate your intentions to contribute to the organization and decide on actions to take. Follow up on your commitments and responsibilities. Share your contributions and comments on the provided or suggested channels. Ask for advice and collaborate as you do so, and ask for suggestions and feedback to ensure you are contributing value and making an impact.

Interview

Ed Burns

Q: Hi, Ed Burns. Why don't you introduce yourself and tell us a little bit about your current role?

A: My current role, as we'll talk about, is a happy extension of my previous roles.

I work at Microsoft and I am the principal architect overseeing how Jakarta EE runtimes can find a home on Azure. In this role, I work with partnerships with the three main commercial Java app server vendors that are still producing well-used products: IBM, Red Hat, and Oracle. These vendors are responsible for multi-million-dollar accounts in the world of running Java EE workloads. They run critical Java EE workloads for all sectors of the economy, from finance to energy, technology, and communications.

We've got customers that are doing all of these things, and they have workloads that they want to continue to derive corporate value from by moving them into the cloud. Moreover, they want to do so in a way that lets them capitalize on the cloud value proposition of transparency, expenditure, and the scalability of workloads so that you're not really leaving any money on the table with regard to runtimes.

Q: You have a vast amount of experience. Tell us a little bit about how you got started and how you got to where you are now, in a high-level role at Microsoft.

A: Well, the thing that I like to realize is what I call the magic triad: right place, right time, right skills. Some of that is luck, some of it is preparedness, and some of it is being able to see an opportunity.

There were two moments in my career where that happened. The first was in college. I happened to be a student at the University of Illinois in Urbana-Champaign as an undergrad in the early 1990s and managed to get involved as a student programmer in NCSA Mosaic, which was the world's first graphical web browser. When I graduated in 1995, there were not that many people in the world at that time that were able to do HTML, understood what HTML authoring was, understood what HTTP and web servers were, and knew how to do Unix socket programming and other web browser basics. It was simple stuff back then: HTTP/1 and 0.9 text-based protocols, nothing like HTTP/2 or HTTP/3 being worked on now. But anyhow, that was one opportunity.

Later, J2EE was invented. The early stages of J2EE were what is now known as Tomcat, and that was two specifications: Servlet and JSP. Servlet was a Java wrapper around `CGI-bin`, which was the HTTP technology whose birth I had witnessed in my undergrad days. JSP was based on a Microsoft idea, Active Server Pages. The combination of these things was the first example of a sweet spot for being able to make a money-making, value-delivering Java application that worked on the web.

With that, you had the concept of a framework, and so one of the early frameworks that combined Servlet and JSP was Struts. Struts was set up by Craig McClanahan. He was hired by Sun, and I joined him to work on a specification to create a standard for doing a web framework thing. This is what became JavaServer Faces.

Through my work on JavaServer Faces, I became more deeply involved in J2EE, Jakarta EE, and Java EE. The key value proposition of this open standard is to empower developers by giving them a core set of APIs that ensures that their skills are portable and not locked into any one vendor's ecosystem.

One of the interesting things I got to see happen was the essential forking of the early version of J2EE into what became Spring. Being able to have a historical perspective of how these two ecosystems diverged and observe the levels of commercial success that they both have in comparison to each other is something that's really interesting.

Q: Definitely. You had the opportunity to work at Sun Microsystems, Oracle, and Microsoft. Tell us a story about your career and, specifically, a moment where you felt like you made an impact based on the work that you did and your involvement with standards where it really made a difference in terms of your career and visibility, or where you felt like you were truly making a difference in the work that you were doing.

A: Well, looking back on the very rewarding history I had with JSF, I tried to bring humility and community to the work and embrace the notion of, "This is a community project, so I want to bring as many people in as possible."

One moment was at JavaOne in maybe 2008. I was approached by two Austrian gentlemen, and they said, "We're excited to meet you, Mr. Burns," in a nice Austrian accent. They said, "We're working on a clean-room open source implementation of the JSF spec." I replied, "That's great! We want to get you on the expert group. We want to get your ideas and make sure that we're developing the new version of the spec in a way that is helpful."

At the time, being able to be a member of JCP, which is the standard body that was doing the spec, wasn't as easy for non-corporate members. Over the years, JCP became much more accepting of committers coming in from the outside, and that process has continued to the point that now, Jakarta

EE is the standard body overseeing the continued development of this technology. They have a range of participants, and so does JCP: individuals, Java User Group members, and corporations. These gentlemen came to me and said, "We're building an independent implementation of the JSF spec," and instead of seeing them as competition, I was able to say, "Great – the more the merrier. We need to have more people to test out the spec."

That became MyFaces. That was the key runtime for JSF in IBM, and a lot of corporate implementations used that. To this day, there are still two main implementations of JSF.

Q: You were basically famous in the ecosystem. These people you'd never met sought you out and were obviously eager and excited to meet you, but you actually had an impact on their business.

A: Right. Here's another moment or impact I wanted to talk about, and it's one I take real pride in.

I believe that much of computing, as it was from the very beginning, is all about automating things and creating the opportunity for people to create more value faster. Unfortunately, the pace of that innovation has often outstripped people's abilities to adapt and learn to ride that crest.

What effectively ends up happening with computing is that yes, there are more opportunities, but the number of hands that can actually reap those benefits is increasingly shrinking. Now, the fruit is out there. You can pick it up off the tree, but it's getting harder and harder and the pace is moving ever faster. People who work in computing could reasonably be tagged as job destroyers: that's one way of thinking about it. If you're an optimist, you might say, "No, we're not job destroyers. We're job creators because we're creating innovation that enables human beings to do more."

I've talked with leaders about this and I see both sides, but in practice, it's more of the job-destroying that's happening. But the case of JSF was a bit of a golden spot where instead of automating and destroying jobs, I actually was able to observe people creating companies – building JSF component libraries, doing consulting, and so on. As I mentioned, the company that did MyFaces built a very successful consulting business on top of it, and it is still operating to this day. Because of the openness of the standard, I was able to be a steward and crank the wheel to produce a small and money-making ecosystem of a lot of different companies: some of which have gone bust, some of which have dissolved, and some of which still exist.

I feel proud of that – it's not easy to do as a corporate individual contributor. I am not a start-up person. I have always worked for a big company, so I'm lucky that I was able to have the chance to do that while still having the security of a big steady corporate paycheck.

Q: Right – you had that impact as well as building on your network. You have the opportunity to do that from inside a large company, working as an engineer.

You started out at Sun Microsystems, and you progressed to the senior levels. How do you think your work as a technical leader (being involved in the standard and defining the standard for JSF) helped your career and your progression?

A: That's a good question. There's a key characteristic of working on a project that is an open source project: the implementation and interface are in one project. There's only so much scale you can get because the work you're doing is going to stay in that project.

However, if you work on an open standard such as the Java EE, JCP, and Jakarta standards, you're going to have a wider impact because there are other vendors that are building on, using, and implementing that specification.

In the case of JSF and JCP in general, I was also involved in one of the iterations of the Servlet specification. This was Servlet version 4, which was the one that introduced HTTP/2. Earlier, I talked about being able to remember when HTTP/0.9 was just a simple text-based protocol with MIME headers, compared to HTTP/2 when you had socket multiplexing, a binary header compression protocol, and much more. I'm very fortunate to have that perspective of things, but to come back to the breadth of impact, working on standards gives you a bigger breadth of impact, but you have to balance that with the corporate model.

The corporate model for a single-vendor implementation such as Spring is a lot easier for many corporations to absorb because they know they have one vendor to deal with – their one support channel – whereas if you go with Jakarta EE, you have to pick a vendor but with an implicit understanding that you might be able to move to other things so that trade-off is something to keep in mind.

At the end of the day, I believe the standards give developers and contributors more ability to grow their careers than a single-ecosystem open source project. Now, there are certainly plenty of examples of people who are successful open source committers that contribute to a wide range of different things. Look at the Node.js community. There's TJ Holowaychuk, who has written a huge number of the things that are in that community, but he's also gone on to do lots of other amazing things and other open standards too.

So, it's not a hard and fast rule, but it's easier to be portable with standards.

Q: In terms of your career advancement conversations, did that come up with your managers when it became time to look at moving to the next level?

A: Definitely.

There is a ramp of increasing responsibility that working on standards naturally affords. This ramp has a shallow enough slope that your managers at the time, as you progress along that ramp, can say, "OK, you climbed up a few steps. Are you still performing well, or do you need to tweak something?" It gives you an opportunity to gradually grow, but it doesn't hold you back because if you see that you're able to master the current level, you can go faster and further too.

Going back to the early days of JSF, I originally worked just as the implementation guy for the first version of JSF, and Craig McClanahan was the main spec lead. As the project got further along, the workload got more and more challenging, and I said, "I think I'd like to offer to be a co-spec lead on this." He replied, "Yes, OK. Let's do that." Then, we were able to get the thing done because the scope was getting more and more advanced, and we had to close it down and ship it. That's an example of where I was able to see what the next step was – to go from implementation to spec lead.

Q: And then inside the company, your level increased as a result of that.

When it came to leaving and looking for external positions, how do you think your involvement in a technical standard contributed to your ability to be seen as a strong candidate?

A: Well, over many years working with JSF, JCP, Jakarta EE, and Java EE, I had interactions with many leaders and technical contributors across many different company vendors. Back in the time when in-person conferences were easier to do, right after joining Microsoft, I had the opportunity to take my new boss around JavaOne and just introduce her to the community. I could say, "Oh, here's so and so. They're the director of engineering for this part of the Java platform," and then have them be able to say, "Oh, you've got a good hire there with Ed. I know him from this and that." That experience was repeated with a large variety of people I knew from the Java ecosystem just at JavaOne. It was essentially me telling my new boss, "Look. I'm solidifying that you have hired someone who has connections at least."

Q: Of course. You are a resource that has more to offer than just your technical skills: there's more to it than that, and that's one aspect that you brought to your role with your experience in technical standards: defining the standard.

Do you want to talk a little bit about becoming an author and some of the books that you've written and your experience with that?

A: Sure. There's a story there too, and it goes back to being able to spot when someone is struggling with their task and effectively help them, but also in a way that helps yourself.

I mentioned observing that Craig needed help getting the JSF spec done. One of the conferences I was at was one that no longer exists – it was called The Server Side Java Symposium. I was already involved in JSF at that time, and I went to The Server Side Java Symposium. It was held at Caesars Palace in Las Vegas, and somehow there was this little white baby grand piano that was sitting at the top of an escalator.

It was a late night. There was some party. I think Mike Cannon-Brookes and Hani Suleiman were there, drinking cocktails Anyway, there was this piano. I sat down. It was late. No one was around. I started just tinkling along on this piano, and this guy came up to me and said, "Oh, I play." He sat down next to me and we played a little together.

It turned out he was this guy Christian Schalk from Oracle, and he also knew me as the JSF guy, but he had been signed up to write a book about JSF with McGraw Hill. As it turned out, his former co-author had left the project and he needed another co-author. That was how I got involved in my first technical book: just being open to it and recognizing an opportunity. There again, it is the right place, right time, right skills.

Q: Right. Then, you went on to write several other books.

Well, thanks so much for sharing your career stories.

Summary

In this chapter, you learned how to make a plan to get involved in standards organizations, how to choose a few organizations to participate in to get started, how to join and participate in the process, how to bring the concerns of your company and team into the process, and how to find ways to get involved on a deeper level.

Next, let's continue the discussion on making an impact in your technical career path by discussing how to build your personal brand and unlock the secrets to being respected and requested as a trusted advisor.

15

Build Your Personal Brand and Become a Trusted Advisor

As we conclude part three of this book, you will use all of the skills you have acquired so far to build your personal brand. You are helping and transforming people's lives, and this builds trust in you. Your personal brand will allow you to expand this trust to more people, help you attract people to your projects and initiatives, and position you as a high-achieving, respected professional. This chapter will help you use all you have done up to now to position your brand in the market. When talking about personal branding, the first thing that comes to mind is the following: *Do I need this? Do I have to build my own personal brand? I don't like to self-promote, so why should I even have a brand?*

The reality is everyone has a brand. You already have your brand. The question is, do you have control over what people believe about you? (See the interview with Yolande later in this chapter.) Further, your core values create a strong personal brand. Your values communicate who you are, who you want to become, and why employers, colleagues, friends, and partners choose you. Try to narrow down your core values to 5 or 10 points that communicate the things most authentic to you. You can start with a larger list and then select the ones that help focus and exemplify your brand – not only who you are now, but who you want to become in the future. Some examples of values are the following:

- Agility
- Accuracy
- Autonomy
- Collaboration
- Efficiency
- Excellence
- Duty
- Fun

- Generosity

- Growth

- Honesty

- Independence

- Innovative

- Integrity

- Perseverance

- Resourcefulness

- Responsibility

- Security

- Service

Take the time to make an inventory of your values as you start to think about developing your personal brand.

Thus, in our quest to create our own brand, we will cover the following in this chapter:

- What is personal branding?

- How to build your professional brand

- How to attract an audience

- How to leverage your personal brand professionally

So, let's begin!

What is personal branding?

We covered storytelling earlier in the book, and to be effective in communicating your personal brand, you are going to need to leverage those skills to share both your personal brand and those stories we talked about developing. Throughout your career, if you have developed an authentic personal brand and you stay true to it, and you consistently and effectively communicate your brand messages, you will build trust and establish a lasting personal and professional brand that can provide opportunities for career growth, advancement, and recognition. Let's start by understanding some of the elements of personal branding.

Building trust

We live in a society that's based on trust. We trust that our company is going to pay our salaries. Our company trusts that we're going to work and build the software. Our customers trust that we're going to deliver high-quality software that will solve their problems. Our customers and all our stakeholders trust that companies and developers will use their data in the right way and not misuse their data.

Especially in the context of jobs, the best way to get an amazing job, be it in your company or any other company, is to have people trust you. When people trust you, they believe that you're going to do good work, and that you will be competent, skillful, focused, and loyal.

The best positions in the market are given to people that we trust. At some point in the past, you have likely recommended someone to your company whom you deeply trusted, or perhaps even hired them on your own team.

Research shows that up to 75% of positions are filled through referrals, which is an indication of the importance of trust. If you want to get an amazing role, you need to be trusted by someone and get invited to apply for this position.

Gaining reputation

We need to think about the factors that contribute to our reputation. *Reputation* is what people believe about you. Thus, reputation is something that depends on what people see and believe you're capable of doing. We should keep in mind that reputation and trust, while very similar, are not the same thing. We can however use them interchangeably in many situations. While trust can be understood at a broader level, reputation tends to have more specific consequences for your career growth and for you personally as well. They are similar concepts that we can talk about in a similar way with regard to careers in general. Reputation is what people believe about you. And if people trust you, you have a good reputation. If people don't trust you, it's probably because you don't have a good reputation.

Increasing visibility

One important thing about this is that for people to believe something about you, they have to know you. They have to have heard of you somehow. We need to determine what makes us visible in our company and the market at large. The fact is that we are responsible for our own visibility. We do not need to rely on others to create our own brand for us. We shape and determine our brand, and we determine how visible we are. Perception is how others perceive our brand – that is outside of our control, but perception is based on how we visibly portray our brand.

Those three concepts, trust, reputation, and visibility, are extremely important. They go hand in hand. Again, they're not the same thing, but they work together to position you in the market.

Your brand is the combination of how visible you are, how trustworthy you are, and your reputation among people.

That is what a brand is. A brand is not a logo or a name or a website – although all of these can be used together to build a good brand for yourself. So if people know who you are, trust you, and believe something good about you, they might come to your website and read more of what you have to say. They might come to a presentation or even a workshop or a course that you run. They might buy your book. All of these factors will help in strengthening your reputation and visibility and enable people to trust you.

Your personal brand is the combination of all those assets you possess that show who you are and how you can help other people throughout the world. One important thing about branding that we discuss in more detail in the interview at the end of this chapter is the idea that you can either control your brand and position yourself in the market, or other people will position you.

People always hold some beliefs about you. If they don't know you, what they believe about you might be little or no significance. If they heard bad things about you, they might believe them, even if they might not be true.

If you don't position yourself in the market and control your brand, then what happens is that the market will position you any way it wants. And of course, people that are not you will never position you as well as you can position yourself.

If you take a hands-off approach to your brand, you leave your reputation in the hands of others. You're never going to have as good a reputation as you could if you don't exert a level of control.

Of course, this control is a limited capability. You cannot have full control of your own brand because people do sometimes believe things that might be untrue or wrong. They might have only a limited idea of what you do. They might not see some parts of you. For example, you might have a great reputation as a Java developer, but people might not see that what you're really very good at is in the area of databases.

But you do have a certain level of control, although the better word might be *influence*. You can influence your brand and how people see you in a way that more people will trust you, and see who you really are. This leads to having a good reputation.

Becoming a trusted advisor

When people trust you, they will undoubtedly listen to your suggestions and willingly follow your recommendations. It could be technical recommendations, or it could be which path to follow at a certain moment. It could be how to make specific decisions. It could be a combination of all of those things. If people decide to follow your advice because they trust you, that's when you become what we call a *trusted advisor*.

A trusted advisor is someone who can work collaboratively with their customers and peers to help them make better decisions and achieve the best possible results. The importance of being a trusted advisor is that when you work collaboratively, you are able to influence much earlier in the process the decisions and paths that people and even organizations take.

While a salesperson, for example, might help someone decide which cloud to acquire, or maybe which language to choose for a specific project, a trusted advisor will work with them way before that decision needs to be taken. By the time a decision like this has to be made, the trusted advisor has already gained the trust of the customer or company such that they have a much larger influence on the final outcome. You can be a trusted advisor for your team, your friends, your company, and your management. You can be that person that is working collaboratively early on in the process in such a way that you have the highest possible influence on future decisions. And that, again, opens up all kinds of amazing possibilities and opportunities to get jobs that give you high levels of autonomy and influence. It gets you working on the types of projects that you really want to work on, instead of being at the mercy of circumstances – you are going to be the person guiding and helping others to decide what the environment will look like.

There are several ways that you can become a trusted advisor, many of which are discussed in this book in specific chapters that you can refer to. Let us mention them here briefly to help you understand how each of these positions can be a stepping stone toward becoming a trusted advisor.

Being a community builder

One way to become a trusted advisor is to become a community builder. A community builder is someone who is responsible for getting a group of people to work together toward a common goal. *Community* is a broad term that can apply to your team in your company. It can also be something broader such as a public community, for example, a user group, a technology user group, a meet-up, or an event. There are all kinds of communities that can be built. The community builder helps everyone make connections and get acquainted, and understands the pros and cons of decisions for the whole team.

And so being a community builder is an amazing position because you become the trusted advisor for a whole group of people. And the fact that when you have one person that reflects in the whole group and that increases the trust that people have in you, increasing your reputation in turn. And because it is a community, such a position naturally also increases your visibility a lot.

Being a contributor

Another possibility, and we talk a lot about this when we speak about open source technologies, is for you to become a contributor. A contributor is someone who contributes to the success of a project or initiative. You can contribute to open source projects, initiatives at your company, and public initiatives such as user groups or events. As a contributor and trusted advisor, you are part of the process. You're not simply someone responsible just for doing an activity; you become part of the organization's story and its pursuit of its goals. The more you contribute to an activity, the more trust you'll have from everyone else on the team, and the more influence you'll have over the decision-making process.

As an example, if you participate in an open source project but are just a sporadic contributor that just contributes from time to time, you might gain some responsibilities, but the people in the project are not going to trust you to be there constantly. The more you get involved and the more contributions you make to the project, the more trust you earn, and the better the reputation you will develop. When you have more influence, you can start making decisions about the architecture of the project, new versions, and new initiatives.

Being a publisher, creator, or influencer

Another way you can become a trusted advisor is by creating your own content – that is, being a publisher, creator, or influencer. Instead of you working with people to get something done, you become a trusted advisor via this route because you have the knowledge and you share that knowledge through content such as blogs, videos, or presentations.

We have mentioned being a creator in many chapters in this book, in particular being a publisher. This allows you to gain influence and become a trusted advisor to the largest amount of people possible, going far beyond a single team and even beyond your company. The larger a publisher you are, the more people in the industry will trust you and come to see you as a trusted advisor, and your reputation will grow accordingly in your industry. One important concept here is that building your personal brand allows you to position yourself as a publisher. A publisher is someone that has an audience. Whether you call it being a publisher, a creator, or an influencer, it means *having an audience*. You have people that trust you and see you as their trusted advisor, seeking you out for your content on that particular type of information or technology. Note also that having this kind of influence over such a large amount of people does come with high levels of responsibility.

It can be extremely rewarding to take this path of being a publisher because it allows you to help a lot of people to achieve better results, transform their lives, and even help other people in turn.

Being a mentor

Another type of trusted advisor, and we have a full chapter specifically about this in this book, is to be a mentor. A mentor is someone who works closely with their mentees to help them overcome their challenges and obstacles and achieve better results. As a mentor, your level of responsibility grows because now you're working specifically with people on their personal dreams and goals, and helping them achieve and advance further. It's also extremely rewarding because you get to see the results of your effort and the value of your contribution. You can mentor people in your company, in your team, friends and acquaintances that you meet at events, or other people from your industry network. You can even be a professional mentor where you open up your services of mentorship for a larger number of people or for people that are not in your immediate circle of networking.

Being a mentor is the highest level of trusted advisor because you are personally and emotionally connected to the people that you're mentoring. You are invested in their goals, their dreams, and helping them achieve the transformation they seek. It is an honor to mentor someone. Such a position should undoubtedly be taken seriously.

Identify your professional brand

To begin, you need to **define your vision and purpose**. Personally and professionally, what values are important to you and how do you want your audience to perceive you? How will you make an impact on them? What skill sets or experience do you have that distinguish you from others who have these same values?

Assess your personal brand inventory. After you establish your purpose, values, and skills, take an inventory of how you are perceived in the industry. Take note of your traits, habits, and characteristics. Make any adjustments necessary to reflect your current reality.

Construct a narrative around this inventory. You should branch out to create narratives for basic questions such as, *"Tell me about yourself," "Tell me about your resume of experience," "Tell me where you are from and where you are going,"* and *"What makes you special?"* Use examples from your experience to share stories that answer these questions and incorporate your brand inventory characteristics.

Once you have established and are aware of your unique offering and characteristics, you are ready to build your brand and attract an audience. The key here is to be authentic in living out your personal brand identity – **be your brand**.

How to build your professional brand

Let us now discuss how to build your professional brand. The following subsections cover four steps that are extremely important in building your professional brand.

The first step is to understand yourself because your brand is already in you. A professional brand is not something that appears out of the blue. It's not something that you decide you want to be or become. It is a construction using everything that you already did and all the reputation you have, all your experience and history combined with the things that you want to do in the future. You always start from where you are right now – from your skills, your projects, your experience, your visibility, and the people that you're ready to help.

You start from where you are right now – and then you look to the future. How do you want to present all of this to your audience and your future connections? The first step is to understand who you are, understand what you have done, and make an assessment of all the projects you have participated in and all the skills you have acquired. Try to create narratives out of this. A great way to create narratives is to use the **Star methodology**.

Star methodology

The Star methodology is a methodology used to create narratives for interviews. All interviewers are familiar with it and will easily understand it. You can also use it to your advantage to organize your abilities, projects, and skills into brief Star narratives, allowing you to better understand yourself and build your brand. It works like this, by breaking your narrative down into four points:

- **Situation**: Describe what the scenario of the narrative is.
- **Task**: What is the task that you had to do or the problem to be solved in this particular narrative?
- **Action**: What is the action that you took to solve the problem and complete the task?
- **Result**: What is the result that you achieved?

By thinking about your narratives in terms of the things that you did and the experience you gained, and then putting them in this Star format, you can develop more clarity and have a better understanding of what you can deliver in future roles and explain this in future interviews. More broadly, it helps you develop a very clear vision of who you are, how you can help people, and how you can really use your reputation to create the brand that you want to build.

Define your brand in an outward-focused way

The second step is to define your brand in an outward-focused way. It's very easy to confuse our brand with ourselves. *It's my brand, it's what I do, it's the things that I'm good at.* We can easily think of our brand as something to do solely with us. *But your brand is not about you.* Your brand is about how you help others to achieve what they want.

The best way for you to plan and define your brand is by thinking of what you can help others achieve, because people don't care about your brand, your logo, or your blog. People don't care about us. People care about how you can help them achieve what they want. Everyone wants to have or become something. Once you understand the service that your brand will provide, and what success looks like, along with the results that people will get by being associated with you (i.e., by buying your services, connecting with your blog, or watching your YouTube content), that's when you have a clear brand that people will choose to follow. Take the phrase, *I help people to do X so they can have or become Y.* It's a very simple phrase that you can use. *People* here are those that you want to attract to become your audience, the people that you want to help. *X* is the thing that you are very good at and that you want to be known for. *Y* is the thing that people want to do, have, or become.

This simple, formulaic phrase can really help you get clarity on creating an outward-focused brand. By focusing on other people and helping them have or become something they want, they choose you as the appropriate person for them to associate with. They then start to follow you, to pay attention to your content, to participate more in your initiatives. You have now formed relationships and created engagement with your audience.

Figure out how you want to help

The next step is to figure out how you want to help. This book mentioned many ways that you can help your audience, from participating in open source projects to building communities, public speaking, or writing blogs and books. All of these techniques help you build a relationship with your audience. There's no right or wrong way here as long as you create engagement. You can also use social media, YouTube, audio, video, or podcasts, any way you want to do it. Each audience has a different preference. Whatever technology or means you choose, you're going to attract people that are interested in the means by which you share your content.

Other options include helping your audience by creating courses, doing live streams, or mentoring people. All of these methods are just ways for you to help them achieve success with the results they want. The more people get results by being close to you, or by being in a relationship with you, the more they're going to trust you, and the bigger your reputation will get. This is a great way of creating engagement.

Be consistent

Another thing that's very important is being consistent. One of the most important things in terms of building an audience is consistency. By consistency, we do not mean that we have to share one article at 2 P.M. every week. What we mean by consistency is that you are constantly talking to your audience, consistently being present. A great way to do this is by using social media because you can share a small piece of content every day. Also having conversations, either in-person live conversations on YouTube or on a podcast, is another great technique because people can have access to you.

Showing up consistently at different events over multiple years is also another way. People will soon expect to see you there. Any way that your community can see you with a reasonable frequency, so they can strengthen their relationship with you, contributes to building that consistency that is fundamental for people to believe that they have a relationship. And it's these relationships that are so important for trust, visibility, and your reputation. The biggest goal of building your brand is to build these relationships with people. One last point that we want to make is that relationships are built with *people*. Even though you might be helping companies to achieve results or helping teams to be more productive, in the end, you're going to be talking and building a relationship with *people*. They could be managers, developers, or your peers. But you need to be looking for people to build a relationship with.

How can we attract an audience?

Now that you see the importance of being a trusted advisor to your audience, the next important step is to attract an audience.

Building a brand is all about successfully attracting your own audience. We are all publishers. Our experience is that attracting an audience is something that technical people are afraid of because developers (and technical people in general) are not looking to be celebrities. They're not trying to promote themselves. When you start talking about attracting people, it always sounds unnecessary and doesn't seem to be connected to your career. Some people think that this is only for people who want to build a product or something like that.

Take responsibility for helping others – leaders take responsibility

In reality, attracting an audience is you taking responsibility for helping other people. Think about it. You have the knowledge, you have the capacity to mentor people, you have the experience, the skills, and all those things can help others to achieve their sought-after results, to be successful, to improve their careers, and to improve their lives. If you don't take responsibility to work with them, how can they ever find you? Attracting people means taking this responsibility to find the people that need you and helping them achieve the things that they need.

Leaders are those that take responsibility, so when you take responsibility to help others, you're being a leader. Even though that might sound scary and unnecessary, it is precisely due to being a leader that this process of building your brand and attracting people to you will have such a large impact on your career. Behaving like a leader will make you more visible and give you a stronger reputation. Being more visible in your community will flow into other aspects of your life as well. For instance, this will lend more visibility to your content, allowing you to meet a wider range of people and opening up more opportunities for yourself and also for others. You will attract more people to the projects and communities that you are involved in.

It will also improve you technically because the more people you attract as your audience, the more people you're going to have a chance to talk to about your technical topics of interest, and the more chances you're going to have to get involved in important projects. The result is that you also increase your technical expertise.

You can't transform people, but they can transform themselves

Once you realize how you can inspire people to transform themselves and their careers, you will see how it can benefit your own career. First, you have to understand how to inspire people. The most important thing in terms of attracting people is understanding that you can't transform people. People transform themselves.

Every time you help someone take an action that helps them transform themselves, you're being a leader to that person. You're being that leader that not only attracts people, but actually helps people to take action and transform themselves, to do something that will deliver them results. The content that we generate, be it articles, books, videos, presentations, or even training courses – that content does not change or transform people. What really transforms them are the actions that they take once they discover your content. Exactly because of that, the focus should always be on helping people take action. The objective of creating content should always be to inspire people to take action. We can create amazing presentations, but if at the end of it, the person consuming our content is not ready to take action, then nothing transformative will happen for them.

We have to recognize that taking action is one of the hardest things for people to do. There are all kinds of reasons that we use to convince ourselves that we don't need to take action. We say things like, *"Oh, I don't need this right now,"* or, *"No, it's too hard for me to do it. It's not going to change my life."* People will create all sorts of excuses to not take action on something that you propose. The challenge is how can we work with people in a way that we inspire them to take action. To do that, there are four steps that we should consider.

Build a better future

Step number one: help them build a better future. People will gravitate toward something that they want. If they can see that your content or the technology you're proposing can bring them a better future, they will be more inclined to take action. So you should always help them build a better future for themselves. However, you don't need to do this by telling them what the better future is.

You usually do this by understanding their needs and problems, and helping them realize what kind of future can materialize once they solve those problems. Thus, they can see that if they learn a given technology, they can get a new job. If they work, if they solve a given challenge, they might get a raise. And by getting a new job or a raise, they might improve their family's life. Each person will have their own dreams, their own goals. And if you can help them imagine and build that better future with your content, with the technology that you're proposing, you're going to help them move toward that.

Help them maximize the current problems

Once you can imagine a better future, the very first thing that your brain is going to do is tell you it is a great future, but right here, right now, it's not so bad. We don't need to move toward that better future right now. You can focus on the second thing you have to do, which is to help them maximize the current problems. People not only move toward something they want, but they actually move faster away from something they don't want. Therefore, by helping them understand the current situation, the problems they're going through, and how bad staying where they are actually is, you're going to help them want to move away from the current problems and toward this better future that you help them create.

Help build a bridge

The third step is to help build a bridge. Because the moment they can see that there is a better place to go and they cannot stay where they are, they're going to start using excuses like, *"Oh, but it's too hard. There's no way to get there. What this person did is different from what I'm able to do."* It's important to build a bridge from where the person is all the way to where they want to get, to this better future that they are looking for. And the way to do that is by using your skills, the technology that you're proposing, and the content that you're creating to lay out a series of steps that the person can see themselves taking. If they take these steps, then they can get to the better place you're talking about. A good example of a series of steps is exactly what we provide here in this book.

This book lays out 15 chapters. In other words, it lays out 15 steps that you can take to get an amazing career and improve your life. As a leader, you have to organize your content in a way that people can see that if they take this series of steps, if they walk that path that you're proposing, they will get to this amazing life that you help them create. The fourth step, then, for people to transform their lives is for them to take a small action.

Take a small first step

Now that the person can see a better future, they recognize that staying where they are is not reasonable, and they see there is a bridge between where they are and the amazing future they want to get to, they will start saying things like, *"Yes, that's great. I'll start this tomorrow. I don't need to do this right now,"* or *"I can wait for a better moment in my life to do something like this."* And they will continue to be stuck in whatever situation they are in right now. You should help them take that first small step because as soon as they start moving, there's a much greater chance that they will continue to take more and more steps in that direction.

Be clear – people in doubt do not take action

Our whole objective with our content in terms of inspiring people to take action is to do these aforementioned four things: build a better place, maximize their problems, build a bridge to the better place, and then help the person take a small step so they can start walking that path. And this fourth step is very, very important because if they represent the content, they are building your brand. If you don't know what step people need to take to walk on that path, how can someone consuming your content really understand what the next step is? You have to be very clear to help them take this first step – and the best step that you can help them take is to build a relationship with you. Once you take the responsibility to attract people to you, you're also taking the responsibility to create this relationship between you and the person. And the longer they stay with you, the more they will consume your content, participate in your activities, use your technology, get involved in your project, and join your community.

The longer they stay close to you, the more they're going to learn and advance in their careers because you have a focus, a brand, and you're going to continue to work in that space. You're going to continue to help them. This step of them building a relationship with you is extremely important – it could be joining a community that you are part of, maybe a Discord server or a Slack channel, or maybe it could be to connect through social media. There are all kinds of easy steps that will help people connect with you. And once they connect, you can continue to provide information, help, and support so they can continue to move on this path, across this bridge that you have to help them create.

Help them help others

One last thing that creates impact is to help your audience help others. We talk a lot in this book about both building and participating in communities. The more you can bring the people that trust you into communities that you're part of, then the more support they're going to have, the more they will be able to help others, and the larger transformation you can help them achieve. Let's look at the various ways in which you can build a community from your audience.

Share their stories (testimonials)

One way is to incentivize your audience to share their stories. It's an easy way to help others by letting them share their struggles, the actions they took, and the results they achieved. All of this helps other people from the community to really want to take those steps and want to be involved.

Promote an environment of support

You can also promote an environment of support. Incentivize and inspire people in your community to support others, welcome new members, help them to find their way around, and really be part of building the community. Once someone joins in, if they can start helping others too, then they will feel part of the community much faster and they'll be more inspired to continue to take action and participate.

Share the successes and the results

Another great way to build community is by sharing successful results from people in the community. So make a point to congratulate people, even if they have only taken a small step.

You can use gamification to do that. You can use a point system, or you can simply tell people that you appreciate and recognize the step they're taking, which will also go a long way toward helping them continue to take the next step, and the next, and the next, and improve their results.

You're also helping them work with other people in your community so they can support each other on this path. Taking action is extremely hard, but if you help people take the first step and you can engage them inside a supportive community to help them continue to grow, then you're setting them up to transform their own lives and improve their whole situation.

Ask for feedback

Once you have established your brand, attracted an audience, and shared your brand, ask your audience for feedback. This will help you to determine if you are delivering on your brand promises. Delivering on your brand promises will establish even more trust in you as a professional to be able to achieve your goals. Be willing to adapt your content and your messaging as needed to remain consistent with your brand. Create a continuous feedback loop to ensure consistent improvement and refine the content and activities you are involved in throughout your professional career. Be generous in your appreciation of the feedback, as well. Feedback is a gift. Create a space for people to feel safe to provide feedback to you. It will help you to grow and engage more deeply with your community. Now let's discuss how to leverage your brand professionally.

Leveraging your personal brand professionally

All of this may sound like a full-time job of helping others and that it will not bring any benefit to you and your career. So let's take a look at how doing everything we've discussed can actually help you professionally.

Trust leads to opportunity

First of all, trust is the best way to create opportunities and get amazing positions. The best-paying, most interesting, and challenging positions in the market are offered to people that we trust. When someone has an interesting position inside their company or is working on an interesting project and needs help from someone, they will invite someone they trust to be part of it. The same thing happens inside companies. When teams, managers, and developers need help to hire someone, they will look for people that they trust. When you build trust with other developers, managers, and people from different companies, you increase the chance that someone that trusts you will invite you to one of these amazing projects. Remember that up to 75% of jobs are in what we call the *hidden job market*.

These jobs are not visible to people that are not in the circle of trust. For you to get access to them, you need to be trusted by a greater number of people. When you build your brand, attract an audience, start to be seen as a trustworthy person, then more people will suggest your name, invite you to a hiring process, and give you access to the most amazing positions in the market.

Trust is the best way to meet amazing people

But not only does it unlock invisible jobs – trust is also the best way to meet amazing people. When people trust you and become your friend, you have a chance to peek inside their head. Instead of you just seeing an amazing developer or someone far away, disconnected from you, you can actually have a connection and a relationship with them. With that, you both share your skills, knowledge, and insights with each other. This mutually beneficial relationship makes both of you stronger, allowing you to tackle harder problems and more complex challenges.

Software development is an environment that requires far too many skills and way too many tools for one person to know it all and be ready to do everything. When you build relationships with more people, you gain access to the knowledge that you need to go after the highest challenge. That will also give you a lot of confidence because once you have friends and know you can reach out to them, you're going to be more confident and actually more open to interesting and challenging projects. This confidence will allow you to work much better in your current project, even if you don't ask for help. So, building trust with a larger community of professional developers will help you become a much better developer by itself. Last but not least, trust is also the best way for you to lead people.

Trust is the best way to lead people

If you want to grow beyond senior positions to positions with more responsibility and autonomy, you require a leadership mentality. And the best way for you to be seen as a leader and really help people achieve results and work together as a team is when you are a trustworthy person. By building your brand, attracting people, and being that trusted advisor that people around you believe and trust, you're going to position yourself to have a larger influence and more responsibilities. With that, you can take on more leadership positions – not necessarily a manager position if you don't want that, but even that could be a reality. Every position beyond the senior level is a position that requires some level of leadership and influence on both the team and the wider company. The more you build trust with people around you, the more you will be prepared for those positions with both your confidence and the network to get invited to those positions. Therefore, building your brand is a great way for you to attract the best people in the market and the best jobs in the market.

Saying this, it sounds like we built our brand only for our own selfish purposes of wanting to grow. But in reality, the only way for you to be a leader is when you stop thinking only about yourself and start taking responsibility to help others to achieve what they want. It's a win-win situation when you take the responsibility to attract people to you. You help them achieve results and success and that will bring back results for your career.

When you are ready to interview for a new role either at your existing company, or at a new company, there are some things to consider. If you have been following the advice in this book, you will already be doing them or have started doing them. You are going to need skills and certifications, a support network, a social network, and a community of like-minded peers. When you are ready to take the next step in your career, sometimes you will not want to make it widely known to others, but there are some times when you may unexpectedly be looking for a new role and it will make sense to share the news broadly and make your intentions known. At some point in your career, you will find yourself in both these situations, or maybe even decide that you want to strike out on your own to be your own boss and start your own company, either solo or as part of a team. This section will prepare you for any of these scenarios. You will need the components discussed in this book, including your personal brand. Your personal brand will set the stage and be the foundation of this endeavor. You will rely on it heavily to make it through these transition points in your career.

The following are some steps in the process of looking for a new opportunity:

- **Resume**: You probably want to familiarize yourself with the process of resume writing. Some things to suggest are to not make it too long, don't use the first person, and make sure to have a section that lists all relevant technologies with your levels of expertise.

- **Recruiters**: Use recruiters to help you stand out from the crowd. With online job listings and job boards, you are like a grain of sand or a needle in a haystack. You can initially locate jobs through online listings and job boards, but then go further and find recruiters to make the introductions for you.

- **Use your network**: Reach out to your contacts in companies where you would like to work. Ask them for personal introductions or referrals to open positions.

- **Online tools**: LinkedIn is a powerful tool. When you are looking for a new position, take a fresh look and clean up your online profiles, adding your most recent accomplishments. Add a summary of your skills and achievements. Use tools such as OneNote to help you keep track of your meetings and contacts. You are going to meet a lot of people on your hunt. OneNote has sections for to-dos, interviews, training, and so on, and you can use *Ctrl + 1* to create and toggle checkboxes.

- **Practice interviews**: Executive coach and author, Mike Minoske, also known as Coach Mike, wrote the book *The Job Search Manifesto* and has developed a model framework for interviews. The framework includes four interview questions: Baseline (questions such as *"Tell us a little bit about yourself"* and *"What do you know about the role?"*, etc), Skills and Experience (questions that allow you to share your knowledge and experience; technical interview questions), Leadership (questions that highlight your leadership abilities, whether through being a direct manager or not – this allows you to demonstrate your potential to lead internally and externally), and finally, Cultural/Behavioral (when you share your successes and failures and your abilities to resolve conflicts, manage time and priorities, and work with too little or too much information).

- **Pay it forward**: Always be ready and willing to help others you know and trust. Make it a priority to thank people for their willingness to help you.

Looking for a new role or starting your own company are both excellent examples of when you will need to utilize your personal brand and put it to work for your career advancement.

Interview

Yolande Poirier

My name is Yolanda Poirier, and I currently am working at Neo4J. I'm in charge of the community there, globally, but particularly in the US. I'm responsible for meetups, websites, forums – you could call it community, but that's a fancy word – everything that touches developer communities and data science. Also, the champion program. We have a Discord account, for example. We are running an online conference in the fall, which I'm also involved with, both promotion and the Call for Papers. I'm part of DevRel, which is really nice as well because my counterparts are technical and they help us with all the initiatives. So that's very nice. And I've been doing all of this for quite a while, as you know.

Q: So, this is my question. You've been working with communities for quite a while. How did you get started? How did you get involved with communities and working with branding, marketing, and DevRel, all of this?

A: I think a lot of people come through the meetups, but first you need to have some passion for communities, for organizing events. Doing that in your free time definitely helps. People have different profiles and in my case, I do community, but I also work very closely with marketing. I was always in a marketing department. Some people are in a smaller company, for example, so they may come from engineering and start with the forum, making sure that people answer questions. Sometimes they will run beta programs, for example. That's a very different profile. It really depends on the size of the company, how it is structured. All those departments are also structured differently. When I was at Oracle, it was engineering. DevRel was more in engineering and I was part of marketing, but I had to go back and forth. So you need to wear multiple hats, that's for sure. I found what was really helpful for me was to understand the different roles and responsibilities in the organization. So understanding what engineers do, how the product is being developed, what's the cycle, but also how corporate marketing works, how events are structured, who is responsible for what, and even branding as well, because branding also has rules. There are also legal needs to be involved at some point. So it's really wearing multiple hats, which I really love.

Q: You mentioned how people can get into this, but how did you get started? How did you get involved? I love what you just said at the end there, that you loved wearing multiple hats. Can you elaborate on this? How did you get started wearing multiple hats? Did you always do that?

A: Actually, I started at Sun Microsystems in product marketing from all places on Java. And, you probably know a little product called JavaFX. Well, a long time ago I started on that. And similarly, product marketing can be structured differently because my role was not very technical. It was more outward facing, with more promotional aspects. So that was also a little bit different. There was an inbound and outbound marketing function, but it wasn't very engineering focused, so to speak. As part of that role, I definitely had to understand everything. And then from there, I moved to an organization that dealt with cloud computing in the early days. And again, there were developer initiatives and some products to work on as well. And I stayed in those developer roles for quite a while, actually. I was on student initiatives, you name it, all of which was similar but very different at the same time. Different players, different activities, different people to deal with.

Q: One of the things that a professional is always worried about is the whole thing that you just mentioned, about wearing too many hats. Lots of people are worried about how many things they need to learn, how many technologies they need to understand, how many things they need to do. How do you handle that? How do you handle knowing lots of people, lots of different things, lots of different skills that you have to have to work on all these things?

A: I think this is something we're all almost always struggling with that because you feel like you don't know enough, which is probably true. I think it's knowing how much depth you need to understand in order to be effective because you have to understand the communities; you have to be able to talk with technical people. You need to understand the key technologies. Making sure that you have some system to understand what your company is doing and how it fits with the rest of the ecosystem – that's a must. There is no way you can bypass that. And for several reasons, you need to understand the community that you're going after. I mean, where are the touchpoints with those communities? And so the more you know about the technology and other related technologies, the better. There are also opportunities for events. Also, as a community manager, you always find yourself mentoring others. You may find somebody who is motivated to talk about your product but doesn't know really how they can actually fit into what you're doing. So it's like a puzzle, a constant puzzle with moving pieces that you need to figure out because otherwise, you can't really help people.

If you see a person, very quickly, you need to understand who this person is. Are they a backend developer or a frontend developer? What are they interested in? Are they interested in blogging, speaking? What are their strengths? You have to empower people. And sometimes they know who they are, sometimes they don't. So you have to be quick to identify that as well. And also whenever possible, make sure that you connect them with the right people so they can also actually move forward in their career, in having fun, all of that. You have to think fast. I think that's what has always helped. You meet someone and you say, okay, I know what kind of person that is. And sometimes you get it wrong, and that's okay too. But I think at least trying to help people grow in your community is key. Don't get me wrong, I love people who are at the top of their field and are champions. They produce content, they are keynote speakers. Those people are fantastic in your community.

So I'm not really worried about those people. I just open doors. I just say, *"Oh, there is an event here. What would you like to do?"* So I just support them. And usually it's with a program, or with money, if we have money. So that's easy. To me, that's the easy part. The more complex and more fun thing is helping more people to be successful via the community that you're building. So it's about going to conferences and figuring out how people are learning about your product, what tools they can use, how easy can you make it for them to use your product. Anything that works for that is gold, because then you can really grow your community. So that's fun. And you can also then mentor those people who are champions to also become mentors with you when you see certain opportunities.

Q: Just as a side note here, I believe in exactly what you said about empowering people so they can move forward and find their own path. I found it fascinating how you described that because that's exactly what I believe. So that's awesome. But I think that ties in very well with branding. You've been a person who has helped other people. You mentioned those top people in the industry, how you've helped them find and build their own brands. When you mentor people, you also help them do the same thing. So what do you think branding is for developers? What is a personal brand? Because one thing – I'm not sure if you've had this experience – but one thing that I have seen a lot is that developers come to me and say, *"Look, I don't want to promote myself."* When you talk about branding with them, they imagine they're promoting themselves and they don't want to do this. Why do you think that's important?

A: First of all, when I do a workshop, the first question I usually ask is: does anybody here have a brand? Even the way I phrase the sentence is a total sap because of course, most people say no. I'm like, well, yes, you do have a brand. No matter who you are, you show up, you have a presence, you have a brand. People will use whatever shortcut they can and will label you in one way or another. So the question is, do you have control over or can you influence how people see you? Or if you think that you don't really care, well, would you show up naked to a party? Well, maybe not, right? Because that wouldn't be comfortable. So that means that you're aware that you make an impression. And I think that's what a brand is. Of course, when we think about brands, we think about the big brands such as Nike and celebrities and so forth. Well, the truth is that we all have a brand, so we have to work on it. And nobody is fully comfortable with it, ever. I don't know. I mean... I'm certainly not.

Summary

In this chapter, you learned key marketing concepts about branding, how to define your own style and attract your audience, how to apply simple marketing concepts to your own brand, how to attract the right people that you can help, and how to use your brand to get amazing internal and external opportunities.

So here you have it: a full Masterplan for the Developer Career. It may look overwhelming right now, but every step listed in the book can be done in small first, and then grow when you have results. Also, there is no need to do it all at once. Your developer career is an infinite game: keep working on it, and it will always improve and grow.

There is just one thing that can prevent this book from helping you - not taking action.

You can do small things. You can do just a few things. You can even decide not to do some, or even many of them. Yet, if you don't take action on any of the things we showed you here, nothing will happen to your career.

We hope that you will take action. And if you need help, follow us on social media, and we will do our best to guide you on the right path.

Thank you and congratulations!

Heather VanCura @heathervc

Bruno Souza @brjavaman

Index

Packtpub.com

Subscribe to our online digital library for full access to over 7,000 books and videos, as well as industry leading tools to help you plan your personal development and advance your career. For more information, please visit our website.

Why subscribe?

- Spend less time learning and more time coding with practical eBooks and Videos from over 4,000 industry professionals

- Improve your learning with Skill Plans built especially for you

- Get a free eBook or video every month

- Fully searchable for easy access to vital information

- Copy and paste, print, and bookmark content

Did you know that Packt offers eBook versions of every book published, with PDF and ePub files available? You can upgrade to the eBook version at packtpub.com and as a print book customer, you are entitled to a discount on the eBook copy. Get in touch with us at customercare@packtpub.com for more details.

At www.packtpub.com, you can also read a collection of free technical articles, sign up for a range of free newsletters, and receive exclusive discounts and offers on Packt books and eBooks.

Other Books You May Enjoy

If you enjoyed this book, you may be interested in these other books by Packt:

Practical Design Patterns for Java Developers

Miroslav Wengner

ISBN: 978-1-80461-467-9

- Understand the most common problems that can be solved using Java design patterns
- Uncover Java building elements, their usages, and concurrency possibilities
- Optimize a vehicle memory footprint with the Flyweight Pattern
- Explore one-to-many relations between instances with the observer pattern
- Discover how to route vehicle messages by using the visitor pattern
- Utilize and control vehicle resources with the thread-pool pattern
- Understand the penalties caused by anti-patterns in software design

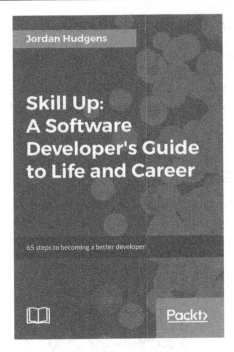

Skill Up: A Software Developer's Guide to Life and Career

Jordan Hudgens

ISBN: 978-1-78728-703-7

- Improve your soft skills to become a better and happier coder
- Learn to be a better developer
- Grow your freelance development business
- Improve your development career
- Learn the best approaches to breaking down complex topics
- Have the confidence to charge what you're worth as a freelancer
- Succeed in developer job interviews

Packt is searching for authors like you

If you're interested in becoming an author for Packt, please visit `authors.packtpub.com` and apply today. We have worked with thousands of developers and tech professionals, just like you, to help them share their insight with the global tech community. You can make a general application, apply for a specific hot topic that we are recruiting an author for, or submit your own idea.

Share Your Thoughts

Now you've finished *Developer Career Masterplan*, we'd love to hear your thoughts! Scan the QR code below to go straight to the Amazon review page for this book and share your feedback or leave a review on the site that you purchased it from.

`https://packt.link/r/1801818703`

Your review is important to us and the tech community and will help us make sure we're delivering excellent quality content.

Download a free PDF copy of this book

Thanks for purchasing this book!

Do you like to read on the go but are unable to carry your print books everywhere? Is your eBook purchase not compatible with the device of your choice?

Don't worry, now with every Packt book you get a DRM-free PDF version of that book at no cost.

Read anywhere, any place, on any device. Search, copy, and paste code from your favorite technical books directly into your application.

The perks don't stop there, you can get exclusive access to discounts, newsletters, and great free content in your inbox daily

Follow these simple steps to get the benefits:

1. Scan the QR code or visit the link below

https://packt.link/free-ebook/9781801818704

1. Submit your proof of purchase
2. That's it! We'll send your free PDF and other benefits to your email directly

Made in the USA
Coppell, TX
09 January 2024

27481554R00171